CRITICAL ESSAYS IN MODERN LITERATURE

CRITICAL ESSAYS IN MODERN LITERATURE

The Fiction and Criticism of Katherine Anne Porter (revised)
Harry L. Mooney, Jr.

Entrances to Dylan Thomas' Poetry
Ralph Maud

Joyce Cary: The Comedy of Freedom
Charles G. Hoffmann

The Fiction of J. D. Salinger (revised)
Frederick L. Gwynn and Joseph L. Blotner

James Agee: Promise and Fulfillment
Kenneth Seib

Chronicles of Conscience: A Study of George Orwell and Arthur Koestler
Jenni Calder

Richard Wright: An Introduction to the Man and His Work
Russell Carl Brignano

Dylan Thomas' Early Prose: A Study in Creative Mythology
Annis Pratt

The Situation of the Novel
Bernard Bergonzi

D. H. Lawrence: Body of Darkness
R. E. Pritchard

The Hole in the Fabric: Science, Contemporary Literature, and Henry James
Strother B. Purdy

Tragic Realism and Modern Society: Studies in the Sociology of the Modern Novel
John Orr

Reading the Thirties: Texts and Contexts
Bernard Bergonzi

The Romantic Genesis of the Modern Novel
Charles Schug

The Great Succession: Henry James and the Legacy of Hawthorne
Robert Emmet Long

The Romantic Genesis of the Modern Novel

The Romantic Genesis
of the Modern Novel

CHARLES SCHUG

University of Pittsburgh Press

Published by the University of Pittsburgh Press, Pittsburgh, Pa. 15260
Copyright © 1979, University of Pittsburgh Press
All rights reserved
Feffer and Simons, Inc., London
Manufactured in the United States of America

Library of Congress Cataloging in Publication Data

Schug, Charles, 1945–
    The romantic genesis of the modern novel.

    (Critical essays in modern literature)
    Includes bibliographical references and index.
    1.   English fiction—20th century—History and
criticism.   2.   Romanticism—England.   3.   James, Henry,
1843–1916—Criticism and interpretation.   4.   Conrad,
Joseph, 1857–1924—Criticism and interpretation.
5.   Woolf, Virginia Stephen, 1882–1941—Criticism and
interpretation.   I.   Title.
PR888.R73S3   823'.03   78-26484
ISBN 0-8229-3397-7

Grateful acknowledgment is made to those who granted permission to quote material used in this book.

From *Mrs. Dalloway* by Virginia Woolf, copyright 1925 by Harcourt Brace Jovanovich, Inc.; copyright 1953 by Leonard Woolf. Reprinted by permission of the publisher, the author's literary estate, and The Hogarth Press Ltd.

From *To the Lighthouse* by Virginia Woolf, copyright 1927 by Harcourt Brace Jovanovich, Inc.; copyright 1955 by Leonard Woolf. Reprinted by permission of the publisher, the author's literary estate, and The Hogarth Press Ltd.

Portions of chapter 3 first appeared as "The Romantic Form of Mary Shelley's *Frankenstein*," *SEL*, 17 (Autumn 1977), 607–19.

For my mother

and

For Linda

Contents

Preface

The word *Romantic* is a dangerous one to use in literary criticism. Despite many attempts to pin it down, it eludes precise definition. Unhappily for those who want neat categories, it is also indispensible for discussion of many writers who lived in the first quarter of the nineteenth century. Because it is both difficult to grasp and unavoidable, there is an understandable desire to impose limits on it; and since they cannot be semantic limits, chronological ones have been substituted, transforming it from a critical or linguistic problem to a historical one. As long as the cloak of literary history is available, critics are protected. To venture beyond the conventional limits is to challenge the compromise by which that protection was extended in the first place. Any study that seeks, as this one does, to examine Romanticism outside its historical bounds is likely to arouse the suspicion or the skepticism of some readers. For this reason alone, a few prefatory remarks are necessary about the nature and scope of this essay.

The fundamental proposition underlying my discussion is that the aesthetic impulses which motivated artists like Wordsworth, Shelley, and Keats did not cease to exist after Victoria ascended the throne. The Romantic era, rather, marks a watershed: a fundamental aesthetic change was effected that continued to shape literature long after the 1820s. I have not set out, however, to argue the case for this general proposition. I do not need to because, luckily, that has already been done by scholars of the calibre of Robert Langbaum, Karl Kroeber, and Northrop Frye. My efforts instead have been to consider how their discoveries might help us to understand a specific body of literature—in this case, the "modern" novel, the novel, that is, at the beginning of the twentieth century.

In consequence, I have drawn more heavily than is perhaps usual for an essay of this nature on the work of those who suggest the ongoing influence of Romanticism. This is especially so of two critics—Robert Langbaum and Karl Kroeber. It was Langbaum's compelling study of *The Poetry of Experience: The Dramatic Monologue in Modern Literary Tradition* (1957; rpt. New York: Norton, 1963) that first opened my eyes to the connections between Romantic and modern literature and gave me a new way to think about the experience of reading modern fiction. It was Kroeber's *Romantic Narrative Art* (1960; rpt. Madison: University of Wisconsin Press, 1966) that at a crucial stage of this essay helped me to understand how the aesthetics of the Romantic poets could be transformed into the aesthetics of modern novelists. My debt to these scholars is enormous and is recorded at considerable length throughout these pages.

I also owe a large debt to a group of critics of Romanticism, among whom are, in addition to Langbaum and Kroeber, Graham Hough, Albert Gérard, Northrop Frye, M. H. Abrams, and Larry J. Swingle. They have produced a substantial body of criticism that allows us at last to get beyond the old formulas to a more solid and comprehensive grasp of the fundamental aesthetics of the original Romantics. From their criticism I have abstracted a working definition of Romantic form. I have done so for several reasons. First, this working definition gives us a quick way of referring to the Romantic aesthetic. This device is especially needful since the aesthetics of modern fiction are complex in their own right. Second, taken together, the ideas of this particular group of critics, if not universally accepted, form a major theory of Romanticism that is impossible to discount. By basing my remarks on their theories, I am able to avoid many of the issues that, although pertinent to considerations of individual Romantic writers, would sidetrack us here. (Of necessity, then, I ask my readers to accept the theories of these scholars.) Third, by relying on what has already been established, I avoid the repetitive and superfluous effort of presenting my own theory of Romanticism. I am thus able to focus attention where it properly belongs, on modern fiction and its aesthetic.

The desire to focus primarily on modern novelists has dictated a second critical shortcut. In order to get right to analysis of particular works, I have had largely to ignore questions of literary history. The gap thus created is substantial, but to fill it would be to write a different, considerably longer essay than this one. I have rested my case, primarily, on a kind of analogy: I suggest that if a selection of major modern novels can be shown to have the same kind of formal and structural attributes that we see in many Romantic poems, then we can safely conclude that a Romantic aesthetic, in part at least, accounts for the special nature of modern fiction compared to, say, Victorian fiction. This may seem a drastically selective approach, but it is the best and most direct way to work a concrete demonstration of my thesis. This essay must accordingly be judged by the results of my readings of the novels.

Nevertheless, one is right to wonder why, if I am correct, there is a delay of fifty years before the Romantic aesthetic began significantly to alter the novel. Because I have specifically excluded consideration of literary history, the reader will find no answer to that question in the ensuing pages. It is certainly a question that merits exploration, however, and I hope that someone will soon tackle it. There are a number of obvious places to begin. Part of the groundwork for a history of the influence of Romanticism on the novel has been laid by Robert Kiely in *The Romantic Novel in England* (Cambridge, Mass.: Harvard University Press, 1972). Many of the novels he examines are out of the mainstream of British fiction, but he does show how Romantic elements can be traced in fiction throughout the nineteenth century. Some of the works he considers can be classified as "gothic," and many gothic novels share and perpetuate Romantic characteristics, especially a discontinuous, nonnarrative structure, a feature I examine below as one of the hallmarks of Romantic fiction. Two novels frequently included on lists of gothic fiction, *Frankenstein* and *Wuthering Heights,* are also the clearest examples we have of nineteenth-century novels with fully Romantic forms. Kiely discusses them both, and I analyze *Frankenstein* below. A study of gothic fiction would thus seem an important part of any effort to trace the impact of Romanticism on the novel.

I have said below, following W. J. Bate's suggestion, that romanticization of subject matter precedes romanticization of aesthetic form. This, too, would be a fruitful area to explore, for there are many signs of Romantic subject matter in nineteenth-century novels. Scott, Dickens, and Charlotte Brontë are the novelists who immediately spring to mind in this regard. The early Hardy might perhaps be worked in here as well. Yet another line of investigation would lead, I believe, from Keats through the Pre-Raphaelite Brotherhood to Walter Pater, whose aesthetic ideas are profoundly affected by Romanticism. Pater's influence on modern fiction, especially on Conrad and Joyce, is in turn significant.

These few remarks suggest the difficulty of the task. Beyond the volume and diversity of the material necessary to be examined, one is faced with the tricky problem of tracing influences. Moreover, it would be misleading to confine the discussion solely to British literature, since the interplay of French, German, and Russian fiction with British novels should not be overlooked, especially because those fictions are themselves shaped by the Romantic movements in their respective countries. The reader will understand if I, like Marlow, have withdrawn my hesitating foot and tread a less arduous path.

Preface

I am aware that some readers may be reluctant to have further ingredients tossed into the soup: there are enough issues raised by modern fiction, they will say, without the complication of Romantic influences. There is certainly merit in any attempt to foster economy and directness in literary criticism. I have pursued this thesis, however, in the belief that a more precise understanding of the way in which the modern novel fits into the ongoing literary tradition of Romanticism will help to clarify, and may actually simplify, the issues that fiction presents. I hope that my analyses of seven major novels by Henry James, Joseph Conrad, and Virginia Woolf justify that belief.

A number of people have assisted me in the writing of this essay, and I should like to thank them here. John Paterson and Thomas Flanagan offered helpful and challenging guidance at several stages during the preparation of the manuscript. I am grateful to them both for their patience and their enthusiasm about the project. An early chapter was read by Stephen Booth, to whom I am indebted generally for advice and criticism and whose own scholarship is a model I can only hope to emulate. Special thanks are due to Hanna Pitkin, who took time out from her own work in political science to read my manuscript and whose "editorial" comments are an intellectual training. Her ear for awkward, infelicitous, or simply unclear writing is infallible, and I have benefited enormously from working with her. Lynn Striegel, James Striegel, and William McCarthy read portions of earlier drafts; I thank them for their comments and suggestions.

I should like also to express my appreciation to the Interdepartmental Program of the graduate college of Iowa State University for funds made available to me for the typing and photoduplicating of the manuscript. In addition, I want to thank my former colleagues Judy Nelson, Linda and Aubrey Galyon, Rachel and James Lowrie, and Dale Ross.

They contributed to the making of this book by helping to make difficult working conditions less difficult.

My greatest debt is to Linda Koenig. She read the manuscript through several times and at all its stages, always offering valuable comments, criticisms, and suggestions. Her thorough knowledge of eighteenth-century fiction and of the gothic novel enabled her to bring a perspective different from mine to bear on my thesis and helped me to strengthen some of the weak parts of my argument. Our extended and far-ranging discussions of literature have allowed me to test out and modify many of the ideas I offer below. Her contribution to this essay is great; so is my gratitude to her.

The Romantic Genesis of the Modern Novel

ONE

Introduction

At the end of the nineteenth century a change occurred that significantly altered the ficitonal world of the English novel. The work of many modern novelists, among them the subjects of this study, James, Conrad, and Woolf, reveals a new attitude toward experience, both actual and aesthetic, that sets it distinctly apart from the work of their earlier novelist colleagues from Fielding and Richardson to Hardy and Meredith. In examining the difference in aesthetic experience in reading a modern and a "traditional" novel, I was reminded of the difference in reading a Romantic and a non-Romantic poem, and I was struck by what seemed a strong similarity between the experience of the Romantic poem and that of the modern novel. I have since come to be convinced that the change that occurred in the form of the novel can be accounted for, at least partially, by the fact that at the end of the nineteenth century the novel became Romantic in form. It is that proposition—that the modern novel has a Romantic form—I wish to explore here.

I am not the first, of course, to have perceived a resemblance between modern literature and Romantic literature in general or even between modern fiction and Romantic poetry in particular. There is a lively and continuing controversy about the relationship of Romanticism to modern literature that was begun in the early years of this century by T. S. Eliot and Ezra Pound, among artists, and T. E. Hulme, Irving Babbitt, and the New Humanists, among critics and philosophers, and that has been refueled of late. Increased interest in the issue stems in part from the publication, starting in the 1950s, of several critical studies exploring similarities between Romantic and modern works of literature. The authors of recent considerations of "modern" literature seem to fall into two camps: (1) followers of Eliot and Hulme who seek to define and locate a modernist tradition that is distinctly set off, on the one hand, from Romantic and Victorian literature and, on the other, from what some have now taken to calling "post-Modern" literature; and (2) critics like Robert Langbaum, Harold Bloom, Northrop Frye, and M. H. Abrams, to name but a handful, who suggest or seek to investigate a continuity between the literature of the nineteenth and twentieth centuries.

With some exceptions, the opinions of Eliot, Pound, and Hulme against what they called Romanticism ("there may be," says Eliot, "a good deal to be said for Romanticism in life, there is no place for it in letters")[1] remained unchallenged until about mid-century. Then, when critics like Frank Kermode and Murray Krieger reexamined Hulme's writings, especially his influential essay "Romanticism and Classicism," they discovered that his ideas were heavily indebted, especially through the influence of Bergson, to that very Romanticism he so vigorously attacked.[2] Kermode indeed goes on, in addition to exploring the underlying Romantic nature of many of Hulme's ideas, to examine in *Romantic Image* some essential points of continuity between the Romantics and modern symbolist poets (Yeats primarily); his analysis relies on isolating a use of imagery that is fundamentally Romantic but which both twentieth- and nineteenth-century poets employ. Similarly, other critics began at that time to make distinctions between the lasting and important contributions of Romanticism and its transitory or peripheral characteristics; such is the effort of Robert Langbaum in *The Poetry of Experience* (1957) or Northrop Frye in *A Study of English Romanticism* (1968). Although poetry remained the center of attention, as further connections between Romantic and modern literature were proposed, some critics began to suggest that modern fiction ought also to be examined in light of the continuing influence of the Romantic aesthetic. In *The Lyrical Novel* (1963), one critic explored a form he said derived ultimately from Romanticism, although he defined the genre closely and made few claims for it beyond three specific novelists (Hesse, Gide, and Woolf).[3] In 1974, David Thorburn published *Conrad's Romanticism*, which he described as a "preliminary effort to locate modern fiction within a territory already mapped out for modern poetry."[4] In the epilogue he proposed that other modern novelists might profitably be analyzed as writers in the Romantic tradition. This study is an attempt to do just that.

Thorburn and his predecessors have by no means convinced the followers of Eliot, Babbitt, and Hulme, however. One critic, Maurice Beebe, an outspoken and, by virtue of his position as editor of the *Journal of Modern Literature* (and before that of *Modern Fiction Studies*), influential representative of the Eliot-Hulme school, argues the case against Romantic influence on modern literature in two recent articles, "*Ulysses* and the Age of Modernism" (1972) and "What Modernism Was" (1974), which appeared in an issue of the *Journal of Modern Literature* devoted to the topic "From Modernism to Post-Modernism." Beebe's comments are worth considering further, for they seem in part founded on a popular misconception about Romanticism that is one source of a continuing hostility toward both Romantic literature itself and those critical studies that suggest an ongoing Romantic influence. Beebe sees in the earlier of the articles four distinguishing elements of "modernism": (1) its formalism ("It insists on the importance of structure and design—the esthetic autonomy and independent whatness of the work of art"); (2) "an attitude of detachment and non-commitment" (what the New Critics called "Irony"); (3) a use of myth as "an arbitrary means of ordering art" rather than "as a discipline for belief or a subject for interpretation"; and (4) Impressionism—"Modernist art turns back upon itself and is largely concerned with its own creation and composition. The Impressionists' insistence that the viewer is more important than the subject viewed leads ultimately to the solipsistic worlds-within-worlds of Modernist art and literature."[5] Arguments could be made to show that each of these features is compatible with Romanticism, but the first and last points are particularly important to our discussion here, especially since Beebe reiterates in "What Modernism Was" his claim that concern for form and technique decisively separates the moderns from the Romantics ("To claim that the Modernists shared this insistence [that technique is more important than subject] with the Romantics would be an act of critical recklessness").[6]

"We find around the turn of the century, in Satie and Pound for example," Beebe notes in *"Ulysses* and the Age of Modernism," "a new and more sophisticated concern for techniques than was apparent during the Romantic decades."[7] No one, I think, will dispute this point: modern writers do express a much more conscious concern about form and technique than the Romantic poets ever did. But self-conscious aesthetic concerns alone are hardly enough in themselves to distinguish one group of writers from another. It is the *nature* of these concerns that matters, and the fact is that many modern writers are consciously grappling with the same or closely related aesthetic issues as Romantic writers. Geoffrey Hartman observes one such similitude underlying a seeming dissimilitude: "It does seem to me that the personal and expressive theory of poetry, ascribed to the romantics, and the impersonal theory of poetry, claimed in reaction by the moderns, answer to the same problem and are quietly linked by the ambiguity in 'unconsciousness.' Both theories value art as thought recreated into feeling or self-consciousness into a more communal power of vision."[8] We ought not in general to be surprised at the possibility that modern and Romantic artists confront the same kinds of aesthetic issues. For as W. J. Bate reminds us in *From Classic to Romantic,* "It should be noted, indeed, that a romanticization of subject matter long precedes the deliberate romanticization of the aesthetic medium."[9] Bate's remark can help us to understand why the Romantics themselves, who had begun the process of "deliberate romanticization of aesthetic medium," should have been less sophisticated in their aesthetics and less consciously concerned about form and technique than artists who followed them by half a century and more. The Romantics, Albert Gérard suggests, "apparently . . . were unaware of the precise nature of the new formal patterns which they were creating—or they would have discussed them. Indeed, it is most probable that those patterns were not immediately perceptible because they did not correspond to the usual criteria of formal structure."[10]

Beebe's proposal that "Modernist art turns back upon itself and is largely concerned with its own creation and composition" helps to support (unawares) my suggestion that modern fiction can be seen, in some ways at least, as the product of a deliberate romanticization of the aesthetic medium: the explicit and conscious concern of modern novelists for the aesthetics of their art in itself does not disqualify them as Romantics but rather could suggest that they are the natural inheritors of a Romantic legacy. Certainly there are many indications of a romanticization of subject matter in the novel during the nineteenth century; Robert Kiely, for one, has discussed some of them in *The Romantic Novel in England.*[11] With the exception of *Frankenstein,* the novels contemporaneous with the great poems of the Romantic period do not participate in the experiments and innovations in form that we see in the poetry. Why it should be the novelists of the late nineteenth and early twentieth century who embody the formal discoveries of the Romantic poets in their work is a question we shall have to leave to literary historians. My immediate concern is to demonstrate the similarity in formal and structural properties between modern novels and Romantic poems. For the moment, however, the least we should be able to conclude is that, since modern novelists inherited a substantial tradition of Romantic literature, both in poetry and in prose, it would not be unexpected for us to discover that their aesthetics are founded on a Romantic base. To validate such an assumption we need not be concerned if the later group of writers has a more self-conscious aesthetic than the earlier one.

Behind Maurice Beebe's claim that conscious aesthetic considerations distinguish the modernists from the Romantics lies another, important issue. He claims "formalism" as a distinguishing element of modern literature and calls James's essay "The Art of Fiction" (1884) "one of the first important manifestoes of Modernism in part because he insisted there that what constituted the *art* of fiction was to be found more in treatment than in content." James found in his "center of consciousness" technique, Beebe goes on, "a way to fuse content and form through the rich vision of a detached observer, but it is clear that for him, as for other major Modernists, technique was more important than subject."[12] As we shall see in chapter four, Beebe has not accurately represented James's position: it is not true to say without more qualification than he offers that technique was *more important* than subject for James. But more significant for our immediate discussion is the fact that Beebe's argument is founded on an apparent misundersanding of the real nature of Romantic poetry and of the Romantic aesthetic in general. Behind his argument lies the implication that Romantic literature is formless, that since Romantic poets rarely expressed concern for structure or form, their poetry is somehow disordered or unstructured. But much modern criticism has been designed to dispel this very misapprehension. "The number of recent learned articles dealing with design, structure, and patterning in romantic poetry attests to the growing recognition," notes Gérard in *English Romantic Poetry*, that "within the poetic mood itself there is an inborn orderliness whose discreet operation is revealed to the watchful reader" (pp. 18, 19). Other critics have different names for this "inborn orderliness"—R. A. Foakes calls it "self-intuition," Graham Hough "an inner organic law," and Gérard himself elsewhere "intuition of unity"—but whatever it is called it speaks to a concern for aesthetic structure and order.[13] The Romantics, Gérard suggests, passed beyond a "concept of unity that was tectonic, mechanical, and stable to one that was atectonic, organic, and dynamic" (p. 239). Moreover, he warns that the Romantic conception of organic form "should not be taken as a gentle euphemism for shapelessness"; in fact, "the romantic inspiration, however emotional in its origin, worked itself into recognizable structural patterns which combine the spontaneity of the creative impulse with the orderliness of the valid poetic artifact" (p. 17). James's concerns in both "The Art of Fiction" and his prefaces are informed by much the same kind of aesthetic issue as Gérard raises here—maintaining the sense of spontaneous life in art. As James remarks: "Catching the very note and trick, the strange irregular rhythm of life, that is the attempt whose strenuous force keeps Fiction upon her feet. In proportion as in what she offers us we see life *without* rearrangement do we feel that we are touching the truth; in proportion as we see it *with* rearrangement do we feel that we are being put off with a substitute, a compromise and convention."[14]

But I anticipate. I shall consider both Romantic form and James's aesthetic ideas at greater length later. It should be evident from the few remarks I quote here that no one need fear calling Romantic a writer who professes conscious or well-developed concerns for aesthetic form or order. If the worries of Hulme and the New Humanists centered on what they conceived of as inadequate or inept Romantic thought or philosophy ("spilt religion"), I suspect the worries of their present-day descendants center on what they conceive of as Romantic formlessness. The impetus for those of us seeking to demonstrate the underlying Romantic nature of modern literature is not to show that it is, as one critic has objected, "merely an extension of romanticism."[15] Rather, we wish to locate modern literature within a larger, Romantic tradition in order to understand it better. I believe that a reevaluation of modern fiction in light of modern theories of Romanticism—a reevaluation such as I am undertaking here—will help fix more firmly not only its place in literary history, but also the complete range of its aesthetic. Rather than blurring distinctions or confusing issues, an investigation of the Romantic traits of modern fiction will help us to see and evaluate more clearly the differences between pre- and post-Jamesian novels and will facilitate a more accurate and comprehensive definition of "modernism" than has been suggested so far. I do not seek to refute or overturn most of what has already been established about modern fiction; my efforts are to broaden our understanding of that fiction and, in some cases, to suggest new readings that clarify or resolve long-standing critical issues.

In a sense, my approach is to conflate two critical ideas already established: that a substantial change occurred in the form of the novel at the end of the nineteenth century and that the Romantic aesthetic exerted a continuing influence on the literature of the last two centuries. I am suggesting that the latter phenomenon is in part a cause of the former. Before we move on to an extended examination of the Romantic aesthetic, let us briefly consider the critical precedents for these two notions.

Three full-length studies of the proposition that the novel changed drastically at the beginning of this century are especially worth mentioning: David Daiches, *The Novel and the Modern World* (first published 1939; revised 1960); Leon Edel, *The Modern Psychological Novel* (originally published as *The Psychological Novel 1900–1950* [1955]); and Alan Friedman, *The Turn of the Novel* (1966).[16] These studies are in general agreement about the phenomenon they examine and suggest complementary explanations of it. Daiches and Edel are concerned with the change in the novel as manifested primarily in new, innovative techniques, while Friedman directs his attention toward structural differences between traditional and modern novels.

Both Daiches and Edel note the influence of William James, Henri Bergson, and Sigmund Freud on the modern consciousness. Edel believes that the writings of these thinkers reflect "the deeper and more searching *inwardness* of our century" (p. 28); partly through the techniques of stream of consciousness and interior monologue, modern writers consequently "turned fiction away from external to internal reality, from the outer world that Balzac had charted a century before to the hidden world of fantasy and reverie into which there play constantly the life and perception of our senses" (pp. 11–12). Daiches' emphases are slightly different. He sees three factors responsible for "a radical redefinition of the nature and function of fiction" (p. 1). The first is "a new concept of time as continuous flow," derived from Bergson and James; the second is "a new view of consciousness deriving in a general way from the work of Freud and Jung but concentrating on the fact of multiplicity of consciousness" (p. 7). The third factor is the one most crucial for our discussion: the "breakdown of public agreement about what is significant in experience and therefore about what the novelist ought to select" (p. 11). Daiches suggests that the traditional English novel "had been essentially what might be called a 'public instrument,' basing its view of what was significant in human affairs on a generally agreed standard. Its plot patterns were constructed out of incidents and situations which were seen to matter in human affairs equally by writer and reader. . . . The correlation between internal and external, between moral or intellectual development and appropriate observable action or inaction, was taken for granted" (pp. 1–2). For the modern novelist, however, "that publicly shared principle of selection and significance is no longer felt to exist, can no longer be depended on" (p. 5).[17]

Alan Friedman in *The Turn of the Novel* argues that the novel "traditionally rendered an expanding moral and emotional disturbance which promised all along to arrive, after its greatest climax, at an ending that would and could check that foregoing expansion"; the traditional novel thus had a "closed form" (p. xi). On the other hand, the modern novel has an "open form"; it presents an ongoing and expanding experience which is not checked at the end of the novel. This shift from a closed to an open form signals a far-reaching alteration in the nature of fiction as it reflects human experience: "It was not merely plot, or characterization, or technique, or point of view, or thought, or symbolic organization that changed; it was not a matter of irreconcilable meanings, conflicting themes, or difficult problems. . . . The process of experience which underlay the novel was itself disrupted and reorganized. The new flux of experience insisted on a new vision of existence: it stressed an ethical vision of continued expansion and virtually unrelieved openness in the experience of life" (pp. 15–16).

Like Friedman, I wish especially to examine the formal or structural change in the novel, although I shall do so from a different perspective. This study ought to complement the work of Daiches, Edel, and Friedman in that I am proposing a new explanation for the phenomenon they examine and a new way of talking about it. Edel does note, although he does not discuss the point in any detail, that "the novel of subjectivity represents historically a return to romanticism" (p. 140). If we turn to the considerable number of recent studies proposing or exploring the continuing influence of Romanticism for a critical precedent, we find an array of diverse critical intelligences and approaches.[18] This study elaborates, with some modification, John Bayley's comment in *The Romantic Survival* that the novel is the primary inheritor of the Romantic legacy. "It is arguable," he writes, "that the novelists rather than the poets of the nineteenth century are the real beneficiaries of the great Romantic endowment. Certainly the novel, and not the long poem, was to become the dominant literary form of the century, and the novel went on to success in a field in which poetry virtually ceased to compete—the relationship between individual imagination and the problems and complications of society. Those who deplore the plight of contemporary poetry often ignore the fact that many of the former functions of the poet have been taken over by the novelist: the change is simply one of form."[19] While I have several reservations about these remarks (since he is primarily concerned with three twentieth-century poets in *The Romantic Survival,* Bayley does not comment further on this point), I do think that his idea that novelists are the "beneficiaries of the great Romantic endowment" is worth pursuing further.

I wish to inquire into the form or structure of the modern novel since I believe that it is through *narrative structure* (to be more specific) that we shall best discern the Romantic aspects of the modern novel. It is a new kind of narrative structure, in fact, that in part prompts Ralph Freedman to advance the idea of a "lyrical novel." In noting that lyrical novels are a "paradox," Freedman remarks: "Novels are usually associated with storytelling: the reader looks for characters with whom he can identify, for action in which he may become engaged, or for ideas and moral choices he may see dramatized. Lyrical poetry, on the other hand, suggests the expression of feelings or themes in musical or pictorial patterns. Combining features of both, the lyrical novel shifts the reader's attention from men and events to a formal design." The lyrical novel is thus for Freedman a "hybrid genre" that "uses the novel to approach the function of a poem" (p. 1). It is thus also a very specialized and limited genre.

Freedman is right to focus on narrative innovations, but I

think there is another way to look at the phenomenon he seeks to analyze. If the genre "lyrical novel" tries to approach the function of poetry, and if "modern lyrical novels are creatures of Romanticism," as he claims (p. 18), then perhaps we can find experiments combining lyric and narrative during the Romantic period itself to help us out. The first thing that springs to mind, of course, is *Lyrical Ballads*. In that volume Wordsworth and Coleridge sought to alter the nature of lyric poetry by introducing balladic aspects, that is, *narrative* aspects, since the ballad is primarily a narrative poem. The best study of the manner in which Wordsworth and Coleridge, as well as other Romantics, experimented with narrative is Karl Kroeber's *Romantic Narrative Art*. "The achievement of Romantic balladry," he writes, "was the establishing of a new form within the lyric mode: the literary ballad. This was part of a new interest in and a new value for a narrative lyricism symbolical rather than rhetorical in structure and purpose." The "literary ballad" he defines as "a symbolic narrative whose value depends not on its historicity but on its success in embodying in plain diction, colloquial rhythm, and a simple metrical form the significance of an intense human experience."[20] Thus where Freedman stops at noticing the "formal design" of the novelistic experiments combining narrative and lyric, Kroeber moves past "design" (the "simple metrical form") toward a more underlying quality to this poetic combination of narrative and lyric—the intense human experience the literary ballad offers as a symbolic narrative.

I would suggest that the modern novel offers something closer to Kroeber's model than to Freedman's. Something in the nature of a "narrative lyricism symbolical rather than rhetorical in structure and purpose" happens in many modern novels by English authors other than Virginia Woolf alone (Freedman's only example from modern English novelists). It would seem therefore that the "lyric novel" is one of the possibilities of fictional form that my category "modern (Romantic) novel" includes. The modern novel does not in general offer a traditional narrative, but rather a new kind of narrative: just as the Romantic lyric poem is really a narrative of experience, as Kroeber suggests and as Robert Langbaum helps demonstrate in *The Poetry of Experience,* so the modern novel, with its Romantic form, offers not a traditional narrative of events and encounters, but a narrative of experience in which events and characters assume a relationship to each other and for the reader different from what we are accustomed to in the traditional novel.[21] Lyrical elements, I would suggest, are but part of the formal means most modern novelists use to embody their visions of reality; those means consistently provide the necessary new (i.e., modern) perspective on experience. The phenomenon Freedman notes is thus more widespread and much more central to the experience of modern fictional worlds than he allows for. Accordingly, the use of lyrical elements is not merely a device a couple of novelists hit upon to express "new" subject matter. In a sense, the subject matter of a modern novel is the same as that of a traditional novel, but the new form of the modern novel obviously alters its content. The relationship between form and content is both circular and reciprocal, but I think one needs to stress the formal change in the modern novel: through the development or elaboration of a number of fictional techniques—point of view, stream of consciousness, interior monologue, use of complex narrative structure, to name but a few—new considerations of familiar fictional material were possible, and the changed perspective resulted in "new" subjects for novelistic consideration at the same time that a new sense of experience prompted the need for the new techniques and thus the new form.[22]

Any discussion of narrative would be incomplete without reference to Wayne Booth's authoritative study, *The Rhetoric of Fiction.* I shall consider some of his ideas at greater length in chapter three, but I mention him now because his criticisms of modern forms of narration help throw my thesis into relief. Booth spends considerable time exploring modern versions of unreliable narration. Although many writers of fiction from the eighteenth century on have used unreliable narration, modern authors have tended to combine it with authorial silence and impersonality. "We are likely to have trouble," Booth says, with such a combination.[23] He thinks that it leads to needless uncertainty about modern fiction as well as to frequent and extended critical contretemps; "the critical disagreement," Booth complains, "revealed to anyone who compares two or more critics on any one story [by Henry James] is a scandal" (p. 315). Moreover, such a combination of unreliable narration and authorial silence encourages what he calls "deep reading" and symbol and irony hunting. It is at this point that Booth's discussion becomes especially relevant to our considerations here. It seems to me that the "deep reading" approach is a method neither unique to criticism of the novel in general nor inappropriate to discussions of the modern novel in particular. The kind of close textual analysis about which Booth complains was not originally a critical method designed solely for modern fiction; poetry, above all lyric poetry, is also susceptible to such an analysis.

Indeed, the kind of critical dispute to which Booth objects in connection with modern fiction is really not very different from the kind of disputes we discover concerning the interpretation of a poem like "Ode on a Grecian Urn." Except for those special problems unique to each literary form, the general issues involved in the disagreement about Keats's poem are similar to those involved in the disagreement about a short story by Henry James—the questions of voice, moral judgment, and determination of "meaning" are central to both disputes. The problem of the governess's innocence or guilt in "The Turn of the Screw" is akin to the problem of the "real meaning" of " 'Beauty is truth, truth beauty'—that is all / Ye know on earth, and all ye need to know" in that a critical method required to provide a "solution" to each problem must be *sui generis*—the genus in this instance being a fairly large one: a critical method that can deal with the whole of Romantic literature. Booth himself comes close to acknowledging the need for a special critical method for modern fiction when he says, somewhat testily, "One of the worst results of all this is that it becomes more and more difficult to rely, in our criticism, on the old standards of proof; evidence from the book can never be decisive" (p. 369). Since the evidence one calls on in literary criticism is not comparable to the physical evidence of an experiment in chemistry, for instance, or even to the evidence at a trial, and can never really be "decisive," we need to look behind Booth's remarks at another issue: the "old standards of proof" were never "decisive," but they were *applicable*.[24] We need to find new standards, and I should like to suggest that a reevaluation of James and other modern novelists as Romantic writers will throw a new light on the critical problems Booth raises and will help to explain, at least in part, the kinds of responses modern fiction has evoked. It seems to me that, allowing for the obvious differences between poetry and prose fiction, one faces similar critical issues in assessing Romantic poetry and modern fiction.

In fact, if we look at Booth's complaints about modern fiction in a larger frame of reference, they turn out to be oddly similar to those some critics have made about Romantic poetry; thus Booth: "In short, we have looked for so long at foggy landscapes reflected in misty mirrors that we have come to *like* fog" (p. 372). Foggy, misty, cloudy, dreamy—words such as these form the core of a Star Chamber vocabulary used by some to try and to convict Romanticism. One is reminded—to choose but the most obvious example—of Hulme's "Romanticism and Classicism," which voices kindred sentiments about Romantic literature, for instance, "So much has romanticism debauched us, that, without some form of vagueness, we deny the highest."[25] Booth accuses modern fiction of a similar debauchery; just as Hulme unfairly denigrates Romanticism in order to exalt his own brand of Classicism, so Booth hands modern fiction the short end of the stick in order to reassert the worth of pre-Jamesian fiction and its predominant narrative styles. Yet, if it is invidious to use modern standards in judging Victorian fiction, there can hardly be virtue in using Victorian standards to judge modern fiction.[26]

The terms of Booth's criticism of the modern fictional experience turn out to be similar to those sometimes applied to Romantic poetry; perhaps the new standards necessary to judge modern fiction would therefore best be promulgated by reference to the standards we use to judge Romantic poetry. Some remarks by John Bayley are worth noting here: "One can hardly emphasize enough how little the early Romantic theories deserve such epithets as dreamy, exotic, eccentric, private, escapist—all the adjectives which have come by association to cling to the word Romantic—nor how much they require, on the contrary, such terms as practical, sensible, unifying, all-embracing, morally aware, and so on. But as the nineteenth century goes on, it is prose that qualifies more and more for these latter attributes of the liberated imagination, and verse the former."[27] Bayley's remarks bring us full circle to my general thesis, since, as noted above, he elsewhere suggests that novelists are the "real beneficiaries of the great Romantic endowment" (p. 15).

What we find in the modern novel is a work of literature closely resembling in its formal and structural attributes the great Romantic poems of the early nineteenth century. To remark the modern novel's Romantic aspects is not to diminish its status or to deny its genuine innovations or original characteristics. It is not to assert the "triumph" of Romanticism or even its "dominion." Metaphors of battle or struggle or mastery are fundamentally inappropriate, despite the belligerance of an Eliot or a Hulme. We have a perspective now that Eliot, Pound, and Hulme lacked. We can brush aside the ephemeral and the peripheral aspects of Romanticism, the misunderstandings of it, to reveal its lasting and far-reaching contributions to our way of perceiving the world. To study the Romanticism of James, Conrad, and Woolf is to acknowledge the significance and importance of their fictional worlds as expressions of, and guides to, the modern spirit.

TWO

Romantic Form: Poetry

Among the numerous modern commentators of Romanticism, a few seem to fall roughly into a group. It is to this "group" that I turn for a definition of Romantic form. I seek not a comprehensive definition of Romanticism, but some shorthand way of isolating and talking about the structural or formal properties that many Romantic works share. Therefore, the critical work that interests me is the work of writers like M. H. Abrams, Robert Langbaum, Albert Gérard, Karl Kroeber, and Northrop Frye, to name but the major figures. There seems to be some measure of agreement among these critics about the general attributes of Romantic form; although each writer sometimes has his own terminology, we can conveniently divide Romantic form into three related aspects—the organic, the experiential, and the creative. I shall offer a brief sketch of each of these aspects, but it is important that we not think of them as totally discrete categories. The requirements of language and the conventions of critical discourse ask us to speak as if the three are distinct from one another, but in reality they are merely ways to label different emphases of the same, single phenomenon. In other words, while we must think of Romantic form as a unified whole, it is sometimes easier to talk about that whole if we pay attention to one particular aspect of it in isolation. Moreover, what we are concerned with at bottom is the *effect* such a Romantic form has on a literary work. We shall therefore not be interested in mechanically cataloguing a work's experiential, organic, and creative aspects. I present this three-part Romantic form merely as a base on which to found my expositions of Romantic works; although I shall not often call attention directly to these specific aspects of Romantic form, they are the implicit focus of our discussion. Our explicit focus will be the consequences of this Romantic form.

The first aspect is the organic, the easiest of the three about which to find agreement, since it is a critical commonplace to consider organicism and Romanticism together. There are grounds for such a connection among both the original Romantics themselves (especially Coleridge) and modern critics. One of the latter has even called "the organicist or evolutionary idea" the "central idea of the nineteenth century."[1] The philosopher Ernst Cassirer assesses the impact of the concept of organicism this way: "The Romantic concept of the organism did not refer to a single *fact* of nature, a specific, limited group of objective phenomena. . . . For [the Romantics], the 'organism' signified not a particular class of phenomena, but a universal speculative principle, a principle which indeed constitutes the ultimate goal and systematic focus of Romantic speculation."[2] Once we grant the importance of organism, another question arises: how do we recognize it in literature? In other words, how does it affect literary form?

Graham Hough provides, in *The Romantic Poets,* the simplest working definition of *organic.* In examining two poems by Coleridge, he says: "They are a perfect type of romantic composition—meaning by romantic here something that grows according to an inner organic law, not something that is composed from outside according to a predetermined scheme."[3] Now there are two applications of this definition. We might apply it to the artist's aesthetic beliefs and conclude that attitude toward composition determines the organic character of the product. Or we might apply it to readers' responses and conclude that when we talk about the organic in literature we are referring to the impression the work makes on the reader. These two applications need not be mutually exclusive; each is valid. The second, moreover, is a logical outcome of the first; it is one consequence—to use again W. J. Bate's words—of a "deliberate romanticization of the aesthetic medium." As a rough generalization we might say that the first application of this definition of organic was the original Romantics' concern (although it did not preclude their revising and rewriting their works extensively) and the second was the concern of those writers, like Henry James, who were the inheritors of the Romantic tradition. Albert Gérard's remarks are especially illuminating here. He notes that although the Romantics often wrote of the problems affecting their work, there is no "concrete, detailed discussion of structure" in their writings. He goes on to consider the reason for this omission:

> Herbert Read's excellent definition of organic form will help us understand why this should be so: "When a work of art has its own inherent laws, originating with its very invention and fusing in one vital unity both structure and content, then the resulting form may be described as *organic*." This implies that the creative process is primarily expressive rather than constructive. In other words, the purpose of the poet is not to fabricate an artifact according to a formal pattern preexisting in his mind; it is to provide a total and accurate rendering of the germinal idea which stirs his imagination. If this is the poet's main preoccupation, the part played by conscious artistry—at least with regard to the overall structure of the poem—is bound to be rather slight, for the work of art in its progress from beginning to end will strive to reflect as faithfully as possible the movements of the artist's mind.[4]

What happens in the process of deliberate romanticization, we can conclude, is that conscious artistry comes to assume a more central position. The goal is still a total and accurate rendering of the germinal idea that stirs the artist's imagination; what is different is the artist's attitude toward the proper methods for rendering that idea. We have something far more complex than a simple return to composition "from outside according to a predetermined scheme," however; the motivating force behind the artist's efforts has changed. As Gérard suggests, if it is "the movements of the artist's mind" that are reflected in the Romantic work of art, then new kinds of organizational patterns will be discernible. While there may be continued or new interest in traditional aesthetic modes, the kinds of ideas or images contained within these modes will no longer be traditional, nor are they likely to be ordered within the work in traditional ways.

A case in point, discussed by Karl Kroeber at length in *Romantic Narrative Art*, is the Romantics' interest in traditional narrative ballads. Kroeber explains that "the evolution of Romantic lyricism is, in some measure at least, the gradual transformation of simple narrative structure as the basis of lyric organization into a discontinuous, non-narrative structure."[5] The logical coherence of Wordsworth's "A Night Piece," for example, "derives almost entirely from the narration of how the traveller's mind moves in harmony with the changes in the night sky" (p. 52). Kroeber calls this poem and others like it, particularly Keats's odes, visionary lyrics; in the best of these visionary lyrics a transmutation occurs of narrative elements into a discontinuous structure so that the images of such a poem "create a self-satisfying inner order, a non-logical continuity" (p. 58). The coherence of "Ode to a Nightingale" thus "derives almost entirely from the unity of [the speaker's] liberated feelings, from the dramatic invasion and counter-invasion of his conflicting sentiments, which do not correlate directly with the objective, external circumstances surrounding his vision" (p. 59).

There are two consequences of these Romantic experiments with narrative. One consequence is a significant impact on poetry in general. "The Romantic visionary lyric, then," Kroeber concludes, "led toward a poetry of intense subjectivity organized solely by the inner logic of vision, a poetry whose discourse transcended rational consistency, a kind of poetry which has perhaps attained its fullest development in our own day, and which found its finest expression during the Romantic age in the great odes of Keats, Shelley, and Wordsworth" (p. 63). The second consequence is the impact on fiction. Northrop Frye assesses part of its impact this way: "In any work of fiction there are two reasons why one episode succeeds another episode. One reason is that it is logically the next episode in the plot: the other is that the author wants it to come next. . . . From the Romantic movement on, the author's desire to have a certain episode come next may be independent of the requirements of the plot; or the plot may disappear in favor of a sequence depending solely on the author's will."[6]

Consequent to a concentration on an inner logic of vision, on the unity of the poet's feelings, must be a consideration of experience (the second important aspect of Romantic form). As Gérard says: "What matters is the idea, and the experience from which it arises. Everything which does not derive from the experience . . . must be rigorously proscribed" (p. 16). Another critic, Larry J. Swingle, sees Romantic poetry embodying "two main movements," one of which is primarily concerned with experience. This movement leads the reader into an exploration, an attempt "to grasp not doctrine but the 'primal stuff' of experience with which one must deal in order to generate doctrine."[7] The best and most important statement of the significance of experience to the Romantic vision, however, is Robert Langbaum's in *The Poetry of Experience*. Since he argues his case persuasively there, all we need do here is to look at his conclusions: the essential idea of Romanticism, according to Langbaum, is "the doctrine of experience—the doctrine that the imaginative apprehension gained through immediate experience is primary and certain, whereas the analytic reflection that follows is secondary and problematical. The poetry of the nineteenth and twentieth centuries can thus be seen in connection as a poetry of experience—a poetry constructed on the deliberate disequilibrium between experience and idea, a poetry which makes its statement not as an idea but as an experience from which one or more ideas can be abstracted as problematical rationalizations." As a result, the Romanticist "discovers through experience the empiric grounds for values" and is thus "always in the process of formulating values, although he never arrives at a final formulation." Moreover, "the process of experience is for the romanticist a process of self-realization, of a constantly expanding discovery of the self through discoveries of its imprint on the external world."[8]

A third and related area of interest is the aspect of Romantic form I have called creative. It derives from an aesthetic theory which, according to M. H. Abrams, sees art as expressive rather than mimetic or pragmatic. In analyzing this expressive theory of art in *The Mirror and the Lamp,* Abrams says: "In general terms, the central tendency of the expressive theory may be summarized in this way: A work of art is essentially the internal made external, resulting from a creative process operating under the impulses of feeling, and embodying the combined product of the poet's perceptions, thoughts, and feelings. The primary source and subject matter of a poem, therefore, are the attributes and actions of the poet's mind; or if aspects of the external, then these only as they are converted from fact to poetry by the feelings and operations of the poet's mind."[9] The point about the artist's mind as central to Romantic poetry is discussed by both Gérard and Kroeber as well. The emphasis is on the aesthetic consequences: the finished work, notes Gérard, "is the outcome of a genuine act of creation by which the idea shapes itself organically into adequate sensuous forms."[10]

There are several other points about Romantic form and

the experience of reading Romantic poetry that we shall need to consider later. For now, however, a conception of an organic, experiential, and creative form ought to suffice as a shorthand way of thinking about the effects of Romanticism on literary structure. To get a clearer sense of what it means to talk of such a Romantic form, let us analyze a representative Romantic poem: "Ode to a Nightingale." I shall offer neither a startling nor a new interpretation. Rather, I want to demonstrate how we can speak of this poem as Romantic in the sense we have just examined and to determine what kind of interpretation we can arrive at by so speaking of it. A useful way to appraise the Romantic nature of Keats's poem, I think, is to compare it to a poem that does not have a Romantic form. For the purposes of comparison, then, we shall also look briefly at Pope's "Ode for Music on St. Cecilia's Day."

The major difference between "Ode to a Nightingale" and "Ode for Music" is very clearly stated by Graham Hough's useful working definition of *romantic* in *The Romantic Poets:* "something that grows according to an inner organic law, not something that is composed from outside according to a predetermined scheme." In *The Romantic Assertion* R. A. Foakes suggests a historical reason for this new, Romantic aesthetic. He notes that poets writing in the eighteenth century and earlier "had been able to assume as their frame of reference a concept of an ordered and stable universe," but "the Romantic poets wrote for a society which could no longer be measured against a concept of order and degree. . . . The destruction of an external frame of reference led them to seek a principle of order within the individual, within themselves, to write of man and the world largely in terms of their own inner life, or their own self-sought, self-created relationship with God."[11] Foakes's "principle of order" is what Hough calls an "inner organic law," and it informs all Romantic poetry. The view of Romanticism enunciated by these two critics in fact comprises all three of our elements. Romantic poets examine their own imaginative experiences to create a work of art that impresses us as having grown organically. This is not to say that the Romantics exercised no aesthetic control or did not consciously order and shape their poetry. Rather, they sought to re-create their intuitive experiences in art. "The Romantic poet," says Foakes, "employed the power of 'self-intuition' to restore order to a world which had ceased to afford ready-made images of order, in the way it had done for Shakespeare and for Pope."[12]

Keeping in mind the general distinction that a pre-Romantic poem impresses us as having been written according to a predetermined outside scheme while the Romantic poem seems composed according to an inner organic law, let us now look specifically at the two poems, beginning with "Ode for Music on St. Cecilia's Day."

"Ode for Music" is an encomium on the occasion of St. Cecilia's Day, cast as an irregular Pindaric ode. While the choice of the Cowleyan variation allows Pope greater leeway in stanzaic structure than a regular Pindaric ode, many of the poem's major characteristics are immediately predetermined by the form he chooses: it will be a long lyric, its subject serious and its style elevated, and it will be composed of stanzas of irregular length and rhyme scheme (in this instance Pope selects a three-stanza strophe, an antistrophe of equal length, and a one-stanza epode). The selection and treatment of a serious subject and an elevated style will in turn themselves be predetermined—by contemporary poetic and social conventions, by the age's conception of order and degree. Since Keats's poem as well is an irregular Pindaric ode, it must be influenced by similar considerations of subject, style, and stanzaic structure; but since it is also an example of a major innovation in the nature of the ode itself, we must give most of our attention to other influences shaping each poet's particular handling of the form.

It is not so much the choice of the ode form, then, as the poetic and cultural values of the time that impose a sense of a predetermined scheme on "Ode for Music." Foakes's general summary of Pope's approach to nature reads like a paradigm for the poem: "Nature is 'methodized' in accordance with an aristocratic scale of order and value in society, which in turn is given the sanction of divine law."[13] In the strophe of "Ode for Music" just such a methodization is begun. In stanza 1, after a conventional opening device—an invocation to the muses: "Descend ye Nine! descend and sing"[14]—Pope introduces the poem's general subject, music and its power and effect, and describes its limitations and range, listing a representative selection of musical instruments (lyre, lute, trumpet, and organ) and kinds of musical sounds ("sadly pleasing," "shrill," "deep, majestic, solemn") which serve as norms against which other instruments and sounds can be measured. In the second stanza a scale of order and value in society is established for music. It becomes a mediator, capable of limiting or correcting ethical extremes: "By Music, minds an equal temper know, / Nor swell too high, nor sink too low" (22–23). Stanza 3 adumbrates the scale by including a permissible and socially desirable exception to music's mediating function: "But when our Country's cause provokes to Arms, / How martial music every bosom warms!" (36–37). These three stanzas—the strophic part of the ode—lay a logical groundwork, establish a scale of social order and value, and provide a conventional framework for the more specific subject the rest of the poem takes up: the antiphonal discussion of two of music's greatest moments, one—Orpheus'—only momentarily successful, the other—symbolized by the devotion of St. Cecilia—potentially humankind's greatest success because it makes possible the soul's entrance into heaven. This last—consideration of St. Cecilia—provides "the sanction of divine law" of which Foakes speaks.

If the strophe of "Ode for Music" embodies contemporary, publicly shared, and conventional sentiments about music and tries to define its universal aspects (rather than its personal or private effects), the antistrophe—stanzas 4 through 6—offers a poetically conventional discussion of a mythological subject. Similarly, the epode offers an acceptably "serious" conclusion to this eulogy of music by considering St. Cecilia and her dedication of music to God's service. It had been customary for poets to write poems honoring St. Cecilia for an annual festival of musicians in London on her name day, 22 November,[15] and as befits a poem for such a public occasion, the persona's voice throughout "Ode for Music" is public and official; it enhances the seriousness of the subject by its seemingly imperious, third-person tone. The persona states conclusions rather than explores elements of the subject, and his statement summarizes and epitomizes the cultural and social values of the time. Here is then the most important way in which we gain a sense of predetermination: we expect the poet to take the preexistent "what oft was thought"—a factor external to the poem—and express it in a way never so well essayed before. Pope does in short what we expect an Augustan poet to do.

Another kind of predetermined scheme informs the poem as well. "Ode for Music" conforms to literary convention in its contrasting of Classical subject matter with Christian material to make a religious or moral point. In this respect it may be likened to medieval *exempla* or to some Renaissance emblems. Although St. Cecilia is mentioned in the title of the poem, the effectiveness of her role in the last stanza depends on this external poetic convention and not on an organic, internal connection to the material of the other stanzas. Lacking knowledge of the convention, the reader might easily be startled at line 124 ("This the divine Cecilia found, / And to her Maker's praise confined the sound"), since so belated an introduction of St. Cecilia near the end of a poem in her honor might otherwise seem odd indeed.

But for the reader familiar with literature in which allusions to mythology are invoked in order to draw a parallel with Christian scripture or history, her seemingly unprepared-for introduction is easily accepted. The previous recounting of the Orpheus legend can then be seen in a new light: Orpheus is a natural choice of a Classical analogue for the Christian patron saint of music, since his feat is surely the most remarkable one concerning music that Classical mythology records. St. Cecilia's achievement, however, is superior, because she gains entrance to heaven while Orpheus fails in his efforts to retrieve Eurydice; in a Christian context, Cecilia's goal is itself also a more formidable and valuable one than Orpheus'. The scheme of the poem becomes lucid in the light of this poetic convention: as glorious as this Classical triumph of mythology is, it can never compare with the triumph of Christianity, a triumph which St. Cecilia's martyrdom well demonstrates.

Thus, while it might be possible to say that the contrasting of the mythological and the Christian in this manner is organic to the history of English poetics, it is not internally organic to "Ode for Music." The recognition that Pope has planned his poem to conform to and rely on this poetic tradition reinforces our sense of his depending on an external, predetermined scheme. Needless to say, this sense is what Pope wants us to feel, for it enriches the impression of universality he seeks to create.

The three, related aspects of Romantic form are clearly inapplicable to "Ode for Music." The predominant sense of an external, predetermined scheme that informs the poem disqualifies it as either organic or creative. It is self-evident that a poem patterned on a predetermined scheme cannot have grown according to an inner organic law. Nor can such a poem be considered creative. A poem composed according to an external predetermined scheme depends on a mimetic aesthetic, not an "expressive" or creative one. For the Romantic, as Gérard notes, "the finished work is the outcome of a genuine act of creation by which the idea shapes itself organically into adequate sensuous forms. And this idea, in its turn, is nothing other than the vision conveyed by the poetic experience."[16] The "idea" does not shape itself thus in Pope's ode, nor is such a vision conveyed by the poetic experience of his ode. For the neoclassic poet, a poem's "unity and ideal quality arise out of a strictly intellectual or technical operation"; they are arrived at "by treating general types according to fixed rules," while for the Romantic they are "the culmination of an organic process in which the poet creates a work which is a symbol."[17] The third aspect of Romantic form—the experiential—can also be eliminated because, as we have seen, Pope seeks to define not a personal, private experience of music but music's universal and public features. Indeed, so far is Pope from being interested in private or personal experience in this poem that he has done what no Romantic poet would ever do: he chooses a topic uncongenial to his own sensibilities. Here is Dr. Johnson on this very poem: "Poets do not always express their own thoughts; Pope, with all this labour in praise of musick, was ignorant of its principles, and insensible of its effects."[18]

If Pope's ode depends on a firmly established literary tradition as well as a set of social and publicly shared values which together impose a predetermined outside scheme on the poem, Keats's ode depends on a different aesthetic entirely: he develops the treatment of his subject in an associative, seemingly haphazard manner, relying on an accumulative process that obeys its own internal logic, creating, in Kroeber's words, a "self-satisfying inner order, a non-logical continuity" (p. 58).[19] The speaker of "Ode to a Nightingale" continually and abruptly shifts from one image or concern to another, letting the poem flow on in an exploratory, apparently unbalanced manner. Yet the poem coheres, its coherence deriving, as Kroeber explains, "almost entirely from the unity of [the speaker's] liberated feelings, from the dramatic invasion and counter-invasion of his conflicting sentiments, which do not correlate directly with the objective, external circumstances surrounding his vision" (p. 59).

The Cowleyan ode Pope is writing represents a fairly substantial break from the strict form of the regular Pindaric ode; the Romantic ode Keats is writing departs further. One might divide "Ode to a Nightingale" into a three-stanza strophe, four-stanza antistrophe, and one-stanza epode, but such an asymmetrical structure alone—Pope's ode is divided 3–3–1—would seem to indicate that the formal requirements of the ode are by no means the primary guiding principle of Keats's poem. Even if its structure were more like a regular Pindaric ode, other aspects of "Ode to a Nightingale" would still remain the center of our attention. Some structural principle other than the one on which Pope based "Ode for Music" is discernible here.

The disparity between Keats's approach and Pope's is immediately apparent in the strophe of "Ode to a Nightingale."[20] I shall therefore spend some time examining the development of these three stanzas to see how they cohere; and for the moment I should like to conduct this examination developmentally, that is, I should like to trace step by step the reader's experience as he or she goes through the poem for the first time, assuming here a reader familiar with Romantic poetry.[21] (By "reader" I also imagine an ideal reader who is able to see connections immediately that in reality might take several readings to perceive.)

Whereas Pope began his poem with a (traditional) invocation to the muses, "Ode to a Nightingale" opens with an intensely personal statement:

> My heart aches, and a drowsy numbness pains
> My sense, as though of hemlock I had drunk,
> Or emptied some dull opiate to the drains
> One minute past, and Lethe-wards had sunk,

(1–4)

followed immediately by a statement of the ostensible cause for the speaker's condition:

> 'Tis not through envy of thy happy lot,
> But being too happy in thine happiness.   (5–7)

The experience here presented is at a polar opposite from the measured and controlled description of music introduced in the first stanza of "Ode for Music." Rather than the ordered and balanced definition of the range and limits of musical effect that we saw in Pope's ode, this stanza offers a deliberately blurred and imprecise evaluation of an experience resulting from (or perhaps it is in conjunction with) a strong reaction to a nightingale's song. Why the persona feels dispirited because he is too happy with the bird's song (or with the bird's ability to sing "in full-throated ease") is not explained or explicitly accounted for; moreover, the nature of that dispiritedness itself is only vaguely evoked—there is a confusion in the opening lines of the poem among physical, spiritual, and metaphorical discomfort, as well as between sleep and death. "My heart aches" could describe a literal situation ("There is a physical pain in my chest") or a figurative one ("I am greatly dispirited"), while "a drowsy numbness pains" is oxymoronic (numbness would normally indicate lack of pain). Similarly, Keats exploits the varying effects of poisons, which, in small dosage, produce a narcotic state ("drowsy numbness"), and, in large doses, death. Moreover, he deliberately confuses the expected effects of different poisons. Hemlock, which is usually considered fatal (i.e., not normally used as a narcotic, as, for instance, belladonna might be), here produces the drowsy numbness, while "some dull opiate," which should normally cause numbness or sleep, leads the persona to an oblivion associated with death ("Lethe-wards").[22]

The connection between the first two stanzas of Pope's

ode was explicit and logical. By contrast, the second stanza of "Ode to a Nightingale" has at first glance only a casual, seemingly nonlogical link to the first stanza, a link that is supplied by the reader's knowledge of the effects of the various drugs mentioned in the poem so far. The bulk of the second stanza (eight lines) comprises an elaborate and ecstatic paean to a "draught of vintage" in specific, sensual detail ("With beaded bubbles winking at the brim, / And purple-stainèd mouth" [17–18]). Now alcohol bears a resemblance to the opiates in the first stanza in that both are drugs used to lessen the pains, physical or psychological, that the world can cause; here is what I call an external link between the first two stanzas, external because the reader supplies a connection based on the ordinary logic he or she might use in everyday life, although as we have seen in respect to the effects of various drugs in the first stanza, the persona of the poem appears not strictly to adhere to such logic. Moreover, in as much as the wine here has the opposite effect from the opiates in the first stanza, the connection can at best be called tenuous. Some link between the first and second stanzas exists in the persona's mind that is not apparent at this point to the reader—at least to readers applying the kind of standard logical requirements that served them well in reading "Ode for Music."

The last two lines of the second stanza, however, present the possibility of a different kind of connection: "That I might drink, and leave the world unseen, / And with thee fade away into the forest dim" (19–20). The drinking of wine appears now designed to effect a union with the nightingale or an approximation of its state. In both the first and second stanzas there is a continuity supplied by the nightingale's song, which has acted as a stimulus to the speaker's thoughts. We can perceive a unifying factor in the speaker's response to the nightingale's song. This is an important discovery because we now recognize that we will be given not what oft was thought but what *once* was thought, uniquely and idiosyncratically, by the persona of this particular poem. The persona's response in stanzas 1 and 2 does not follow a predictable or inevitable pattern, and his thoughts are not expressed or conceived as conventional or publicly shared notions about one's response to the song of birds or to music. The poem grows by, through, and with the persona's private experience. It grows, in other words, according to an inner organic law created by the persona's imagination.

If the conclusions so far are correct, they ought to be confirmed by stanza 3, and indeed this stanza adds a new dimension to the reader's slowly increasing knowledge of the connection between persona and nightingale that helps put the poem into clearer focus. The persona envies the nightingale for what it has never known and he desires to forget

> The weariness, the fever, and the fret
>   Here, where men sit and hear each other groan;
> Where palsy shakes a few, sad, last gray hairs,
>   Where youth grows pale, and spectre-thin, and dies.
>   (23–26)

This stanza suggests, then, a reason for the persona's desire to join the nightingale—to escape from an unhappy world of human suffering, where death is everpresent. In retrospect, the persona's discomfort in stanza 1, as well as his admiration in stanza 2 for the anesthetic properties of wine, seems to be clarified and made relevant by this exposition of human woe. A clearer sense of what this poem is about begins to emerge for the reader—or at least the several threads of ideas with which the persona has been working appear to be combining to form a single strand. The song of the nightingale, which the persona imagines to lead an innocent, happy, and charmed existence, prompts him to speculate on oblivion and forgetfulness and ways to escape from the physical and psychological ills of the world. Furthermore, the discussion of wine can now also be seen as a preliminary (perhaps unconscious) testing of a different method (other than through external physical stimuli) to escape—through the imagination.

Just as the general subject of the strophe—the relationship between persona and nightingale—grows and develops slowly over the course of the first three stanzas, so too are the topics and concerns of the remaining stanzas explored and constructed according to an internal, organic logic. On the surface, the four stanzas of the antistrophe deal randomly with disparate material: stanza 4 specifically considers the power of poetry to offer transcendence from ordinary thinking ("though the dull brain perplexes and retards" [34]), and to effect an instant and magical transformation from physical to imaginative reality ("Already with thee!" the persona exclaims as he joins the nightingale in an imaginative world populated by the "Queen-Moon" and her "starry fays"). Stanza 5 offers an imaginative reconstruction of the nightingale's thicket in highly sensual terms, while in the sixth stanza the persona abruptly expresses an intense, overt death wish. The last stanza of the antistrophe contrasts the ability of the nightingale's song—which is evidently at this point a surrogate for an object of art—to endure through time with the individual's mortality and frailty. There is yet another shift in the epode as the persona breaks his reverie and the nightingale flies away.

Despite an initial, surface impression of a kind of incoherence here, these stanzas—and the whole poem—do hang together. Why? Because the local shifts and changes of topic are dependent on a larger, internal frame of reference that reveals their organic relationships to the whole and to each other. [23] Once the poem is considered in its entirety, what may have struck us at first as abrupt shifts in the persona's focus of attention can be perceived as integral, organic parts of his exploration of the relationships between not only himself and the nightingale but also human suffering and the means to escape it, and between imagination and reality, the eternal and the finite, art and life, the self and the world. The poem has a kind of systolic movement, so that, while the death wish in stanza 6 may seem suddenly introduced—because it follows a stanza that has just dealt with a sensual awareness of nature and life—in a larger frame of reference the concentration on the desire to die, coupled with questions of mortality and immortality in the following stanza, is a natural subject for this poem to take up: death and dying have been important considerations all along. The treatment of death here, however, can in no way be called systematic, as might Pope's discussion of death and immortality in "Ode for Music."

While the various subjects that Pope takes up are ordered around the conventional poetic scheme of the contrast between the Classical and the Christian, the persona of "Ode to a Nightingale" does not arrange the subjects he deals with in a predetermined pattern. He does not subordinate one of his subjects to any of the others—each is examined for itself and seems to develop moment by moment, the persona granting each new thought equal consideration. This is not to say that the structure of "Ode to a Nightingale" is haphazard or accidental. There *is* a guiding principle: the persona's individual and idiosyncratic experience (the very particular, personal speculations prompted by his hearing the nightingale) is the center of the poem. Here is the larger frame of reference which puts the individual elements of the poem into perspective and which enables us to see coherence in it. Here also is the second of our three elements of Romantic form, the experiential. This second element is intimately connected to the first since, as we have seen, the exploration of the persona's experience is conducted organically.

This focus on experience automatically shapes the persona's outlook—changes the way in which he sees reality—in a manner that would have been impossible for Pope. As

Robert Langbaum tells us in *The Poetry of Experience*, for the poet who adheres to what Langbaum calls the doctrine of experience, "the imaginative apprehension gained through immediate experience is primary and certain, whereas the analytic reflection that follows is secondary and problematical" (p. 35). One might almost say that the imaginative apprehension gained through immediate experience is the guiding principle of every stanza of "Ode to a Nightingale"; never does the persona seem to rely on an *analysis* of his experience to guide him. He comes closest to offering an evaluation of the total experience of the poem in the last stanza: "Adieu! the fancy cannot cheat so well / As she is fam'd to do, deceiving elf" (73–74). This thought might have been the occasion for a discussion of aesthetics, of fancy and imagination (neither of which topics would be irrelevant to the rest of the poem), but instead the persona avoids any attempt to analyze the experience. Unlike the epigrammatic, conclusive, climactic last lines of "Ode for Music"—"His numbers raised a shade from hell, / Hers lift the soul to heaven"—which summarize that poem's central contrast, the ending of Keats's poem is uncertain and inconclusive. The persona cannot assess his experience, cannot draw from it the same kind of neatly balanced statement that Pope's speaker does. The persona of "Ode to a Nightingale" ends tentatively with two questions: "Was it a vision, or a waking dream? / Fled is that music:—Do I wake or sleep?" (79–80). Without analytic reflection and without a reliably fixed external framework, distinctions of this kind—was it vision or waking dream?—are difficult, if not impossible, to make.

But such distinctions are never the issue for Keats in the first place, as they might be for Pope. As Langbaum says, Keats's persona penetrates the nightingale's song imaginatively until he gains a "new intensity of understanding" in stanza 7, when "in the vision of the 'magic casements,' he achieves the insight which includes all the others, which, including both joy and pain and standing both inside and outside the world of sense and time, is finally adequate to the original perception." But, Langbaum continues, the insight is enigmatic and lasts only an instant. The final stanza seems to deny the rest of the poem unless we recognize that "the thing we are left with is the thing the observer is left with—a total movement of soul, a step forward in self-articulation" (p. 51). As Langbaum says elsewhere (of "Tintern Abbey"): "The meaning of the poem is in all that has accrued since the original vision, in the gain in perception. But the gain is rather in the intensity of understanding than in what is understood" (p. 46). Here is the crux of the difference between Keats and Pope. For Pope the reverse of this situation applies: the intensity of understanding (in the sense that Langbaum means it) is irrelevant or even undesirable.

Inherent in our discussion of the poem's organic and experiential nature has been an assumption of its creativeness as well. That is, the poet's activity in attempting to define and explore his own experience is a creative rather than a mimetic one. He does not seem to be recording reality but discovering it. He has not set out to imitate or to copy nature but to discover, to see things anew, to express his experiential reality in a "new" language. In stanza 1 we saw him defying the logical requirements of our everyday language in the discussion of death and sleep and the various narcotics that could produce each state. Our ordinary frame of reference was momentarily jarred out of focus, while the poem created what we might call a new linguistic reality, the linguistic reality of the poem's persona, the logic of his mind as it responds, uniquely, to experience.

THREE

Romantic Form: Fiction

It is self-evident that a literary form like the novel must meet structural requirements different from those of a lyric ode. Our efforts now must be to determine in what ways it is possible and profitable to speak of Romantic form as a fictional phenomenon as well as a poetic one. That is to say, at which aspects of a novel must we look to decide if its form is Romantic? Karl Kroeber gives us a clue in *Romantic Narrative Art*. "Movement of perspective or point of view," he notes, "appears to be the narrative equivalent of the dialectical tensions so important to lyric and dramatic poetry."[1] I suggest that the area in which Romantic form is best to be discerned in fiction, and through which we may best approach it, is that of the more inclusive category under which movement of perspective and point of view are included: narrative mode. The kind of narrative mode chosen to convey the fictional world has been recognized, since the appearance of Wayne Booth's *Rhetoric of Fiction*, as perhaps the most sophisticated tool that novelists have at their call. The choice of narrative mode ranks equally with other aspects of technique like characterization, plot development, imagery, and diction; or perhaps it surpasses them, since the type of narration necessarily determines to a large extent how these other aspects are perceived by the reader.[2] Let us, then, consider some general and theoretical features of the narrative aspects of fiction and of their relationship to Romanticism.

The obvious place to begin is with Wayne Booth. He replaces conceptions like "omniscient narrator" and formulations like "exit author" with a whole range of considerably more sophisticated categories: narrators may be narrator-agents or observers (i.e., dramatized or undramatized), who are reliable or unreliable, commenting or silent, self-conscious or naive, isolated or supported, and who "can be either privileged to know what could not be learned by strictly natural means or limited to realistic vision and inference" (the category "complete privilege" coincides with what is usually called omniscience).[3] Booth also introduces the idea of the "implied author," an element essential to an understanding of a narrator's reliability. The passage in which he explains his use of *reliable* and *unreliable* is worth quoting at some length:

> For lack of better terms, I have called a narrator *reliable* when he speaks for or acts in accordance with the norms of the work (which is to say, the implied author's norms), *unreliable* when he does not. It is true that most of the great reliable narrators indulge in large amounts of incidental irony, and they are thus "unreliable" in the sense of being potentially deceptive. But difficult irony is not sufficient to make a narrator unreliable. Nor is unreliability ordinarily a matter of lying, although deliberately deceptive narrators have been a major resource of some modern novelists. . . . It is most often a matter of what James calls *inconscience*; the narrator is mistaken, or he believes himself to have qualities which the author denies him. Or, as in *Huckleberry Finn*, the narrator claims to be naturally wicked while the author silently praises his virtues behind his back.
> Unreliable narrators thus differ markedly depending on how far and in what direction they depart from their author's norms; the older term "tone," like the currently fashionable terms "irony" and "distance," covers many effects that we should distinguish. Some narrators, like Barry Lyndon, are placed as far "away" from author and

reader as possible, in respect to every virtue except a kind of interesting vitality. Some, like Fleda Vetch, the reflector in James's *The Spoils of Poynton,* come close to representing the author's ideal of taste, judgment, and moral sense. All of them make stronger demands on the reader's powers of inference than do reliable narrators.

(Pp. 158–59)

While unreliable narration, as Booth goes on to suggest, is symptomatic of modern fiction in general and, I should add, of novels with a Romantic form in particular, an unreliable narrator *per se* is not an indication of Romantic form. Rather, the way in which narration (reliable or otherwise) is used determines whether a novel has a Romantic form. We need to decide not whether the narrator speaks for or acts in accordance with the norms of the work, but whether the implied author believes that she or he speaks for or acts in accordance with public values shared by his or her contemporaries. Here in another guise is the point Daiches makes in *The Novel and the Modern World.*[4] The major pre-Jamesian novelists—Fielding, Richardson, Austen, Dickens, Thackeray, Eliot, Trollope, Hardy, Meredith—tend to leave us with a sense of public significance, a sense that objective moral judgment is both possible and necessary, a sense that the norms of their (fictional) worlds share a common ground. On the other hand, the novels of many modern writers—James, Conrad, Ford, Lawrence, Woolf, Joyce—tend to leave us adrift, to cut us off from judgments based on shared moral standards. If these modern novelists are united, it is by a recognition that they cannot share joint solutions to moral problems held in common, but must each seek unique solutions to self-defined moral questions. Modern novelists favor unreliable narration because it more accurately reflects that uncertainty of modern life they portray in their fiction. In its ordinary sense, reliability is precisely one of the things that existence in the modern world makes untenable, and one can hardly adopt the pose of narrative reliability to announce that reliability is impossible. In contrast, to use one of Booth's examples, the unreliability of Barry Lyndon is employed as a counterpoint to the values Thackeray knows the reader will share with the implied author. The narrator's unreliability, like that of the unreliable narrators of most other pre-Jamesian novels which employ such narration, throws into relief the implied author's "reliability."

The distinction between the possibility of moral judgments based on shared public standards in the pre-Jamesian novel and its impossibility in the post-Jamesian novel should in no way be thought rigid or absolute, for, as both Daiches and John Bayley point out, the loss of a publicly shared principle of selection and significance occurred not at one distinct historical moment but gradually over the course of the nineteenth century.[5] For example, despite a number of readings, both contemporary and modern, to the contrary, I would argue that *Vanity Fair*, in its demonstration of the inadequacy of Victorian moral standards, comes close to developing what today we might call an existential view of reality.[6] A similar sense of the inadequacy of popular moral standards—of their hypocrisy[7]—can be felt in the novels of Dickens and Eliot, although, unlike *Vanity Fair*, their novels are informed by a sense that, while popular standards are perhaps not functioning properly, some kind of shared standard, based on a humanist world view, is possible and operable—that, in other words, what is necessary is the replacement, the revision, or the upgrading of current standards. Thackeray's novel, like many modern novels, seems to deny the relevance of publicly shared standards to the human condition at all and to suggest the impossibility of maintaining such a shared social morality.

Even though the values of the implied author must be the general and overriding object of our consideration, the necessary final check in determining Romantic form, the implied author remains just that—implied. Both the presence and the values of the implied author are an implicit rather than an explicit part of the novel, and in order to gain a focus on what is implicit, we need to pay a good deal of attention to what is explicit: the narrator. We should not forget that it is the relationship between the narrator and the implied author that determines the former's reliability. Keeping in mind the qualifications of the preceding paragraph, we may venture some generalizations about the kinds of narrators we are likely to meet in pre- and post-Jamesian novels.

The narrator of a typical pre-Jamesian novel might be described this way: reliable (in Booth's sense); the most knowledgeable "character" in the novel; capable of judgment, a faculty he or she does not hesitate to exercise; the arbiter of morality and correct behavior for the world of the novel, who consciously and explicitly sets the standards by which we are to make our own judgments, which presumably will agree with the narrator's for the most part. As we shall see in a moment, the narrator of *Adam Bede* is a representative example of this kind of pre-Jamesian narrator. An important variation is the dramatized, first-person narrator of novels like *Jane Eyre, Great Expectations,* or *The Way of All Flesh,* who, because she or he is a participant in the events related, functions as judge or moral arbiter in a somewhat different manner. In each of these last examples, a special relationship exists between the "I" who tells the story and the "I" who has lived the story, so that the narrator is able to judge the actions of his or her own younger self and to provide a final moral balance to the novel. But, again, as in the case of unreliability, the larger context must be examined: the total effect of this kind of narrator is much the same as the dramatized third-person or undramatized third- and first-person narrators of other Victorian novels; they share a similar sense of common public moral standards. By way of comparison, we might consider the role of Marlow in *Heart of Darkness.* While on the surface he resembles Pip, for instance, in that he seems to offer judgments of his younger self, the cumulative effect of the elder Marlow's remarks is to cloud the issues he raises and to heighten, rather than relieve, his and our uncertainty. He admits his inability to evaluate or even fully to comprehend his experience in the Congo and by this admission blocks any simple or easy assessment of it on our part.[8]

The narrator of a typical modern novel, like Marlow, is either incapable of or uninterested in making judgments that the reader can be expected to endorse. The flux of modern experience—as has been noted many times before—seems to yield no moral order at all, invalidating as well the traditional morality that some Victorians vainly sought to preserve. The modern narrator seems only infrequently to be the most knowledgeable character in the novel; she or he is often unreliable (in both Booth's and the ordinary sense). Consequently, the narrator's function as moral arbiter becomes untenable. In the case of these kinds of unreliable narrators, like John Dowell of *The Good Soldier,* the moral judgments they make are discovered to be misguided or even willfully incorrect, because of their personal limitations and their vested interest, as it were, in the story they tell. In instances of impersonal narration—where a third-person narrator restricts us to another character's single point of view ("The Aspern Papers" is a good example)—the narrator often makes no explicit moral evaluations at all; sometimes he or she leaves the reader to depend on the "lucid reflector," who is frequently unreliable in very much the way that Dowell is in *The Good Soldier.*

If one way in which we can identify the Romantic form of a novel is to see whether the implied author speaks for or acts in accordance with public values shared by his or her contemporaries, a second way is to consider the consequences of narrative experiments prompted by the Romantic aesthetic. There is, to use Karl Kroeber's terms, a "gradual transformation of simple narrative structure" in the modern novel "into a discontinuous, non-narrative structure" (p. 51). Henry James begins the change with his experiments with point of view and unreliable narration (especially in his short stories), while Conrad and Woolf, among others, help to complete the transmutation "of narrative elements into a discontinuous structure," to bring about the creation of "a self-satisfying inner order, a non-logical continuity" (p. 58) in the structure of the novel. The effect of Woolf's fiction, as Ralph Freedman suggests, is sometimes quite similar to the effect of a lyric poem. To be more particular still, I would say the effect is not of just any lyric, but of Romantic lyrics, of the poems Kroeber calls visionary lyrics. The effect is present not just in *Mrs. Dalloway* or *To the Lighthouse,* but in *Heart of Darkness* and *Lord Jim* as well. In other words, allowing for the change in genre, we can recognize that the structural properties of many modern novels are similar to those of many Romantic poems.

The best way to see the consequences of the Romantic aesthetic on the form of the novel is to consider a specific example of a novel with a Romantic form. For this purpose I shall analyze Mary Shelley's *Frankenstein.* This work is a good choice because if we examine a novel contemporary with Romantic poetry, questions of "modernism" and what it is will not confuse the issue at hand—how we can talk about a novel's form as Romantic. Fortunately, such a contemporary novel with a Romantic form does exist; most other "Romantic" novels, as Robert Kiely defines them, share "some of the thematic and stylistic characteristics evident in the new poetry and drama of the time,"[9] but they are not fully congruent in form or structure in the way that *Frankenstein* is. We can again benefit from a comparison, however, so that I shall discuss Shelley's novel in conjunction with a novel that does not have a Romantic form, George Eliot's *Adam Bede.*

Frankenstein and *Adam Bede* are a logical choice of novels to consider together in that both make explicit use of Miltonic echoes and parallels. The way in which the two novelists work this Miltonic material into their narratives very clearly distinguishes one from the other. Shelley uses it in a typically Romantic fashion, and Eliot uses it to reinforce a narrative mode antithetical, as we shall see, to the Romantic aesthetic. The Miltonic parallels in *Adam Bede* are a contribution of the implied author rather than the narrator. Although the narrator does mention Milton in passing, he does not himself point out any likenesses or draw any contrasts between the central figures in the novel and the characters of *Paradise Lost*.[10] The presence of the Miltonic parallels emphasizes the fact that Eliot's novel is constructed to give the reader a sense of a complete moral universe, one in which she or he will have no difficulty distinguishing commendable behavior from unacceptable or disreputable actions. Eliot's use of literary reference works along side narrational commentary to reinforce a sense of operable public moral standards.

In *Frankenstein* the Miltonic material is a matter for the attention of both the implied author and the several narrators. It is the implied author who arranges to have the monster find a packet containing, among other books, a copy of *Paradise Lost*. However, the monster himself comments in his narrative to Frankenstein on the similarity of his position to that of both Adam and Satan: " 'Remember that I am thy creature; I ought to be thy Adam, but I am rather the fallen angel, whom thou drivest from joy for no misdeed.' "[11] And it is not only the monster who defines himself in terms of Milton's Archangel; near the end of the novel Frankenstein himself notes: "All my speculations and hopes are as nothing; and like the archangel who aspired to omnipotence, I am chained in an eternal hell" (p. 200). Now, whereas we might describe Eliot's use of Milton as an attempt to establish fixed points of outside reference through which the judgments of the narrator are silently endorsed by the implied author, Shelley's use of Milton is shifting, nondefinite, inconclusive. In *Adam Bede*, these literary allusions provide external standards—they work in conjunction with the outside social and moral standards the implied author creates and uses—while in *Frankenstein* they have significance primarily as internal reference points through which the various characters attempt to define themselves. Their meaning is relative, not intrinsic; they have value insofar as they are tools of self-exploration.

If *Adam Bede* seeks the fullest possible illumination and explication of moral experiences through a continual measuring of individual situations against an internal social standard, the total narrative movement of *Frankenstein* is directed elsewhere: Frankenstein's extreme pride in seeking to create life ultimately yields no abstractable conclusions for us about human nature, except perhaps a reiteration of human fallibility. It is difficult to extract a usable "moral" from this tale. "Don't try to give life to inanimate objects" speaks to a specific situation in which scant few of us can expect to find ourselves, while anything more general— "The search for knowledge is fraught with peril" or "One must bear the responsibility for the consequences of his or her search for knowledge"—would require a great deal of preparatory qualification and explication to be made specifically relevant to the novel and would have severely limited value outside its particular embodiment within it. No good literature can be easily reduced to a one-line moral, but some literature, like *Adam Bede*, because it keeps reminding the reader of external social values, can be profitably examined in the light of a general moral proposition like, for example, pride goeth before a fall.[12] The point here is that some works, *Adam Bede* for one, ask us to think of the situations they contain in terms of such moral formulations, while other works, like *Frankenstein*, present the situations within them as starting points for the examination of human experiences, experiences which fail to yield conclusive results but which continue to open out into new areas and further mysteries. Despite E. M. Forster's contention that death is congenial to a novelist because it provides a finality,[13] death offers no true finality, as we shall see, to Frankenstein's moral quest as far as the reader is concerned. To speak in the terms Alan Friedman uses to discuss the modern novel, we could say that the ending of *Frankenstein* is open: at its end the moral experience of the novel seems to continue rather than to conclude.

Having established a general difference between the two novels, let us now look at each individually. The narrator of *Adam Bede*, in Wayne Booth's terminology, is an undramatized, but commenting, first-person narrator, who is both partially privileged, since he does not have complete omniscience about the characters in the novel, and isolated, since he does not have support from the other characters and does not converse with them but instead functions outside their world (with the exception that the narrator says he has spoken with Adam; see chapter 17). Moreover, the narrator is reliable; his values are consonant with those of the implied author. It is through the establishment of the narrator's reliability—that is, through the means by which the reader sees the narrator speaking for or acting in accordance with the norms of the implied author—that a sense of public significance and selection is generated in this novel; and it is this sense that prevents us from calling *Adam Bede* Romantic in form. There are two closely related facets to the creation of this public sense; both are functions of the implied author's endorsement of the narrator. One is the narrator's comments, the other the shaping and patterning of and within the chapters.

Authorial or narrational intrusion is a much-discussed topic in studies of the novel; Booth's *Rhetoric of Fiction* is the buoy at the edge of the cove alerting us to the complexities of the subject. An equally insightful contributor on this issue is W. J. Harvey. Writing before the appearance of *The Rhetoric of Fiction* and hence unable to take advantage of the subtleties of Booth's approach, Harvey examines, in *The Art of George Eliot*, the narrational intrusions in *Adam Bede* and reaches several conclusions relevant to my particular point here. Harvey makes no distinction between narrator and implied author or between implied author and the actual author herself, but if we read "narrator" where he writes "omniscient author" we can give a new validity to his observations. He contends that the "omniscient author" is a bridge or link between "the fictional microcosm of the characters and the macrocosm of George Eliot and the real world," that what might seem a "clumsy intrusion of the author" has a "necessary function in establishing the kind of 'reality' of the story being told"; it is an "illusion of reality"

> not of a self-contained world, a fictional microcosm intact and autonomous as in the Jamesian mode, but a world coterminus with the "real" world, with the factual macrocosm. . . . George Eliot speaks of life as a "mixed entangled affair" and that phrase aptly expresses not only the nature of life within the fictional microcosm but also the relationship of that microcosm to the real world that you and I and George Eliot inhabit. She is not aiming at the insulations, the self-sufficiency of the Jamesian novel; no sharp boundaries between real and fictional are to be drawn here; the edges are blurred and the author allows us easy transition from one world to the other.[14]

But in order for this kind of illusion of reality to be successful, the intrusive moral comments must have an intrinsic value. "If they repel the reader or provoke his dissent they will fail in their purpose" (p. 81). Upon close examination we discover that "most of them are commonplaces, truisms, platitudes about life and human behavior"; they are "generally neither dramatic gestures, rhetorical embellishments demanding an overwrought emotional response from the reader, nor are they the dogmatic assertions of a particular philosophy; rather they are, in the main, the sober, unemphatic and mature statement of those great commonplaces of human nature, those basic facts of life that underlie all human situations, real or imaginary" (pp. 82–83).

I think Harvey is correct in identifying the comments of the narrator as commonplaces, although, as he notes, while they express commonplaces, they are not themselves commonplace (p. 83). That these comments are truisms or platitudes is *prima facie* evidence of a common agreement between Eliot and her readers on what is significant in human experience and what ought to be selected for embodiment in her novel. They cannot be commonplaces without common agreement; part of the reason some modern readers react so adversely to such narrational comments is precisely that they are no longer the expressions of a common agreement between author and reader. If asked why James would not—or could not—aim at a fictional microcosm like Eliot's, we would need to seek more than an aesthetic answer; the reason must be philosophical as well. In his and our real world we can no longer be sure of the "basic facts of life that underlie all human situations," can no longer be sure, for that matter, that there are any such basic facts in the first place. It is not that there can be no agreement at all about the significance of an experience but that no agreement can be taken for granted. Eliot does take such an agreement for granted. She endows her narrator with sagacity, confident that the reader will not question his credibility as long as his remarks are commonplace and not "idiosyncratic or tendentious," qualities which "would draw his reader's attention away from the proper object of his contemplation" (Harvey, p. 82).

In the introduction to his edition of *Adam Bede,* John Paterson says: "We must fully believe in such fictional existences as Adam's and Arthur's, Hetty's and Dinah's, by virtue of the fact that a narrative presence and voice we've learned to trust so obviously does."[15] I suggest that there are two reasons for granting that trust. First, the narrator's comments carry "the 'weight of lived experience' in a way that guarantees their validity" (Harvey, p. 83). Second, the implied author endorses and supports the narrator's remarks; that is, the narrator is reliable. In this instance, the narrator's literary reliability, in Booth's use of the term, reinforces our own sense of his personal reliability, that is, his trustworthiness. The clearest example of this reinforcement is the manner in which the pervasive theme of appearance versus reality figures in the novel.

Throughout *Adam Bede* the appearance—of a character, an event, a physical place—is never sufficient for judgment; our sight must be keener, we must look deeper, past the surface. What we see there need not automatically contradict the appearance, but it will almost always modify it. Mrs. Irwine articulates the extreme statement of the position which the weight of the novel seeks to correct: " 'Nature never makes a ferret in the shape of a mastiff. You'll never persuade me that I can't tell what men are by their outsides. If I don't like a man's looks, depend upon it I shall never like *him*. I don't want to know people that look ugly and disagreeable, any more than I want to taste dishes that look disagreeable. If they make me shudder at the first glance, I say, take them away. An ugly, piggish, or fishy eye, now, makes me feel quite ill; it's like a bad smell' " (ch. 5, pp. 56–57). The fates of the major characters in the novel demonstrate the inaccuracy of Mrs. Irwine's manner of judging people. Hetty Sorrel is irresistibly agreeable to look at, but the outward shell conceals the inner weakness: she has never developed any inner resources with which to resist her vain aspirations of becoming Arthur's wife or from which to draw strength during her ordeal on the road and at the trial. Arthur Donnithorne's outer appearance as well augers strength of character, yet the exterior is misleading: like Hetty, Arthur is weak, deluded by the deference of his friends and tenants into mistaking the appearance of his being a good, upstanding squire for the reality of it. The qualities impressed upon us by Adam's and Dinah's outward appearance are also modified during the course of the novel but in less violent and more subtle ways. Adam's physical strength turns out to be a fair corollary for an inner resilience. Although as severely tested as Arthur, Adam pulls through, a better person because less proud and more cognizant of human fallibility, his own as well as others'. Dinah learns that it is better to be less zealous in her Evangelism, since too fiery a zeal is ultimately a vanity as bad as Hetty's. Dinah learns to be less the religious fanatic and more the religious humanist.[16]

Now this facet of the theme of appearance and reality in the novel is part of the ethos of the implied author. Since the narrator claims to be merely reporting events he has heard, the material and the shape of those events result from Eliot's efforts, not her narrator's. Eliot's construction of the novel's plot reinforces the narrator's comments. When the narrator suggests a contrast between Hetty and Dinah in chapter 15, for instance, the point he makes is confirmed by subsequent events. So also is his judgment of Parson Irwine validated by the Parson's actions in the novel.

The narrator himself calls our attention to other aspects of this theme of appearance and reality, aspects which, again, the implied author makes sure are supported and verified. For example, in the chapter "The Hall Farm," the narrator explicitly remarks the disparity between the farm's apparent physical age and state of disrepair and its occupants' vitality; we are not to judge the life at the farm by a rusty gate or a broken pane. The most important discussion of this theme occurs in chapter 17, "In Which the Story Pauses a Little," perhaps the most famous chapter in the novel. Here the narrator argues for realism in art, an aesthetic position which is a logical counterpart of the ethical position which the novel takes on outward appearance. If we judge only on appearance, then we will come to prefer, like Mrs. Irwine, surface beauty, and we shall run the risk of mistaking the shallow for the ideal. No, rather the ugly but true picture, proclaims the narrator, than the handsome but false. Beauty will follow truth, the truth of human sympathy: "human feeling is like the mighty rivers that bless the earth; it does not wait for beauty—it flows with resistless force and brings beauty with it."

> All honour and reverence to the divine beauty of form!
> Let us cultivate it to the utmost. . . . But let us love that
> other beauty, too, which lies in no secret proportion,
> but in the secret of deep human sympathy. . . . In this
> world there are so many . . . common coarse people,
> who have no picturesque sentimental wretchedness! It is
> so needful we should remember their existence, else we
> may happen to leave them quite out of our religion and
> philosophy, and frame lofty theories which only fit a
> world of extremes. Therefore let Art always remind us of
> them; therefore let us always have men ready to give the
> loving pains of a life to the faithful representing of com-
> monplace things—men who see beauty in these com-
> monplace things, and delight in showing how kindly
> the light of heaven falls on them.   (Ch. 17, pp. 152–53)

Many critics cite this chapter to elucidate Eliot's position on realism in fiction; I quote this passage for another reason. The remarks in this chapter may be vital and useful to an examination of Eliot's aesthetics, but they are also vital and useful in establishing the narrator's reliability. The novel itself strives to achieve the Wordsworthian goals the narrator enunciates in the passage above: his comments and the implied author's goals are here interlocked. This is what reliable narration is—a reinforcement of the norms of the implied author's world by those of the narrator, and vice versa. The jointure is so smooth that it is sometimes difficult to talk about the implied author's goals and those of the narrator in different terms. Nevertheless, there is a distinction to be made, and we see it quite clearly here: the narrator announces Wordsworthian goals but it is actually the implied author who effects them.

As it happens in this case, the manner in which the narrator's reliability is affirmed also reinforces our sense of Eliot's dependence on a public agreement about significance and selection. The narrative movement of *Adam Bede* is directed toward illumination of moral situations and social experiences, and Eliot endeavors to construct for the reader a sense of a complete moral universe in which proper and commendable actions are easily distinguished from suspect and unacceptable ones. Necessary for such completeness, as Harvey explains, are those bridges and links to the real world. Such purposes as these must be founded on well-established common grounds; they must start with common assent, else the mode of narration, instead of creating the necessary link with the external world, will turn "into a cul-de-sac, leading us nowhere, or worse, [will turn] into a path leading us away from the novel into an area of intellectual discourse remote from the body of the particular life in the novel" (Harvey, p. 81). Without a common agreement about what is significant in experience and what should be selected for a work of art, the narrator's comments, so necessary for the effective creation of Eliot's fictional world, would be misread and misunderstood, in perhaps the way some twentieth-century critics, applying criteria derived from James for a world without such common agreement, have indeed misread and misunderstood them.

Although the sense of public significance and selection on which *Adam Bede* depends is enough to disqualify its form as Romantic, specific reference to the three elements of that form will reinforce the point. Like Fielding's narrator of *Tom*

Jones, the narrator of *Adam Bede* tells us that he is reporting history. He is at pains throughout the book to keep us conscious of the sixty-year difference between the occurrence and the narration of the novel's events. Several critics have commented on this emphasis on time in *Adam Bede*.[17] Karl Kroeber notes its influence on characterization: "Time, in past's relation to the present, is of overwhelming importance in *Silas Marner*. In Eliot's other novels time is only slightly less important. . . . For Eliot, characterization is temporal. Even her minor, consistent, or 'flat' characters (such as Mrs. Poyser) are consistent because they adhere to historically determined attitudes and codes of behavior. And all of Eliot's protagonists have an individualized history both 'in' and 'outside' the action of their novels." Hence time has a strong patterning effect on her novels; "Eliot's fictional worlds," Kroeber says, "are composed of multiple decorums . . . diversely articulated patterns [which] are regarded by Eliot as historical phenomena. . . . Eliot frequently draws our attention to the typicalness of her characters, though most often the character is representative not of a general type but, instead, of a specific pattern of historically determined social circumstances."[18]

Concentration on specific patterns of the kind illustrated here destroys any sense of organic or creative form. Adherence to historically determined attitudes or codes of behavior in the development of fictional characters is antithetical to aesthetic organicism because "history" implies that some sort of predetermined scheme has been identified on which events and characters will be shaped and that the narrative mode of the novel will seek the illusion of reportage rather than imaginative discovery. Even if the selected historical scheme were, say, the organic growth of personality, the reader might have little sense of the novel itself growing organically since its own form might in fact have been externally predetermined. This is not to say that a novel with an organic form could not have a very carefully shaped pattern; what is important is our sense, at least on first reading, of that pattern's having grown according to an inner organic law which is apprehended imaginatively. No such illusion is present in *Adam Bede;* in fact, an opposite effect is consciously aimed at.

Harvey suggests two possible relationships between reader and novel, "contemplation" and "imaginative participation." The latter is "appropriate to the Jamesian mode" (and to Romantic literature), the former to George Eliot's novels: "The fictional microcosm that George Eliot creates is, as Leavis would say, *there* in all its rich truth and complexity, but it is a world surely designed for our contemplation, not for our imaginative participation" (p. 79). If contemplation is the activity Eliot solicits from the reader, an organic or creative form is of no particular necessity; such a form might even hinder her purposes since it could divert her readers by forcing them to spend time and energy on identifying the idiosyncratic, nonlogical order the author has bestowed on the work of art (idiosyncratic comments by the narrator are one of the things that threaten to "draw the reader's attention away from the proper object of his contemplation" [Harvey, p. 82]). Contemplation, as Harvey defines it in opposition to imaginative participation, would not be a particularly useful way of approaching a work with a form like that of "Ode to a Nightingale," for instance, because for Keats, in Robert Langbaum's words, "the imaginative apprehension gained through immediate experience is primary and certain, whereas the analytic reflection that follows is secondary and problematical."[19] It is just this analytical reflection—contemplation—that Eliot seeks.

Moreover, Eliot herself helps us to eliminate the creative part of our triumvirate through the narrator's insistence that he will "mirror" reality. Such a mimetic approach is suggested in the very first lines of the novel: "With a single drop of ink for a mirror, the Egyptian sorcerer undertakes to reveal to any chance comer far-reaching visions of the past.

This is what I undertake to do for you, reader" (ch. 1, p. 5). This approach is elaborated further in chapter 17 when the narrator contends that his "strongest effort is to avoid any . . . arbitrary picture, and to give a faithful account of men and things as they have mirrored themselves in my mind. The mirror is doubtless defective; the outlines will sometimes be disturbed, the reflection faint or confused; but I feel as much bound to tell you precisely as I can what that reflection is, as if I were in the witness-box narrating my experience on oath" (ch. 17, p. 150). In a word, the narrator seeks as best he can to report faithfully what happened; he will not try to interpret or shape history to make a specific point or push a particular thesis about human nature. This effort is consistent with his moral commentary because, as we have seen, his "intrusions" function more to blur the edge between fiction and reality than to point a simple moral. *Adam Bede* very definitely asks us to contemplate moral positions, but the thrust of the novel is to embed our considerations in a properly complex and subtle context that has a historical and social validity.

We cannot, then, call this novel's form organic or creative. Nor can we describe it as experiential, for reasons suggested by John Paterson: "All great art was by definition didactic, George Eliot believed. Every great artist was inevitably a teacher. What he was asked to teach, however, was not the facile and arbitrary truth of the self but the mixed and mysterious truth of the world, not his own narrow and eccentric morality but the more generous and inclusive morality inherent in life itself" (p. xii). If one sees the truth of the self as facile and arbitrary and its morality as narrow and eccentric, then one would be unlikely to seek a model for aesthetic form, as the Romantics did, in a process of discovery through experience. Experience, in one form or another, is the material of all literature; but some writers, whom we can call non-Romantic, tend to treat experience as a given, a *fait accompli*, a human fact which we need to study and interpret almost as we would an archeological artifact; while other writers, Romantic writers, use experience as a starting point, a means, a tool for a continuing process of self-exploration and self-discovery. For the Romantic the "mixed and mysterious truth of the world" is inseparable from the "truth of the self." The non-Romantic writer seeks to interpret existence in the light of a given structure of social and moral values, but the Romantic, to quote Langbaum again, is "always in the process of formulating values, although he never arrives at a final formulation" (p. 26). *Adam Bede* gives us no sense of a continual formulation of values; rather, it gives us the application of commonly agreed-upon moral and social values to the rich and complexly unfolding lives of its protagonists.

The most obvious feature of the narrative structure of *Frankenstein* is the use of three separate narrations, Walton's in the letters to his sister and his journal, Frankenstein's to Walton, and the monster's to Frankenstein. Its narrative structure might be thought of as a box within a box within a box or a series of concentric circles. Perhaps the latter image is the better since the monster's narrative at the center of the novel acts as a kind of vortex for the conflicts and dilemmas the novel embodies. One recent critic of Gothic fiction, J. Douglas Perry, Jr., considers a structural vortex (in which "the fear of being drawn in and the image of the whirlpool find their expression") to be "the over-all gothic structure."[20] Perry goes on to cite J. Hillis Miller's remarks on the effect of such concentricity in fiction: "To watch a play within a play is to be transformed from spectator into actor and to suspect that all the world may be a stage and the men and women merely players. To read a narration within a narration makes all the world a novel and turns the reader into a fictional character."[21] To turn "the reader into a fictional character" is another way of referring to the relationship between reader and novel that Harvey calls "imaginative participation," although such participation may be achieved without the use of a narration within a narration. Imaginative participation is an essential element of Romantic literature; therefore, the narrative frame of *Frankenstein* is important in establishing its Romantic form, as necessary to Shelley's purposes as the sagacious first-person narrator of *Adam Bede* is to Eliot's. But the value of the narrative framework lies in more than fostering the reader's imaginative participation: it serves as well as an important controlling device.

Karl Kroeber makes a point in *Romantic Narrative Art* especially pertinent here. He suggests that "narrative as it appears in [Romantic] lyrics is an element of logical or rational organization; it implies a conception of experience as objectively apprehendable: 'If I tell you what occurred you will know what happened to me.' But the experiences which are the sources of the poems' energy are purely subjective and creative; they cannot be told about; we must be made to participate in the poet's vision" (p. 58). Mary Shelley sets herself a task that she approaches in a way similar to that of the Romantic poets of whom Kroeber speaks: she tries to talk about—and thus to define, to set the boundaries of, to limit—what is essentially a purely subjective and creative experience and hence an ultimately indefinable, illimitable, objectively unfathomable experience, that is, Frankenstein's creation of life and his subsequent struggle to cope with the consequences of this act. As Robert Kiely notes, "If the phenomenon itself [i.e., the monster] cannot be named, neither can the feelings it evokes in its maker. No one can know what it is like to be the monster or its 'parent' " (p. 159).

Shelley's task is not unlike that facing other novelists who choose similar narrative forms. At least two writers who have used elaborate narrative structures like that of *Frankenstein* come to mind immediately: Emily Brontë in *Wuthering Heights* and Joseph Conrad in *Heart of Darkness* and, especially, *Lord Jim*. Each of these works, like Shelley's novel, has at its center an explosive, potentially unwieldly, and uncontainable moral experience. The complicated narrative structure of *Frankenstein*, like that of *Wuthering Heights* and *Lord Jim*, is necessary to keep the violent material of the novel—its moral experience—within bounds. Otherwise, the novel threatens to fly apart, to burst out of the bounds of its formal requirements altogether. The moral consequences of Frankenstein's actions are not containable and they eventually consume him, just as Catherine and Heathcliff's love cannot be limited by the grave but smolders within Heathcliff until it burns him out, and just as a moral force within Jim cannot be satisfied but compels him to self-destruction on Patusan.

In *Frankenstein*, as in Brontë's and Conrad's novels, no one consciousness within the novel is really able to encompass the whole story or to measure its full import. Shelley's three narrators are in the same position that she herself is in: each of the narrators confronts events from a particular vantage point and a limited perspective; each tries to force the reader into participation in his vision, just as Shelley seeks to force the reader into participation in hers; and each seeks to do internally in the novel what Shelley tries to do for the reader: to use narrative to establish a sense of order, of logic and rationality. Walton, Frankenstein, and the monster all pretend (in Kroeber's words), "if I tell you what occurred you will know what happened to me," but the real source of each narrator's vision of experience is purely subjective and creative and cannot be told about. In this respect, *Frankenstein* is like a Romantic poem.

The similarity of the novel to a Romantic poem will be even clearer if we look at a passage from *The Poetry of Experience* in which Langbaum is speaking of "Frost at Midnight": "The meaning of the poem is in all that has accrued since the original vision, in the gain in perception. But the gain is rather in the intensity of understanding than in what is understood. . . . For here, as in *Tintern Abbey*, the revelation is not a formulated idea that dispels mystery, but a perception that advances in intensity to a deeper and wider, a more inclusive, mystery. The sudden advance in intensity gives a dynamic effect, a sense of movement, of the moving, stirring life of the mystery" (p. 46). Most of what Langbaum says of Coleridge's poem is true of *Frankenstein* as well; we can especially see the relevance if we look specifically at the monster's narrative and its function in the novel. It works in the same way that the final vision of "Frost at Midnight" does. Although he purports to explain how he has become a homicidal fiend, the monster does not dispel any mysteries in his narration; rather, it is a revelation "that advances in intensity to a deeper and wider, a more inclusive, mystery."

The crux of the monster's Godwinian apologia is that while he was basically good to begin with, the hostility of other people, and particularly of his creator, forced him to become evil; their rejection of him wrought a severe and hideous change in his nature. "I was benevolent and good," he says; "misery made me a fiend" (pp. 95–96). The monster's situation certainly appeals to the reader's sympathy, and the sympathy he gets is well deserved; but his narrative fails to convince nevertheless. First, no amount of misery can justify his murdering William and his framing of Justine, a totally innocent bystander. Second, the monster has himself told us of an exception to the bleak picture of human nature he offers in De Lacey, the blind man who remains kind and generous despite a life of considerable misfortune. The monster's explanation does not clear up the mystery of his actions: Frankenstein is right to distrust his motives. Far from settling any moral questions, the monster's narrative complicates Frankenstein's own moral dilemma as well as our task as readers.

Without the monster's narrative, the moral experience embodied in Frankenstein's fate, while still difficult and resistant to easy solution, is at least fairly simply defined: he must face up to the consequences of his attempt to usurp the power to create life. He has blundered frightfully, creating a soulless, heartless, homicidal monster whose repulsive exterior mirrors an inner evil and blackness, the natural result, one might conclude, of the tampering of a mere fallible human with divine prerogative.[22] With that narrative—the plangent cry of a sensitive, intelligent, morally aware, initially well-intentioned being who has suffered cruel rejection by his own creator as well as by those from whom he sought love—the moral problem Frankenstein faces takes on almost limitless complexities. In the light of the monster's request for a female companion and threat of violence if his wish is not granted, there can be no thought that Frankenstein's problems will ever be manageably limited or even that they will ever be easily defined. Frankenstein's bizarre pursuit of the monster—bizarre in that the hunter cannot always be told from the hunted—is evidence enough of this point. What is more, the moral problem at the heart of Frankenstein's experience is not ended—that is, not limited—by death: for the reader, this moral experience goes on after Frankenstein's death, it continues after the novel stops. The power of the novel lies in this sense of an ongoing moral experience.

The sense of an ongoing moral experience demonstrates another of the novel's similarities to Romantic poetry. The ideas of responsibility and corrupted innocence are its central moral questions, what Larry Swingle would call its "doctrinal elements." Such a doctrinal element in a Romantic poem "functions as part of a piece of data, and works to create questions in our minds"; it functions "as a means of raising questions not only about itself but about matters beyond itself."[23] Thus do the doctrinal elements of this novel function as well: the monster's narrative raises the question of Frankenstein's responsibility in a dramatic manner and forces us to question our own notions of moral responsibility. One result of the questioning which his narrative prompts, and which the structure of the novel makes unavoidable, is a disruption of the reader's equilibrium; this too is a feature of Romantic poetry. One "main movement" of Romantic poetry "is an attempt," says Swingle, "to disrupt a reader's equilibrium, to break down his sense of order and cast doubt upon the doctrines he holds when he comes to poetry. The effect is to gain a suspension of the reader's sense that the cosmos is well and solidly structured and that he has a good grasp of that structure" (p. 977). It would be hard to imagine a reader of *Frankenstein* whose sense that the cosmos is well or whose grasp of its structure was not threatened by this novel.

Both Swingle (p. 980) and Kroeber (p. 58) stress the reader's participation in Romantic poetry; as we noted above, the same participation happens in *Frankenstein*. But the nature of the reader's participation in a novel is bound to be quite different from his or her participation in a lyric poem. In this instance, the reader must take on a role none of the narrators is equipped to perform. As we said, no one consciousness in *Frankenstein* is really able to encompass the whole story or to measure its full import. Moreover, none of the three narrators is reliable—that is, none acts or speaks in accordance with the values of the implied author. The reader, turned into a fictional character by the narration within the narration, must assume the function of the reliable narrator instead. Readers of the novel, then, make connections no individual narrator or consciousness within it can make, and thus, although the final moral experience of the novel is immeasurable, they are granted a momentary power to glimpse, to hold in mind, the immeasurable, the unfathomable, by virtue of their role as reliable narrator. Despite its occasional awkwardness or patches of poor writing, the effectiveness of the novel stems in part from the power it thus grants its readers.

Now the question of moral experience is a complex one for this novel; it is also essential to our understanding. Here again, the narrative structure must be our guide. None of the novel's narrators represents the norms of the work; each is limited in his understanding of the others' experience and of the total import of the novel. But each narrator interprets his experience in moral terms, and each takes a strong moral position that is inadequate to encompass the experience of the other two. The novel nevertheless seems cast as a moral tale, a fact emphasized by Shelley in her additions to the third edition. In that edition Frankenstein ostensibly agrees to tell Walton his story in the first place so that the younger man will not make the same mistakes that he has: " 'I imagine that you may deduce an apt moral from my tale, one that may direct you if you succeed in your undertaking and console you in case of failure' " (p. 28). But note the ambiguous "I *imagine* that you" and the flexibility of the deduced moral that will serve not as a guide, a principle to live by, but as a rationalization of a completed event, functional whichever way Walton's fortune may go. Just as this "moral" is no moral at all—nor was it meant to be—the other instances of conventional morality in the novel function only to create an illusion that the events narrated are subject to ordinary moral standards, some publicly agreed-upon system of values applicable to human behavior. As I have already suggested, this illusion is necessary to impose a sense of order required by the nature of the novel's subject matter, which might be too easily seen as blithering fantasy instead of a serious attempt, as Percy Shelley tells us in his 1817 preface, to use the supernatural to afford "a point of view to the imagination for the delineating of human passions more comprehensive and commanding than any which the ordinary relations of existing events can yield" (p. xiii). Thus, because of the manner in which the novel is constructed, the real moral problem of *Frankenstein* is an experiential problem: it cannot be comprehended or even approached outside its embodiment in Frankenstein's, the monster's, and Walton's experiences; it cannot be apprehended outside the reader's direct experience of it.

If the reader is to become a "reliable narrator," then his or her experience must be consistent with the implied author's values. But if each of the novel's three narrators is unreliable, where are we to look for the norms of the work? How are we to determine what the implied author's values are? The answers to these questions are already at hand: since *Frankenstein* works like a Romantic poem it will have the same goal. The goal of a Romantic poem, according to Langbaum, is in part "to establish the reader's sympathetic relation to the poem, to give him 'facts from within' ": "For to give facts from within, to derive meaning that is from the poetic material itself rather than from an external standard of judgment, is the specifically romantic contribution to literature; while sympathy or projectiveness, what the Germans call *Einfühlung*, is the specifically romantic way of knowing" (pp. 78–79). Thus *Frankenstein*, like the particular kind of Romantic poem Langbaum wishes to trace, the dramatic monologue, will exploit "the effect created by the tension between sympathy and moral judgment" (p. 85); indeed, both Frankenstein's and the monster's narrations are themselves types of dramatic monologues. The norms of the novel, then, will be similar to the values a typical dramatic monologue embodies: "Arguments cannot make the case in the dramatic monologue but only passion, power, strength of will and intellect, just those existential virtues which are independent of logical and moral correctness and are therefore best made out through sympathy and when clearly separated from, even opposed to, the other virtues" (p. 86).

Now passion, power, and strength of will and intellect are precisely the virtues with which *Frankenstein* asks us to sympathize, but here's the rub: if both Frankenstein and the monster possess these virtues, and both do, with which character are we to sympathize? It cannot be both, since to sympathize with Frankenstein is to disbelieve, as he does, the sincerity of the monster's promise to exile himself with a newly made bride far from human society, while to have sympathy for the monster is to brand Frankenstein heartless and cruel for his skeptical treatment of him—yet this is exactly what the novel asks us to do: sympathize with both characters. As Langbaum says of Cain and Faust: "Our only course is to build a new moral world with them, to see what they see and learn what they learn with as unreserved a sympathy as we give to Wordsworth in *Tintern Abbey* or *Resolution and Independence*" (p. 60). I think it is this paradoxical situation that has driven several critics, notably Richard Church, Muriel Spark, and Harold Bloom, to conclude that Frankenstein and the monster are in some way two halves of the same being.[24] It would certainly help to resolve the paradox if we could interpret *Frankenstein* this way, but I do not believe the novel supports such a reading; we shall not so easily get round the problem.

It is an experiential problem we need to face directly. One might conclude that here is a flaw in the novel, for what Shelley has done is to offer competing claims on our sympathy. It is one thing to have only Frankenstein or only the monster to hold our undivided attention and sympathy, but another thing altogether to have to choose between Frankenstein and his creation. Yet if it is an aesthetic mistake to evoke strong sympathies for both Frankentein and the monster but not offer unequivocal grounds for a final moral judgment of one character over the other, the mistake is entirely consistent with the values the novel argues for: sympathy, compassion, suspension of moral judgment, the need to value life and people as they are rather than as we would ideally like them to be—in short, the values that the dramatic monologue in particular and Romantic poetry in general seek to endorse. A common experience in Romantic poetry, as Larry Swingle says, is the author's "catch[ing] the reader up in open-ended questions and expanding possibilities" (p. 978). Such a catching the reader up is one result of the competing claims for sympathy embodied in *Frankenstein*.

If the reader is caught up in "open-ended questions and

expanding possibilities" and if the poetry of experience is a "poetry constructed upon the deliberate disequilibrium between experience and idea, a poetry which makes its statement not as an idea but as an experience from which one or more ideas can be abstracted as problematical rationalizations" (Langbaum, pp. 35–36), so is *Frankentein* constructed on such a disequilibrium between experience and idea as well. Any comment predicated on the notion that the novel makes its statement as an idea, such as this one by a recent critic, that *Frankenstein* is "an extended homily on the dangers of ambition," is bound to sound false.[25] This critic has been led astray, perhaps, by what Swingle calls the "doctrinal assumption"; the novel certainly exploits the experiential consequences of various characters' ambitions, but if we are to address ourselves to the question of ambition at all we must do so with full knowledge that we are confronting a problematical rationalization about each character's experience, not an explanation of it. As Swingle says: "Rather than raising questions in order to move toward a presentation of doctrine, Romantic poetry tends to do quite the opposite: it employs doctrine in order to generate an atmosphere of the open question"(p. 975). So too is an atmosphere of the open question generated in *Frankenstein* by the discussion of ambition. Moreover, to consider this novel a homily on anything is to accept at face value the idea that Frankenstein has a moral purpose in telling Walton his story; it is to ignore Frankenstein's plea that after his death Walton pursue and destroy the monster, a plea only halfheartedly retracted later; it is to ignore as well his equivocal final words, which undermine whatever moral force his advice might seem to have: " 'Seek happiness in tranquility and avoid ambition, even if it be only the apparently innocent one of distinguishing yourself in science and discoveries. Yet why do I say this? I have myself been blasted in these hopes, yet another may succeed' " (p. 206). If this be homily, heaven help the reader seeking spiritual edification.

Romanticism informs every aspect of the novel; the aesthetic properties of the novel as a whole are mirrored in the experiential problems of its characters. If the novel uses narrative as an element of logical and rational organization, so does each of its narrators. If the novel works the way a dramatic monologue does, so do the "monologues" of Frankenstein and the monster and even, in a slightly different way, Walton's letters. The implied author of *Frankenstein* impresses us with a sense that the formulation of values is continuous, that we can never achieve a final formulation (this is the position of the Romanticist). Frankentein himself is in the same situation: he recognizes that his pursuit of the monster is both futile and compulsory. It is futile because its ultimate aim is to achieve a finality that is impossible, since what he is chasing is not really his physical creation, the monster, but some solution to the terrible and monstrous moral questions that he has previously tried to avoid but which were merely exacerbated while the monster one by one murdered the people Frankenstein loved. It is compulsory because only through his pursuit will he be continuously forced to live up to the responsibility of formulation and reformulation of values. Frankenstein's final speech to Walton seems to sum up very neatly the moral dilemma he faces: is he responsible to his own creature or to the rest of humanity? But both his need to articulate again a position he has stated several times before and his tentatively proposed, tentatively withdrawn request that Walton continue where he has left off indicate his inability to reach a final formulation of what he calls his duty. The process of formulation goes on for Frankenstein right up to the moment of death:

"Think not, Walton, that in the last moments of my existence I feel that burning hatred and ardent desire of revenge I once expressed; but I feel myself justified in desiring the death of my adversary. During these last days I have been occupied in examining my past conduct; nor do I find it blamable. In a fit of enthusiastic madness I created a rational creature and was bound towards him to assure, as far as was in my power, his happiness and well-being. This was my duty, but there was another still paramount to that. My duties towards the beings of my own species had greater claims to my attention because they included a greater proportion of happiness or misery." (Pp. 205–06)

Walton may wish to take this at face value, but we cannot. In the first place, there is no way of knowing whether Frankenstein's "higher" duty would have been necessary at all had he met the requirements of his first duty toward his creation instead of being sickened and running away the moment the monster opened his eyes. In fact, as Ellen Moers points out, the emphasis of the novel "is not upon what precedes birth, not upon birth itself, but upon what follows birth: the trauma of the afterbirth."[26] It is this trauma, his own as well as the monster's, that Frankenstein refuses to confront directly and honestly. In the second place, for all practical purposes Frankenstein has failed his second duty as well as his first: once the monster has eliminated all the people Frankenstein held dear he is no longer a threat to "beings of [Frankenstein's] own species." The monster chooses from the beginning to wreak revenge on his creator, not humankind at large. Frankenstein's real duty was to William and Clerval and Elizabeth, not to his species. Moreover, it is astonishing that Frankenstein finds his past conduct blameless. Is his sin that in a fit of enthusiastic madness he created a rational creature or is it that in a fit of repulsion and irresponsibility he abandoned that creature—ill-prepared though he was—to himself?

Frankenstein's inability to reach a conclusive stance toward the proper course of action, toward his own responsibility, is further illustrated by his request of Walton to finish what he has begun. First he renews the request: " 'When actuated by selfish and vicious motives, I asked you to undertake my unfinished work, and I renew this request now, when I am only induced by reason and virtue.' " Then immediately follows a retraction: " 'Yet I cannot ask you to renounce your country and friends to fulfill this task.' " But Frankenstein seems less concerned with the moral propriety of his request than with pragmatic considerations: " 'Now that you are returning to England, you will have little chance of meeting with him.' " Having presented some of the facts, he backs off altogether, leaving Walton with the burden of the choice: " 'But consideration of these points, and the well balancing of what you may esteem your duties, I leave to you' " (p. 206). Luckily for Walton, the immediate arrival of the monster resolves the issue for him.

The larger issue, however, is not resolved for the reader, just as such larger issues are never "resolved" in Romantic poetry. "The major difficulty Romantic poetry presents to many readers," notes Swingle, "is its open-endedness. The poetry offers questions, exposes problems, uncovers data. It casts doubt upon supposed certainties, and it suggests possible new directions for thought. Romantic poetry stirs the mind—but then it leaves the mind in that uneasy condition" (p. 980). *Frankenstein* presents the same difficulty of open-endedness. The subsequent appearance of the monster after Frankenstein's death—an appearance in which the monster offers a kind of minor reprise of his earlier narrative at the center of the novel—reaffirms the dialectic and reestablishes his claims on our sympathy. For despite the omissions, misinterpretations, dodges, and incorrect evaluations in Frankenstein's deathbed speech, his position remains generally valid: the monster has performed cruel and inhuman deeds of violence and evil in murdering Frankenstein's friends and relatives, and we have no sure way of establishing the credibility Frankenstein refuses to grant him. Forewarned by Frankenstein, Walton is suspicious of the monster's "powers of eloquence and persuasion" (p. 209), but these powers, precisely those of a dramatic monologue, carry the day for the monster, at least as far as the reader's sympathy is concerned. By acknowledging the horror of his deeds, attributing them to a force beyond his control, and effectively rendering his own remorse and suffering (" '[Frankenstein] suffered not in the consummation of the deed. Oh! Not the ten-thousandth portion of the anguish that was mine during the lingering detail of its execution. . . . My heart was fashioned to be susceptible of love and sympathy, and when wrenched by misery to vice and hatred, it did not endure the violence of the change without torture such as you cannot even imagine' " [p. 208]), the monster wins our sympathy even while denying that anyone could sympathize with him (" 'Yet I seek not a fellow feeling in my misery. No sympathy may I ever find' " [p. 209]). Walton, who earlier has felt indignation "rekindled within me" at the monster's words, offers no final comment or assessment of the monster's remarks but merely describes his departure, "borne away by the waves and lost in darkness and distance," thus ending the novel.

But as I have said before, if this is the end it is not the conclusion. While the monster gains sympathy he does not establish unimpeachable credibility. If he was "the slave, not the master, of an impulse which I detested yet could not disobey" (p. 208) in his determined effort to destroy his creator, then perhaps Frankenstein was right in fearing for the safety of all humankind. Just as we sympathize with Frankenstein's motives for denying the monster's request while we acknowledge his guilt in failing to assure for his creature even a modicum of happiness and well-being, so do we sympathize with the monster's plight in being rejected by all whom he encounters while we condemn his revenge and distrust the sincerity of his motives. And there, inconclusively, the situation stands at the end of the novel. Or does it? *Frankenstein* is not after all so unlike

"Ode to a Nightingale" in this respect. In a way the rings of narration impose a systolic action on the novel: we move from Walton's introductory letters to half of Frankenstein's story to the monster's narrative, then back through the rest of Frankenstein's story to Walton's final letters, which contain a brief recapitulation of both Frankenstein's and the monster's monologues. The change back and forth from one narrative consciousness to another offers the reader an experience similar to the experience of moving through the vacillating moods and ideas of the persona of Keats's poem. In both cases, it is the total step forward in articulation and understanding that counts, the accrual of meaning and experience, the gain in perception—in this instance, for the reader to a greater extent than for any individual consciousness within the novel.

The vortical structure of the novel, the pattern imposed on it by the concentric narrations, might be considered the "configurations of particular content" that "reveal a certain temporal *gestalt,* a coming and going, a rhythmical being and becoming" (to use the words of Ernst Cassirer).[27] This experience of rhythmical being and becoming is deeply organic and creative in nature. It takes its shape from a natural object, a whirlpool, and it depends for its effect on the establishment of an essentially nonlogical continuity built up gradually one step upon the other. By his or her active participation the reader creates the novel along with the implied author. Because of this creation through the reader's imaginative participation, commonly agreed-upon external standards are inapplicable to the novel. Indeed, given its extraordinary subject matter, one would be hard put to find appropriate external standards in the first place. Like "Ode to a Nightingale," *Frankenstein* creates its own moral priorities.

FOUR

Henry James

With the appearance of Henry James on the literary scene, the novel came into its own. His career marks a change in both the novel itself and its position on the scale of aesthetic value; a fictional form was altered and critical perceptions and judgments about fiction were given new shape and direction. James was responsible for the novel's beginning to receive serious critical attention, attention which has continued and intensified. If there were temporary excesses (e.g., the dismissal of Victorian narrative modes as crude or inept) the balance has been amply redressed in recent years by critics like Wayne Booth and W. J. Harvey. Indeed, I think we can easily put aside the question of Victorian versus Jamesian modes of fiction altogether and go on to suggest some possible reasons for the fictional differences wrought by James and other novelists contemporary with him.

It is appropriate that we begin our consideration of Romantic form in the modern novel with James. He is the transitional figure: his earlier novels, like *The American*, are brilliant examples of the traditional novel of the nineteenth century, while, starting with the shorter experimental stories of the 1890s—stories that developed fictional ideas and techniques some of which were first masterfully suggested in *The Portrait of a Lady*—and culminating in the three major novels of his career in the opening years of the new century, his later work gives us the first examples of the refashioned novel, the preliminary modern attempt to embody a vision of experience in the novel that had formerly been primarily the domain of poets. James was one of the first novelists to feel the sense of public agreement about what was significant in experience ebbing away, one of the first to realize that the old fictional forms would no longer do and that new ones would have to be evolved to keep pace with the new vision of society and the individual's role in it (new, that is, for novelists). In a sense, society as a whole was beginning to catch up with the Romantic avant-garde of the early nineteenth century: James intuitively recognized the path that novelists had to take to do so as well. Yet he had lived most of his life in the nineteenth century, and he still clung in his fiction to certain conventions and ideas, to a certain sense of social structure, that had very little relevance for younger novelists like Conrad, Woolf, Joyce, and Lawrence. On the surface, then, James's novels will appear at times to be of the old school, but their vision of experience and the deeper impulses of their structures mark them as belonging to the new one.

James and the Romantic Aesthetic

If, as I have suggested, James's critical discussions mark the initiation of a deliberate romanticization of the aesthetic medium of the novel, we should be able to recognize our three aspects of Romantic form in those discussions, although we can expect some modifications or alterations, both because of the change in form from poem to novel and because of the new element of conscious aestheticism. It also follows that someone engaged in such an endeavor will emphasize manner more than matter, technique more than subject. James does exactly this in "The Art of Fiction." But it would be a mistake to assume that an emphasis on technique necessarily implies a new or different aesthetic. Nor should we think that such an emphasis means per force that the writer believes, as Maurice Beebe says of James, that technique is "more important" than subject.[1] James specifically wants "to guard myself from the accusation of intimating that the idea, the subject, of a novel or a picture, does not matter."[2] " 'The story,' if it represents anything," James says, "represents the subject, the idea, the *donnée* of the novel; there is no 'school' . . . which urges that a novel should be all treatment and no subject." He goes on to stress this point:

> This sense of the story being the idea, the starting-point, of the novel, is the only one that I see in which it can be spoken of as something different from its organic whole; and since in proportion as the work is successful the idea permeates and penetrates it, informs and animates it, so that every word and every punctuation-point contribute directly to the expression, in that proportion do we lose our sense of the story being a blade which may be drawn more or less out of its sheath. The story and the novel, the idea and form, are the needle and thread, and I never heard of a guild of tailors who recommend the use of the thread without the needle, or the needle without the thread. (AF 400)

What James seems to be getting at in this passage, and in the essay as a whole for that matter, is a concern for the paramount importance (in Karl Kroeber's phrase) of the artist's "inner logic of vision." If he insists on anything in "The Art of Fiction," it is the division between the writer's proper task as artist and the reader's as critic. James exalts the artist's freedom: "The good health of an art which undertakes so immediately to reproduce life must demand that it be perfectly free. It lives upon exercise, and the very meaning of exercise is freedom"; we must therefore "grant the artist his subject, his idea, his *donnée:* our criticism is applied only to what he makes of it" (AF 384, 394–95). To grant artists their freedom, their *données*, is to respect their imagination and their aesthetic integrity, the inner logic of their artistic visions. We may criticize them harshly if they fail, but "if we pretend to respect the artist at all, we must allow him his freedom of choice, in the face, in particular cases, of innumerable presumptions that the choice will not fructify" (AF 395). Such an aesthetic concern could not have been enunciated before the latter part of the eighteenth century; it is at bottom the same issue Wordsworth raised in the Preface to *Lyrical Ballads* in 1800. Wordsworth says there that the poet is someone who "has acquired a greater readiness and power in expressing what he thinks and feels, and especially those thoughts and feelings which, by his own choice, or from the structure of his own mind, arise in him without immediate external excitement."[3] To argue that the poet should express things "by his own choice, or from the structure of his own mind" is to say that we should grant "the artist his subject, his idea, his *donnée*."

Both Wordsworth and James also emphasize that the determining factor in our judgment of the artist's worth is not freedom of choice but quality of intellect: although artists are free to pursue whatever interests them, only the best minds will produce good art. For Wordsworth, "poems to which any value can be attached were never produced on any variety of subjects but by a man who, being possessed of more than usual organic sensibility, has also thought long and deeply" (p. 735); for James, "there is one point at which the moral sense and the artistic sense lie very near together; that is in the light of the very obvious truth that the deepest quality of a work of art will always be the quality of the mind of the producer. In proportion as that intelligence is fine will the novel, the picture, the statue partake of the substance of beauty and truth. . . . No good novel will ever proceed from a superficial mind" (AF 406). Now, such arguments would not contradict neoclassic doctrine— certainly Dr. Johnson for one would agree with the general import of these remarks—but what allies them as Romantic is the use to which their authors put them. If the best art arises from the best minds, the Romanticist suggests, then the purpose of the artist, in Albert Gérard's words, "is to provide a total and accurate rendering of the germinal idea which stirs his imagination." That is a notion Dr. Johnson would reject out of hand.

James goes beyond Wordsworth, as we should expect him to, in proposing that we apply what he calls "the test of execution" in measuring and judging the total and accurate rendering of the germinal idea that stirs the artist's imagination. Much of James's critical focus is on the tools for carrying out this test of execution, since the critic's attention is quite different from the artist's. It is only in the very limited sense that technique and form are the outward signs of the artist's "execution," the things by which we measure aesthetic success, that James could be said to value technique more than subject. If we grant artists their subjects, then necessarily technique is the critic's only legitimate area of investigation: "We may believe that of a certain idea even the most sincere novelist can make nothing at all, and the event may perfectly justify our belief; but the failure will have been a failure to execute, and it is in the execution that the fatal weakness is recorded" (AF 395). James took his own remarks seriously when he came to write the prefaces to the New York edition of his works, for their overriding concern is execution. In the case of each volume, James tries to reconstruct the circumstances surrounding the composition of the individual work and then to call our attention to particular matters or problems of execution, such as the "makeshift middle" of *The Wings of the Dove*. He focuses especially on structural issues in his fiction, and here, as in "The Art of Fiction," the artist's inner logic of vision is the ultimate guide; the critic's task is to uncover and expose that inner logic, to find the figure in the carpet. In the following passage, for example, James speaks of the artist's "one logic" in a way that makes it clear he is referring to the same phenomenon Karl Kroeber calls "the inner logic of vision": "[The artist] remains all the while in intimate commerce with his motive, and can say to himself—what really more than anything else inflames and sustains him—that he alone has the *secret* of the particular case, he alone can measure the truth of the direction to be taken by his developed data. There can be for him, evidently, only one logic for these things; there can be for him only one truth and one direction—the quarter in which his subject most completely expresses itself."⁴ If "one logic" guides the artist in James's view, there are at least three major areas into which the scrutiny of the critic should fall. These areas, I suggest, in turn conform to the three traits of Romantic form at which we have already looked.

James specifically raises the issue of organicism in "The Art of Fiction." I have already quoted the passage in which he speaks of a novel's "organic whole" and expresses the relationship between a novel's subject and form through the organic metaphor of the needle and thread (AF 400). Elsewhere in this essay he elaborates on the organic nature of art, noting that some people talk of description, dialogue, and incident in a novel

> as if they had a kind of internecine distinctness, instead
> of melting into each other at every breath, and being
> intimately associated parts of one general effort of ex-
> pression. I cannot imagine composition existing in a
> series of blocks, nor conceive, in any novel worth dis-
> cussing at all, of a passage of description that is not in
> its intention narrative, a passage of dialogue that is not
> in its intention descriptive. . . . A novel is a living
> thing, all one and continuous, like any other organism,
> and in proportion as it lives will it be found, I think,
> that in each of the parts there is something of each of
> the other parts. (AF 391–92)

James's concern for the organic is equally prominent in the prefaces, where I have counted twenty occasions on which he uses the word *organic* in regard to literary creation.[5] There is a striking example in the preface to *The Tragic Muse* that can stand for the others: "There is life and life, and as waste is only life sacrificed and thereby prevented from 'counting,' I delight in a deep-breathing economy and an organic form" (p. 84).

Surely James's concern for the organic allies him solidly with the Romantics. And surely his judgment in this area has had significant impact on later novelists as well as critics. If we exempt Leavis and the *Scrutiny* crowd, we should have to say that James's critical ideas about fiction held sway for more than half of this century. His criticism of Victorian novels as "large loose baggy monsters" (p. 84), for example—a logical extension of a demand for organic form even if this criticism is neither completely fair nor always appropriate—has only been most consistently and seriously challenged since about 1960.[6] Moreover, there have been relatively few serious attempts by novelists to return to pre-Jamesian novelistic forms. One thinks perhaps of John Barth's *Sot-Weed Factor* or John Fowles's *French Lieutenant's Woman*, but in both these cases there is a self-conscious playing upon conventions rather than a serious effort at reviving previous novelistic modes. James's ideas have decisively limited the scope and direction of fictional experiments in the twentieth century (at least until the 1960s): his beliefs in "a deep-breathing economy and an organic form" and in the novel as "a living thing, all one and continuous" have been articles of faith for modern writers of fiction. I think one can safely conclude that James's restatement of the (Romantic) concern for organic form has been a major influence on modern fiction and that therefore in this one respect at least we shall have to agree that Romanticism has exerted a significant influence on modern fiction.

But organicism alone is not Romanticism; the organic is

only one of three elements composing Romantic form. We discover, however, that James is as insistent on the second element, the experiential, as he is on the first. Experience is inclusive for James. He speaks of a "cluster of gifts" that can almost be said to constitute experience: "The power to guess the unseen from the seen, to trace the implication of things, to judge the whole piece by the pattern, the condition of feeling life in general so completely that you are well on your way to knowing a particular corner of it" (AF 389). Therefore, he advises the novelist to "try to be one of the people on whom nothing is lost," since "experience is never limited, and it is never complete; it is an immense sensibility, a kind of huge spider-web of the finest silken threads suspended in the chamber of consciousness, and catching every airborne particle in its tissue. It is the very atmosphere of the mind; and when the mind is imaginative . . . it takes to itself the faintest hints of life, it converts the very pulses of the air into revelations" (AF 388). Experience is the very foundation upon which the novelist's art must be built. It is what allows novelists to impose "an air of reality" on their work, and "the air of reality (solidity of specification) seems to me to be the supreme virtue of a novel—the merit on which all its other merits . . . helplessly and submissively depend. If it be not there they are all as nothing, and if these be there, they owe their effect to the success with which the author has produced the illusion of life. The cultivation of this success, the study of this exquisite process, form, to my taste, the beginning and the end of the art of the novelist" (AF 390). Thus experience in the most basic sense informs the novel.

James considers the issue of experience in the prefaces as well, as the following samples show.

There is, I think, no more nutritive or suggestive truth in this connexion [the question of "moral" or "immoral" subject matter] than that of the perfect dependence of the "moral" sense of a work of art on the amount of felt life concerned in producing it. (P. 45)

Experience, as I see it, is our apprehension and our measure of what happens to us as social creatures—any intelligent report of which has to be based on that apprehension. (Pp. 64–65)

The thing of profit is to *have* your experience—to recognize and understand it, and for this almost any will do; there being surely no absolute ideal about it beyond getting from it all it has to give. The artist—for it is of this strange brood we speak—has but to have his honest sense of life to find it fed at every pore. (P. 201)[7]

The question of experience for James, as these selections indicate, is wrapped up in questions of feeling ("felt life"), of the emotional impact of both the writer's inspiration and the work of art itself. Harold T. McCarthy effectively summarizes James's position this way: "In the long and multicoloured shadow which fell between the *donnée* and the novel, James recognized feeling as the cohesive and impelling force. To deviate consciously from this felt power, to add or detract from the dictates of aesthetic feeling, was to run the risk of appearing 'written,' of appearing to be mechanically ordered. The story lost its life-giving principle and became, however life-like, a marionette show. No amount of planning could substitute for the role of feeling in the creative process. No matter how much an author might plot and plan and calculate, what determined the nature of his work was the way he felt and saw and aesthetically conceived it."[8]

James's attitudes toward feeling and experience are thus similar to those of many Romantics. The similarity is borne out especially in his insistence on intensity as an important aesthetic effect. I have noted over twenty instances in the prefaces where James expresses or implies a belief in the importance of intensity as an aesthetic goal.[9] A few examples will suffice:

> What a man thinks and what he feels are the history and the character of what he does; on all of which things the logic of intensity rests. Without intensity where is vividness, and without vividness where is presentability? (P. 66)

> [on "The Turn of the Screw"] Only make the reader's general vision of evil intense enough, I said to myself—and that already is a charming job—and his own experience, his own imagination, his own sympathy (with the children) and horror (of their false friends) will supply him quite sufficiently with all the particulars. (P. 176)

> [on the employing of one center for *The Ambassadors*] It would give me a large unity, and that in turn would crown me with the grace to which the enlightened storyteller will at any time, for his interest, sacrifice if need be all other graces whatever. I refer of course to the grace of intensity. (P. 318)

We might almost be listening here to Wordsworth, or to Keats in his letters, or even to Percy Shelley. Compare these selections from the prefaces to this from Shelley's "Defence of Poetry": "A man, to be greatly good, must imagine intensely and comprehensively; he must put himself in the place of another and of many others; the pains and pleasures of his species must become his own. The great instrument of moral good is the imagination; and poetry administers to the effect by acting upon the cause."[10] Or compare them to this remark by Keats (in the same letter in which he speaks of "Negative Capability"): "The excellence of every Art is its intensity, capable of making all disagreeables evaporate, from their being in close relationship with Beauty & Truth."[11] We might also recall Robert Langbaum's comment about "Tintern Abbey," a comment which applies to Romantic poetry in general, that "the gain is rather in the intensity of understanding than in what is understood."[12] And James even assesses the impact of intense experience on himself as artist in a manner strikingly similar to that of Wordsworth. In a famous phrase from the preface to *Lyrical Ballads*, Wordsworth speaks of poetry as emotion recollected in tranquility; James says: "I have ever, in general, found it difficult to write of places under too immediate an impression—the impression that prevents standing off and allows neither space nor time for perspective" (p. 27).

The creative nature of James's aesthetic is not so easily demonstrated as its organic or experiential aspects. James uses the word *creative* infrequently and seems at times to describe his work in terms of a development (of an idea or "germ") rather than a creation. But if we take care to examine the assumptions behind James's statements about the writing of his fiction, we can see the creative aspect of his aesthetic. When he notes, for example, that the source of an artist's interest in a subject "resides in the strong consciousness of his seeing all for himself" (p. 122), what he is really saying is that artists have to create every aspect of their fictional worlds. In other words, as in the case of the "germ" of *The Spoils of Poynton*, while the inciting incident may be a snatch of overheard dinner conversation, in the making of the work of art the germ is developed and grows entirely under the conscious control of the artist's mind and imagination. It becomes subject to the artist's "one logic." From one overheard remark James literally creates a whole novel. He is especially insistent, moreover, about the irrelevance of the actual circumstances to which that remark refers. He recounts the incident that led to the writing of *The Spoils of Poynton* this way: "There had been but ten words, yet I recognized in them, as in a flash, all the possibilities of the little drama of my 'Spoils,' which glimmered then and there into life; so that when in the next breath I began to hear of action taken, on the beautiful ground, by our engaged adversaries . . . I saw clumsy Life again at her stupid work. For the action taken, and on which my friend, as I knew she would, had already begun all complacently and benightedly further to report, I had absolutely, and could have, no scrap of use" (p. 121). If we did not know from the rhythms of the prose that Henry James was speaking here, we might almost confuse this with the descriptions of creative inspiration we usually encounter—or expect to encounter—in the letters and journals of Romantic poets. There is a Shelleyan disregard for the actual in the face of the imaginative here, and the experience James describes is reminiscent of Wordsworth's "spots of time." James's "germ," like Woolf's "moment" or Joyce's "epiphany," might be said to be a deliberately aestheticized version of the "spot of time": James's perception leads to the making of art instead of to a deeper intuitive understanding of the self and one's relationship to nature, as in Wordsworth.[13] What for the poet is a "renovating virtue" from which "our minds / Are nourished and invisibly repaired" (*The Prelude*, XII, 214–15) is for the novelist a "flash" by which his aesthetic powers are aroused and nourished; for both the experience is a "creative" one.

We will remember that the creative aspect of Romantic form is grounded in the aesthetic theory M. H. Abrams calls expressive ("All art is expression," says James [p. 324]), that the expressive theory of art is in turn dependent on the artist's embodying the "combined product of [his or her] perceptions, thoughts and feelings."[14] ("The very source of interest for the artist," as James notes, "resides in the strong consciousness of his seeing all for himself" [p. 122].) The prefaces are in this sense the record of James's examination of his own artistic perceptions and of the workings of his imagination; viewed this way they argue very powerfully for the supremacy of creativity in the aesthetic process. Moreover, it should be an obvious conclusion that any writer as concerned with technique as James so evidently is would have to acknowledge at some point how "creative" his or her work is. The more writers become conscious of technique and of the means to create various effects, the closer they come to outright espousal of a creative aesthetic. As Harold T. McCarthy says: "[James] described the act of writing as an 'act of life,' and it was an act that was creative in two ways: it created a work of art that bore in every part the evidence of his personal sense of things, and as a result of the deep, intense probing of his personal values, it inevitably created afresh his ethical ideal and its claim upon his self-identity."[15]

We have seen thus far three major similarities between James's aesthetic, as set out in "The Art of Fiction" and in the prefaces to the New York edition of his works, and the Romantic conception of form. One other important similarity needs to be mentioned: the question of reader participation. We said above that both of the Romantic works we analyzed, "Ode to a Nightingale" and *Frankenstein,* required the reader's active imaginative participation, while "Ode for Music" and *Adam Bede* relied rather on what we called (after W. J. Harvey) contemplation. Although we compared Eliot with an earlier writer, Mary Shelley, Harvey in fact established this distinction between imaginative participation and contemplation by comparing Eliot to Henry James. Imaginative participation, for Harvey, is "appropriate to the Jamesian mode."[16] Few people, I think, would dispute his point; the thrust of most of James's theoretical experiments, of his interest in intensity in the aesthetic experience, is toward involving the reader actively in the fictional experience. Such an aesthetic interest, as should be more than apparent by now, is the direct legacy of the Romantic impulse.

The decision to determine Romantic form by examining narrative structure is also supported by James's critical discussions. An acute sense of structure is pervasive throughout the prefaces and it is closely allied to the question of narration. His discussion of structure is in fact developed by and through consideration of important narrative devices and methods (thus James's interest in *ficelles,* reflectors, narrative centers, central consciousnesses, etc.). Out of this concentration on various matters connected to narrative technique his concern for larger structural patterns, like the "roundness" of a work or its "makeshift middle," emerges. What is central to James in all of this, at least implicitly, is movement of perspective (which is, Karl Kroeber reminds us, "the narrative equivalent of the dialectical tensions so important to lyric and dramatic poetry").[17] Most of his literary efforts from the time of *The Portrait of a Lady* on are directed at mastering the skills necessary to control perspective; nearly all his fictional experiments from the later 1880s until the early years of the new century are exercises in the creation and manipulation of perspective for diverse literary effects. In a sense, then, the body of James's literary output, both fiction and critical writings, confirms the importance of studying narration above all else to determine the proper perspective for understanding a work of fiction. It suggests as well that my contention is right that we shall best discern Romantic form in fiction if we approach it through narrative structure.

Freedom in *The Ambassadors*

We have now a theoretical groundwork from which to explore the question of Romantic form in James; let us see how he handles that form in practice. I shall examine the three novels of his major phase, *The Ambassadors, The Wings of the Dove,* and *The Golden Bowl,* in order to reveal both their own Romantic form and any new meanings or resolutions of established critical issues that a knowledge of their form as Romantic might offer. To analyze fully all three of these novels would require a prohibitive amount of space for a study of this nature. Nevertheless, I think something ought to be said about the (Romantic) form of each. I propose, then, to consider selected aspects of each novel that show us the Romantic nature of its form.

One of the most illuminating discussions of James's fiction is an article by Leo Bersani, "The Jamesian Lie," which appeared in *Partisan Review* in 1969. Bersani offers there a vital clue toward our understanding of the Romantic form of James's fiction. He makes this assessment:

> By retracing the structural opportunities (for roundness, for antithesis, for producing illusions of mass without illusions of extent) which allowed each of his works to take shape, James provides the model for a critical complicity with the novelist's experiment. His technical interest in the expanding surface of each work illustrates his sympathy with the most profound intentions of his fiction. For the recurrent Jamesian subject is only superficially the international theme, or the confrontation of innocence and experience, or the conflict of acquisitive and self-renouncing impulses. His subject is freedom.[18]

Why and how James's subject is freedom we shall consider at length; what is necessary to note first is that freedom as a recurrent and basic subject is inherently and profoundly a Romantic attribute. We saw a twofold sense of freedom in both "Ode to a Nightingale" and *Frankenstein,* which were distinguished from "Ode for Music" and *Adam Bede,* in one respect at least, by a powerful sense of aesthetic possibility in both subject matter and structure. Aesthetic innovation and new formal possibilities are impossible without a genuine sense of freedom; and such a sense becomes, significantly, the subject as well as the impulse for much Romantic literature. "A central and persistent concern of Wordsworth's *Prelude,*" M. H. Abrams tells us in *Natural Supernaturalism,* "is to investigate the cardinal value he calls 'genuine freedom.' . . . This Wordsworthian *topos*" is "a prominent aspect . . . in Romantic thought and imagination."[19] We saw above that James's primary concern in "The Art of Fiction" was this same Wordsworthian *topos*. That essay was written in response to Walter Besant's pamphlet of the same title whose main fault lies "in attempting to say so definitely beforehand what sort of an affair the good novel will be" (AF 384). James thus seeks to limit the critic's sphere of activity to allow the novelist complete freedom, especially in the choice of subject. "A novel," James goes on to say, "is in its broadest definition a personal, a direct impression of life: that, to begin with, constitutes its value, which is greater or less according to the intensity of the impression. But there will be no intensity at all, and therefore no value, unless there is freedom to feel and say. The tracing of a line to be followed, of a tone to be taken, of a form to be filled out, is a limitation of that freedom and a suppression of the very thing that we are most curious about" (AF 384).

In *The Ambassadors* that "critical complicity with the novelist's experiment" for which, according to Bersani, James provides the model, is to be found in the twofold nature of the novel's aesthetic experience. There is the experience of the characters in the novel and there is the experience of the readers of the novel. As James himself says: "In every novel the work is divided between the writer and the reader; but the writer makes the reader very much as he makes his characters. When he makes him ill, that is, makes him indifferent, he does no work; the writer does all. When he makes him well, that is, makes him interested, then the reader does quite the labour."[20] For both characters and readers, then, as for writers, questions of freedom are central to the fictional experience. Like other kinds of Romantic literature, James's later novels try as much as possible to weld the experiences of characters and readers; the reader is asked to participate in the characters' experiences—not to share the actual experiences but to share *in* them. In other words, the reader's experience becomes the affective equivalent of the verisimilitudinous ones of the characters. Thus,

in *The Ambassadors,* Strether reaches his final conclusion
that Chad must stay in Europe, must, moreover, remain
faithful to Mme de Vionnet, through a series of encounters
in which new perspectives are gradually presented to him,
consciously or otherwise, while readers of the novel un-
dergo an equivalent or at least similar change or development of perspective through a series of highly structured
and ordered books, chapters, and incidents. The equating
or paralleling of characters' and readers' experience is made
possible in this case by James's decision to remain as much
as possible within Strether's consciousness.

On close examination *The Ambassadors* can be seen as theo-
retically, stylistically, and structurally concerned with freedom. Its thematic concern with the question of freedom,
freedom of various kinds on various levels, from the particular to the abstract, is its most immediately striking aspect.
The words *freedom* and *free* are used often in the novel, especially at crucial points in the development of the plot.[21]
Strether's famous "Live!" speech in Gloriani's garden is the
keynote to the novel's consideration of freedom:

> "It's not too late for *you,* on any side, and you don't strike
> me as in danger of missing the train; besides which
> people can be in general pretty well trusted, of course—
> with the clock of their freedom ticking as loud as it seems
> to do here—to keep an eye on the fleeting hour. . . . Live
> all you can; it's a mistake not to. . . . The affair—I mean
> the affair of life—couldn't, no doubt, have been different
> for me; for it's at the best a tin mould, either fluted and
> embossed, with ornamental excrescences, or else smooth
> and dreadfully plain, into which, a helpless jelly, one's
> consciousness is poured—so that one 'takes' the form, as
> the great cook says, and is more or less compactly held by
> it: one lives in fine as one can. Still, one has the illusion of
> freedom: therefore don't be, like me, without the memory
> of that illusion." (V.ii.131–32)

As it turns out, the "illusion of freedom" becomes ultimately the argument that persuades Strether he must stick
to his original conviction that Chad is better off to stay in
Europe. Moreover, Strether does come in fact to experience
a kind of freedom of his own. After what he calls the
"crash," that is, after Sarah Pocock leaves him no alternative but to make a clear-cut statement of his position to her
and to Mrs. Newsome, Strether stands on the balcony of his
rooms and muses on the changes the previous three months
have wrought. He tries to recapture the "voice" in which
his rooms spoke to him:

> That voice, he had to note, failed audibly to sound;
> which he took as the proof of all the change in himself.
> He had heard, of old, only what he *could* then hear;
> what he could do now was to think of three months ago
> as a point in the far past. All voices had grown thicker
> and meant more things; they crowded on him as he
> moved about—it was the way they sounded together
> that wouldn't let him be still. He felt, strangely, as sad
> as if he had come for some wrong, and yet as excited as
> if he had come for some freedom. But the freedom was
> what was most in the place and the hour; it was the
> freedom that most brought him round again to the
> youth of his own that he had long ago missed. (XI.i.281)

This illusion of freedom, a kind of vicarious participation in
Chad's youth to replace the lost opportunities of his own,
endures even the final testing that his accidental meeting
with Chad and Mme de Vionnet by the river forces.

Chad's goal for himself also is freedom, as little Bilham
explains: " 'He wants to be free' " (IV.ii.112). Strether respects that desire almost from the beginning, although he
does not realize quite what that freedom in fact entails until
the end of the novel ("It hadn't at any rate been in the least
his idea to spy on Chad's proper freedom" [V.ii.128]).[22]

Moreover, his own recognition of the tenuous nature of Mme de Vionnet's freedom significantly affects Strether's decision to urge Chad to stay. In their final meeting, after the encounter by the river, Mme de Vionnet reveals to Strether the true depths of her emotions. He is moved by her plight and perceives a new and unexpected facet to the situation—that Mme de Vionnet is trapped: "It was of Chad she was after all renewedly afraid; the strange strength of her passion was the very strength of her fear; she clung to *him*, Lambert Strether, as to a source of safety she had tested, and, generous graceful truthful as she might try to be, exquisite as she was, she dreaded the term of his being within reach. With this sharpest perception yet, it was like a chill in the air to him, it was almost appalling, that a creature so fine could be, by mysterious forces, a creature so exploited" (XII.ii.322).

What makes this perception so sharp is a sudden sense of the ambiguous, perhaps the anomalous, nature of freedom itself in social situations. Strether had earlier been concerned whether Mme de Vionnet was "free" to carry on a "virtuous" attachment with Chad, "free" here referring only to her marital status (IV.ii.117 and VI.iii.168). But the nature of her freedom in connection with her husband is quite different from the nature of her freedom as it concerns Chad. Ironically, while some thought her shockingly "free" because of the affair with Chad, she is really less free because she is dependent on Chad's willingness to continue the relationship. It is this situation to which she refers when she explains to Strether in their final meeting: " 'I'm old and abject and hideous. . . . Abject above all. Or old above all. It's when one's old that it's worst. I don't care what becomes of it—let what *will*; there it is. It's a doom—I know it; you can't see it more than I do myself. Things have to happen as they will' " (XII.iii.324).

Mme de Vionnet's freedom thus cuts both ways, as does social freedom in general. Mastery of social conventions and ease in social intercourse give a powerful sense of control in James's world and consequently they impart a sense of freedom, but they are also constricting: they prevent certain things from being said or examined freely, except insofar as they are part, as David Lodge notes, "of an in-group game which consists in managing to discuss, or at least to suggest, infinite complexities and discriminations in a vocabulary that is on the face of it remarkably impoverished." Lodge perceptively assesses the consequences this way: "The value attached to this kind of discourse is equivocal. Clearly, James admires it as a form of linguistic virtuosity which has the social usefulness of enabling delicate subjects to be discussed publicly—a problem which preoccupied him as a professional writer; and on a more profound level he undoubtedly held that there were few things that were both true and simply statable. On the other hand the language of heightened cliché is a treacherous medium of communication, concealing as much as it reveals. It is certainly a double-edged weapon in the hands of an innocent like Strether."[23]

If freedom is an important thematic consideration in the novel, Lodge's observation of the "language of heightened cliché" shows us a second area in which the question of freedom—and necessarily its opposite, restriction—figures prominently: in the novel's style. Readers of James's late fiction in general are in the same position as the characters of that fiction. Both readers and characters must learn to participate successfully in the linguistic world James has created, must learn how to "read" his language.[24] More specifically, readers of James's fiction are initially in the position of his American characters. They are typically thrust into the midst of a society whose rules are alien to them. This situation is common throughout James, *The American* and *The Portrait of a Lady* being perhaps the most famous early examples, but the elements of the pattern change from early to late James. Background and social manner are the areas in which Christopher Newman primarily differs from the Europeans he encounters, but from the time of *The Portrait* on the ability to master or control the verbal nuances of social intercourse becomes the talent on which James places the highest premium. Strether, for instance, is deceived through a portion of *The Ambassadors* because he lacks the experience necessary to interpret correctly little Bilham's remark that Chad and Mme de Vionnet's relationship is "virtuous." Similarly, Maggie Verver and her father are at a decided disadvantage in dealing with the European, Amerigo, and the experienced and knowledgeable American, Charlotte Stant, in *The Golden Bowl* because of their linguistic innocence, an innocence that sets the tone for their other "American" characteristics.

Commencing in *The Portrait* the process the "successful" Americans go through is one of internalization of European social language and conventions. For Isabel Archer the social behavior indigenous to the world of Osmond and Mme Merle looms in front of her as a cage, limiting the freedom she has come to Europe to exercise; in an action typical of James's ironic fictional world, Isabel eventually internalizes the cage, thus in a Pyrrhic sense triumphing. We as readers must in a somewhat related way internalize the conventions and linguistic reality of the Jamesian universe. We should be familiar with the required "method" for dealing with the Jamesian universe, moreover, because of our reading, for one thing, of Romantic poetry. The need to participate in the linguistic world of *The Ambassadors* or of *The Golden Bowl* is really no different from the need to participate in the new linguistic reality Keats tries to establish in "Ode to a Nightingale." The scale is different, since the adjustment from lyric poem to novel is substantial, but the aesthetic experience is similar, at least in general. We are really touching here on a matter I raised in connection with Wayne Booth's remarks about James when I suggested that the best way to confront the ambiguities and unresolved issues of the Jamesian fictional world was to treat them in a manner similar to the critical approach required to understand and appreciate a poem by Keats. I suggested that examination of narrative technique was the best path to that confrontation. We have considered theme and style in connection with the question of freedom versus restriction in *The Ambassadors;* let us look now at its narrative structure.

Technically, we have a first-person narration, although the narrator of *The Ambassadors* only rarely refers to himself in the first person, just once that I could find in the first-person singular.[25] There are perhaps half a dozen references to the first-person plural. We would never seriously consider this novel in company with other first-person narrations, however. Instead, our proper course, as virtually all critics of this novel have recognized, is to take our signal from James himself and concentrate on Strether as narrative center. In the preface to *The Ambassadors* James notes:

> Every question of form and pressure, I easily remember,
> paled in the light of the major propriety, recognised as
> soon as really weighed; that of employing but one
> centre and keeping it all within my hero's compass. The
> thing was to be so much this worthy's intimate adven-
> ture that even the projection of his consciousness upon
> it from beginning to end without intermission or devia-
> tion would probably still leave a part of its value for
> him, and *a fortiori* for ourselves, unexpressed. I might,
> however, express every grain of it that there would be
> room for—on condition of contriving a splendid particu-
> lar economy.   (P. 317)

Apart from the obvious interest in perspective here, the noteworthy thing about this passage is James's own awareness of the limitations, the restrictions, of his method. It is important that these limitations be of the right sort. He rejects the possibility of making Strether "at once hero and historian," of endowing him with "the romantic privilege of the 'first person.' " "Suffice it, to be brief," he says, "that the first person, in the long piece, is a form foredoomed to looseness, and that looseness, never much my affair, had never been so little so as on this particular occasion. All of which reflexions flocked to the standard from the moment—a very early one— the question of how to keep my form amusing while sticking so close to my central figure and constantly taking its pattern from him had to be faced" (p. 320).

James goes on to ask why an author "shouldn't throw the reins on his [hero's] neck and, letting them flap there as free as in 'Gil Blas' or in 'David Copperfield,' equip him with the double privilege of subject and object." He answers predictably, saying that "one makes that surrender only if one is prepared *not* to make certain precious discriminations." His summation makes a point pertinent to our discussion:

> The "first person" then, so employed, is addressed by the author directly to ourselves, his possible readers, whom he has to reckon with, at the best, by our English tradition, so loosely and vaguely after all, so little respectfully, on so scant a presumption of exposure to criticism. Strether, on the other hand, encaged and provided for as "The Ambassadors" encages and provides, has to keep in view proprieties much stiffer and more salutary than any our straight and credulous gape are likely to bring home to him, has exhibitional conditions to meet, in a word, that forbid the terrible *fluidity* of self-revelation. (P. 321)

"Strether . . . encaged and provided for as 'The Ambassadors' encages and provides." Here then is James himself endorsing the very point I have suggested, endorsing it, moreover, in the context of possible responses by the reader. Just as it is important that Strether be "encaged"— in order for the thematic questions of freedom to be prop-

erly set off—so is it equally important that the reader respect, indeed, participate in, the encagement which the
narration of *The Ambassadors* provides. If James opposes
"looseness" in narration, he does so to avoid, in part, a
"loose" response from his readers; they must, as I said,
experience aesthetically what Strether experiences, else
James fails in his intentions, as he so obviously failed for
the *Harper's* reader of James's "project" for *The Ambassadors*
who ignored Strether in his report altogether.[26]

Harper's chose a reader who was unfortunately dense; for
the rest of us, at least those of us who are willing to grant
James his basic premises, it is a different story. Since we are
nearly completely restricted to Strether's point of view, our
complicity with James's narrative experiment is immediate
and intense. The novel is constructed as a series of encounters between Strether and the other characters in which
his consciousness is slowly and painstakingly altered and
enlarged. As Strether becomes aware of the complexities of
the situation, so do we as readers: our experience is tied
every step of the way to his, and even when we suspect
things Strether does not, when they are revealed their emotional impact is as great on us as it is on him. The famous
scene "Strether by the River" is the best example. Although
many readers will have guessed what Strether here discovers, this scene has, as David Lodge says, a "tremendous
force," in part because we realize along with Strether the
true nature of Chad's relationship with Mme de Vionnet.[27]

If I have equivocated somewhat in speaking of the reader's
experience as equivalent or parallel to the characters', I have
done so because of the complex nature of the narrative experience of a novel—of this novel in particular. While it is true
that the reader's experience is linked directly and immediately to Strether's, it is also true that the implied author's
values are not identical with Strether's; the reader must recognize this situation for the novel to succeed. We are dealing
here with a reliable narration: the narrator, the infrequently

appearing "I," can safely be assumed, I think, to have the same values as the implied author; but since that narrator spends so much time inside Strether's consciousness, we end up in effect confronting a kind of unreliable narration. Here is the challenge that so excited James: keep us inside Strether's consciousness but make us see his limitations and inadequate point of view.

The primary way that James meets this challenge is through the frequent use of juxtaposition. The novel is filled with arranged meetings, surprise visits, delayed encounters, planned confrontations, and unexpected arrivals and departures, which are either the work of the characters themselves (such as Chad's appearance in the box at the Opéra) or of the implied author (Strether by the river or the first encounter in the novel, his meeting with Maria Gostrey). One result of this juxtaposition is the creation of the proper and complex attitudes toward, and perspectives for, the experience of both characters and readers. The effect is prismatic: the characters see each other and we see them from a seeming multitude of angles, each meeting, encounter, or analysis reflecting on one or more of the others. James accomplishes in this way, albeit on a grander and more complex scale, something similar to what Keats does in his odes—an immediate and intense aesthetic experience; and he does so by using the novelistic equivalent (tight manipulation of perspective through use of point-of-view techniques) of Keats's device of systolic action, what Kroeber calls "dialectical tensions." Just as we must participate fully with the persona of "Ode to a Nightingale," learn what he learns, experience what he experiences, enmesh ourselves in his consciousness in order to experience the freedom that he knows and is creating for and with us, so must we ally ourselves with Strether, learn what he learns, experience what he experiences, in effect encage ourselves in the novel as Strether is encaged, in order to experience a final freedom along with him when the full truth of the entire situation is revealed. The only difference is that our experience of freedom is perhaps less ironic than Strether's, since he chooses to leave Maria Gostrey to return to Massachusetts.

The Romantic Imagery of *The Golden Bowl*

" 'I see. You must have had things to be beyond them. It's a kind of law of perspective,' " Adam Verver says to his daughter in chapter 10 of *The Golden Bowl*.[28] Perspective, as his remark suggests, plays as important a role in this novel as it does in *The Ambassadors,* as it does in fact in virtually all of James's fiction. Instead of limiting the point of view to a single center like Lambert Strether, James chooses a more flexible narrative mode for *The Golden Bowl.* Again we have a first-person narration with an infrequently appearing "I," but the narrator makes his presence more strongly felt here than in *The Ambassadors.*[29] In fact, the narrative presence in *The Golden Bowl* in some ways resembles that in a typical Victorian novel. For instance, the narrator remarks at one point: "We have each our own way of making up for our unselfishness, and Maggie, who had no small self at all as against her husband or her father and only a weak and uncertain one as against her stepmother, would verily at this crisis have seen Mrs. Assingham's personal life or liberty sacrificed without a pang" (II, 101; ch. 30). This comment is similar to the kinds of things a narrator might say in a George Eliot novel or in some other novel that displays, as James puts it in his preface to this novel, the "mere muffled majesty of irresponsible 'authorship.' " James himself acknowledges the "embarrassing truth" that he has partaken of this "muffled majesty" in the work at hand—"It 's not that the muffled majesty of authorship does n't here *ostensibly* reign" (James's emphasis)—but he excuses himself by noting that he has "held my system fast and fondly, with one hand at least, by the manner in which the whole thing remains subject to the register, ever so closely kept, of the consciousness of but two of the characters" (pp. 328–29). These two characters, of course, are the Prince, for whom the first half of the novel is named, and the Princess, who gives her name to the second half. The Colonel and Fanny Assingham are available to provide other perspectives, and James's narrator also enters Adam Verver's and Charlotte Stant's consciousness at times.

By James's own admission, then, we are dealing here with a novel that is constructed in some ways like a traditional novel. We should not be surprised by this situation since, as I noted at the outset of this discussion, James is a transitional figure and his fiction shares many of the qualities of the traditional novels of the nineteenth century. There are a couple of important ways, however, in which *The Golden Bowl* is Romantic. For one thing, this novel is as much concerned with freedom, in subject matter and style, as *The Ambassadors,* and the emphasis on freedom, as I noted above, helps distinguish *The Golden Bowl* from other traditional novels.[30] It is important as well that the reader participate actively in the experience of the novel; James's handling of the point-of-view technique fosters such active participation fully as much with two or more "registering consciousnesses" as with one center such as Strether. If *The Ambassadors* is "about" what Strether learns and how he learns it, this novel might almost be subtitled, *What Maggie Learns,* a matter I shall consider in detail below.

If *The Golden Bowl* shares with *The Ambassadors* a concern for freedom, an interest in the use of perspective, and the need for reader participation, it also goes further than the earlier novel in at least one important respect: it is structured around a pervasive and resonant symbolism, that of the golden bowl as well as that of images of cages. It is in the handling of this symbolism that the underlying Romantic nature of *The Golden Bowl* is best to be seen.

The manner in which the image of the golden bowl informs the novel's structure need not detain us here; it has been amply considered by James's critics, from F. O. Matthiessen in *Henry James: The Major Phase*,[31] still the point of departure for any consideration of James, to Laurence Holland in *The Expense of Vision.* Holland's summary statement will suffice to represent the general nature of the function of the bowl imagery in the novel: "The symbol of the bowl helps govern the novel because the bowl and the act of buying it or possessing it, of breaking and salvaging it later, inform each other, and the bowl itself does not stand as a merely referential or imposed symbol but serves as part of a profoundly creative act to constitute a field of form, a formal nexus."[32] I should like to suggest that in addition to the bowl itself James uses explicit images of encagement as part of this formal nexus, that he uses this imagery in *The Golden Bowl* to impart to an already symbolic work a special kind of symbolic significance. I believe that James expanded his aesthetic exploration of the idea of freedom and restriction in *The Golden Bowl* by using encagement imagery in the same way that a poet like Yeats, for example, uses certain images in his poetry: James, like Yeats, uses what Frank Kermode has called the Romantic Image. Since contemporary poets were experimenting with symbols at the time James was writing this novel and since their experiments, as Kermode demonstrates, represent the "flowering" of the Romantic Image, it seems profitable to explore James's use of symbols from the point of view suggested by Kermode.

In analyzing Yeats's "In Memory of Major Robert Gregory," Kermode suggests that Gregory "becomes . . . a symbol; the poem about him is for Yeats one of those victories by which the artist lives in tragic solitude. He reconciles the opposites of action and contemplation; and this reconciliation of opposites, very properly in a Romantic poet, is the purpose of the Yeatsian symbol, which is the flowering of what I call the Romantic Image."[33] The image as Henry James uses it embodies opposites as well, although like most other things in the Jamesian world the reconciliation it offers is likely to be ironic. As Kermode notes, however, there is already an irony inherent in the artist's relationship to the Romantic Image. He focuses on the artist's sense of separateness, of isolation from other people, and suggests that this belief "in the necessary isolation or estrangement" of those who can perceive the poetic Image is "inextricably associated" with the belief "in the Image as a radiant truth out of space and time" (p. 2). Now, what Kermode analyzes as the sense of reality expressed by artists in their poetry finds, I suggest, a corollary in what James offers in *The Golden Bowl* as his characters' sense—especially Maggie's sense—of reality. James gives us a fictional equivalent of Kermode's biographical or poetical fact. Kermode stresses the cost that such beliefs exact ("the Image is always likely to be withdrawn, indeed almost any normal biographical situation is likely to cause its withdrawal") and notes: "When poetry is Image, life must, as Yeats said, be tragic" (pp. 90–91). Much of the power of *The Golden Bowl* stems from Maggie's experience of the tragic, expressed first in her discovery of Amerigo's infidelity and then in the permanent separation between her and her father that she must accept to win and hold her husband. Her domestic tragedy is the direct consequence of the knowledge she gains through the golden bowl itself. The bowl thus functions for the reader, through Maggie, like a Romantic Image. Consider it more specifically: whole the golden bowl represents the freedom to maintain the fiction of a viable and happy four-way relationship between Maggie and Amerigo and Adam and Charlotte, but broken it represents the ultimately unviable three-way relationships between Maggie, Amerigo, and Adam; Charlotte, Amerigo, and Maggie; and Maggie, Charlotte, and Adam. At the same time, the golden bowl whole, its flaw concealed under the layer of gilt, is the symbol of the flawed relationships Maggie unwittingly condones and maintains; and broken, the bowl becomes the symbol of Maggie's new knowledge, her new awareness that eventually leads to the cementing of her re-lationship with Amerigo and the severing of her relation-ship with her father. The symbol that gives the novel its title has thus a strong affinity to the Romantic Image in that the bowl symbolizes the reconciliation between Maggie and Amerigo and the break between, on the one hand, Char-lotte and Amerigo and, on the other, Maggie and her father.

James uses another kind of imagery in *The Golden Bowl*, however, one that is not as pervasive as the bowl imagery but which appears at an important moment and is perhaps equally telling because of its strategic placement. It surfaces initially in Maggie's consciousness and later, in a slightly altered form, in the narrator's.[34] We first see it as an image of a caged beast released, and it signals Maggie's newfound strength and commitment to her "plan" to save her mar-riage. Later it comes to symbolize what is for Maggie the entire focus of her efforts: to ensnare Charlotte, who is and represents all of the danger to Maggie's marriage. Amerigo and Charlotte, who were lovers before their marriages to Maggie and Adam Verver, have resumed their old relation-ship, having persuaded themselves that their adultery is of little real consequence to Maggie since she seems more in-volved in her relationship with her father than in that with her husband. But because of the golden bowl Maggie has discovered their adultery and sets out with new and (for her) unprecedented determination to salvage her marriage even though it means the severing of her close relationship with her father. She feels trapped in a situation from which she will require all her effort to escape. Maggie, the guile-less American, must use the weapons of the sophisticated European, weapons which Charlotte and Amerigo have em-ployed expertly to keep her innocent of their affair. But if Maggie is to succeed she must conceal from Charlotte both her knowledge and her determination. The crucial en-counter between the two women occurs late in the novel at Fawns, Adam Verver's country estate.

The two couples, along with the Assinghams, have been playing cards. Maggie goes out onto the terrace while Adam, Charlotte, Amerigo, and Fanny are at the bridge table. Charlotte suddenly becomes aware that Maggie is no longer in the room and, asking Colonel Assingham to take her place, leaves the table to seek her out. Maggie has been observing her through the windows and is intensely aware of her movements. She surmises what has happened and a striking image occurs to her:

> [Colonel Assingham] had taken her chair and let her go, and the arrangement was for Maggie a signal proof of her earnestness; of the energy in fact, that, though superficially commonplace in a situation in which people were n't supposed to be watching each other, was what affected our young woman on the spot as a breaking of bars. The splendid shining supple creature was out of the cage, was at large; and the question now almost grotesquely arose whether she might n't by some art, just where she was and before she could go further, be hemmed in and secured. (II, 238; ch. 36)

This image of the caged beast released conveys the full intensity of the moment, and it proves prophetic, for Maggie succeeds precisely in "hemming in" Charlotte. Maggie does this artfully as well, ironically employing the same "art" of concealment that Charlotte herself practices expertly. But the irony is even fuller: the image here is of an escape, a breaking of bars, yet it signals for the escaped creature, Charlotte, her eventual encagement.

The image of broken bars and escaped creatures is applicable to some degree to three of the major characters of this novel, since each struggles for some kind of freedom and against restrictions of differing sorts. Maggie wants the freedom to have both her new relationship with her husband and the old relationship with her father, relationships which are to a great extent mutually exclusive. Charlotte Stant wants the freedom from monetary problems that marriage to Adam Verver can provide but she wants as well to be free to continue her affair with Amerigo, which was broken off precisely for financial reasons. Amerigo wants personal and financial freedom also. Of the major characters, only Adam seems both free and content, although as we shall see he too shares in the restricting of Charlotte. With the exception of Adam, then, images of encagement are appropriate for virtually all the characters I have named: if they break their bonds they almost inevitably threaten some other character's freedom, becoming then like some wild beast who needs to be caged, since the smooth operation of the social world in which they live depends on the maintenance of restrictions, of the social proprieties that govern both private and public lives. Caged, one desires freedom; free, one needs to be caged.

The image of Charlotte as a caged beast released functions for Maggie in a way similar to the way in which the image of Robert Gregory functions for Yeats in his poem. Frank Kermode proposes that "In Memory of Major Robert Gregory" is "Yeats's first full statement of what he took to be a complex and tragic situation: the position of artists and contemplatives in a world built for action, and their chances of escape, which are in effect two, the making of Images, and death" (p. 30). Since Gregory was both a man of action and an artist, he offers a way for the poet to embody his sometimes contradictory responses to that complex and tragic situation to which Kermode refers. Maggie's response to Charlotte assumes a similar ambivalence, since Charlotte has been her best friend. However much a threat she is, she is at the same time "splendid" and "shining." But what Maggie needs to do is to use Charlotte's own methods against her. Once Maggie envisions her friend as a caged beast released, that image becomes for her—as Yeats's image of Gregory becomes for him—"a radiant truth out of space and time" (Kermode, p.

2). From the moment the image occurs to her, Maggie is resolved to carry out her plan determinedly, despite any sympathy she might feel for Charlotte. If Maggie's life is split apart when the golden bowl comes into her possession, when more specifically Fanny Assingham dashes it to the floor in Maggie's and Amerigo's presence, the most vital step in salvaging her marriage is accomplished shortly after, and as a direct result of, her imagining Charlotte as an escaped beast. Maggie's crisis is initiated through a Romantic Image of the author's creation—the golden bowl—but she takes charge of her fate through an image (of encagement) that the narrator attributes directly to her consciousness and which he later endorses by extending it himself to cover Adam and Charlotte. This image of Maggie's, moreover, has great resonance because, like Yeats's image of Gregory, it is a profoundly ironic one that expresses opposite experiences, in this case the experiences of freedom and restriction for the central characters of the novel.

To see how it functions in the novel, let us look more specifically at the context from which the image of encagement emerges. It is localized in the novel, appearing in just three chapters of book 5 and one of book 6 (chapters 35, 36, 38, and 41). James prepares the way for it at the end of chapter 35. Maggie has realized at this point that the prime requisite for her plan must be Charlotte's ignorance; in musing on the situation Maggie concludes that "Charlotte could all the while only be struggling with secrets beyond guessing." She wonders how her husband, Amerigo, "put the haunted creature off with false explanations, met her particular challenges and evaded—if that was what he did do!—her particular demands."

> Even the conviction that Charlotte was but awaiting some chance really to test her trouble upon her lover's wife left Maggie's sense meanwhile open as to the sight of gilt wires and bruised wings, the spacious but suspended

cage, the home of eternal unrest, of pacings, beatings, shakings all so vain, into which the baffled consciousness helplessly resolved itself. The cage was the deluded condition, and Maggie, as having known delusion—rather!—understood the nature of cages. She walked round Charlotte's—cautiously and in a very wide circle; and when inevitably they had to communicate she felt herself comparatively outside and on the breast of nature: she saw her companion's face as that of a prisoner looking through bars. So it was that through bars, bars richly gilt but firmly though discreetly planted, Charlotte finally struck her as making a grim attempt; from which at first the Princess drew back as instinctively as if the door of the cage had suddenly been opened from within.   (II, 229–30; ch. 35)

It is only natural that having conceived this image in response to the situation Maggie should envision Charlotte from the terrace at Fawns as an escaped creature, for it is during their encounter there that Charlotte in fact makes her "grim attempt" to force the issue and Maggie manages to best her, to drive her back into the cage that has begun to form about her.

"The cage was the deluded condition," James says (through Maggie's consciousness), and Maggie "understood the nature of cages." Knowledge thus constitutes freedom, and ignorance—which results in delusion—the cage. From the point Maggie chances on the golden bowl and learns in the process that Charlotte and the Prince knew each other before her marriage to him, Maggie's and Charlotte's positions begin to switch; the cage imagery in chapter 35 and later signals the exchange. Maggie's greatest test, to use the langage of chapter 36, is "by some art" to "hemm in" and "secure" the "splendid shining supple creature" by keeping her in the dark, preventing her from gaining the knowledge she needs to figure a way out of her fate, hence ensuring her powerlessness. The only way to achieve this end is for

Maggie to lie, to lie with assurance and ease, and it is not easy to lie successfully to one so accomplished and perceptive as Charlotte. Maggie is admittedly the underdog in the encounter: "Oh the 'advantage,' it was perfectly enough, in truth, with Mrs. Verver; for what was Maggie's own sense but that of having been thrown over on her back with her neck from the first half-broken and her helpless face staring up?" (II, 242; ch. 36).

Despite her disadvantaged position, Maggie succeeds in turning the tables on Charlotte during this, their most crucial, encounter. Charlotte manages to manoeuvre Maggie from the terrace to the drawing room and announces that she wishes to put a question to her:

> "Have you any ground of complaint of me? Is there any wrong you consider I've done you?. . ."
> Maggie summoned all her powers. "What in the world *should* it be?"
> "Ah that's not for me to imagine, and I should be very sorry to have to try to say! . . . If I've been guilty of some fault I've committed it all unconsciously, and am only anxious to hear from you honestly about it. But if I've been mistaken as to what I speak of . . . why obviously so much the better. No form of correction received from you could give me greater satisfaction."
> (II, 247–48; ch. 36)

Charlotte here employs all her skill, speaking of being anxious to hear from Maggie "honestly" while she herself lies outright in concealing her adulterous relationship with the Prince, which we have seen plotted and executed skillfully; but Maggie knows what she must do:

> " 'If' you've been mistaken, you say?"—and the Princess but barely faltered. "You *have* been mistaken."

Charlotte looked at her splendidly hard. "You're perfectly sure it's *all* my mistake?"

And so it *is* Charlotte's mistake—in underestimating Maggie and failing to realize how much she has learned and grown—although Charlotte is ironically unaware of the accuracy of her comment. Irony in James's world is frequently double-edged.

" 'All I can say is that you've received a false impression,' " Maggie replies, demonstrating how consummately she has learned the Jamesian language. Charlotte has not in truth been mistaken as to Maggie's preoccupation, and so her impression is not false; but Charlotte has been mistaken in her assessment of her friend and of Maggie's abilities, not believing her capable of deceit. Charlotte continues: " 'Ah then—so much the better! From the moment I *had* received it I knew I must sooner or later speak of it—for that, you see, is systematically my way.' " Maggie does "see," more clearly than her friend suspects:

> Her companion's acceptance of her denial was like a general pledge . . . ; it positively helped her to build up her falsehood—to which accordingly she contributed another block. "I've affected you evidently—quite accidentally—in some way of which I've been all unaware. I've *not* felt at any time that you've wronged me."
>
> "How could I come within a mile," Charlotte enquired, "of such a possibility?"
>
> Maggie, with her eyes on her more easily now, made no attempt to say; she said after a little something more to the present point. "I accuse you—I accuse you of nothing."   (II, 249–50; ch. 36)

With this lie, sealed shortly by a pledge (" 'Upon my honour' ") and a kiss, Maggie ensnares Charlotte, dooming her to return to American City with Adam. Charlotte is quite effectively "hemmed in" after this exchange; not knowing how to proceed or what to do, she resembles a trapped or caged animal.

The image of the caged beast appears again shortly, in chapter 38, when Maggie begins to consider the consequences of what has passed between her and Charlotte:

> She had had, as we know, her vision of the gilt bars bent, of the door of the cage forced open from within and the creature imprisoned roaming at large—a movement on the creature's part that was to have even for the short interval its impressive beauty, but of which the limit, and in yet another direction, had loomed straight into view during her last talk under the great trees with her father. It was when she saw his wife's face ruefully attached to the quarter to which in the course of their session he had so significantly addressed his own—it was then that Maggie could watch for its turning pale, it was then she seemed to know what she had meant by thinking of her, in the shadow of his most ominous reference, as "doomed." (II, 283; ch. 38)

Maggie begins to pity Charlotte, who is trying to grapple with a situation she knows distressingly little about ("Something indubitably had come up for her that had never come up before; it presented a new complication and had begotten a new anxiety"). The futility of Charlotte's search for an answer, since it is impossible for her to get all the information she needs to deal with it (Amerigo has maintained complete silence to her), "might have been grotesque to a more ironic eye," the narrator notes, "but Maggie's provision of irony, which we have taken for naturally small, had never been so scant as now" (II, 284; ch. 38).

The "intrusion" of the narrator at this point is significant because it prepares the way for another image of ensnarement, this one his own. It is one which endorses the validity of Maggie's original image of encagement. During her observation of her father and stepmother, Maggie notes a new relationship between them as they walk together around Fawns; notice that it is the narrator here who supplies the metaphor for Maggie's perception: "Charlotte hung behind with emphasised attention; she stopped when her husband stopped, but at the distance of a case or two, or of whatever other succession of objects; and the likeness of their connexion would n't have been wrongly figured if he had been thought of as holding in one of his pocketed hands the end of a long silken halter looped round her beautiful neck. He did n't twitch it, yet it was there; he did n't drag her, but she came" (II, 287; ch. 38). Mattheissen judges this image "nothing short of obscene" in its neglect of the cruelty it implies, but I am not at all sure that James can fairly be accused of neglecting the cruelty in it.[35] It is perfectly consistent with the other images we have been examining and is no more "cruel"—if cruelty is really the issue—than the others. I suspect that Matthiessen singles out this one, however, because it is clearly at this point the narrator's image and not just one of the characters'; it thus carries a different kind of weight and chillingly fixes Charlotte's fate. It also indicates that Adam Verver is not as unperceiving as we might have thought until this point, for Maggie begins to read much into certain of his "facial intimations" (she also now considers the narrator's metaphor herself):

> They amounted perhaps only to a wordless, wordless smile, but the smile was the soft shake of the twisted silken rope, and Maggie's translation of it, held in her breast till she got well away, came out only, as if it might have been overheard, when some door was closed behind her. "Yes, you see—I lead her now by the neck, I lead her to her doom, and she does n't so much as know what it is, though she has a fear in her heart

which, if you had the chances to apply your ear there
that I, as a husband, have, you would hear thump and
thump and thump. She thinks it *may* be, her doom, the
awful place over there—awful for *her;* but she's afraid to
ask, don't you see? just as she's afraid of not asking;
just as she's afraid of so many other things that she sees
multiplied all about her now as perils and portents.
She'll know, however—when she does know."

(II, 287–88; ch. 38)

Such are the consequences of failure in the Jamesian world.
If Charlotte has played for high stakes, and she certainly
has, her penalty for losing is also mercilessly high. The
chilling effect of Charlotte's defeat is accomplished in part
by the conjunction of the narrator's and Maggie's perceptions. The sealing of her fate thus carries a greater intensity
than it might otherwise have had; and the grace of intensity, as James reminds us in the preface to *The Ambassadors*,
is the "grace to which the enlightened story-teller will at
any time, for his interest, sacrifice if need be all other graces
whatever" (p. 318). James uses the Romantic Image in this
novel, however, in a way which allows him to preserve
those "other graces" while still attaining intensity.

There is one other significant occurrence of the cage image in the novel, in chapter 41 (the second chapter of book
6).[36] The Ververs have just sent a telegram arranging for a
last meeting with Maggie and Amerigo before their departure for the United States. Maggie goes into the Prince's
room, where he has secluded himself:

She knew herself suddenly, almost strangely glad to be
coming to him at this hour with nothing more abstract
than a telegram; but even after she had stepped into his
prison under her pretext, while her eyes took in his face
and then embraced the four walls that enclosed his rest-
lessness, she recognized the virtual identity of his con-

dition with that aspect of Charlotte's situation for
which, early in the summer and in all the amplitude of a
great residence, she had found with so little seeking the
similitude of the locked cage. He struck her as caged,
the man who could n't now without an instant effect on
her sensibility give an instinctive push to the door she
had n't completely closed behind her.   (II, 338; ch. 41)

Amerigo's position is not really the same as Charlotte's,
however: "There was a difference none the less between his
captivity and Charlotte's—the difference, as it might be, of
his lurking there by his own act and his own choice; the
admission of which had indeed virtually been in his starting at her entrance as if even this were in its degree an
interference." The difference is in fact total: whereas Charlotte is doomed, Amerigo is reprieved, and whereas Maggie's task was to encage Charlotte, it is now to release Amerigo: "Of a sudden somehow, and quite as by the action of
their merely having between them these few written words,
an extraordinary fact came up. He was with her as if he
were hers, hers in a degree and on a scale, with an intensity
and an intimacy, that were a new and a strange quality, that
were like the irruption of a tide loosening them where they
had stuck and making them feel they floated" (II, 338–40;
ch. 41). Thus through the agency of the same image with
which Charlotte's defeat is signaled, so is Maggie's victory.
With the same image she encages Charlotte and frees Amerigo. Like the Romantic Image of a poem by Yeats, James's
cage image "reconciles" opposites, the opposites of freedom
and restriction. The reconciliation is for Maggie an ironic
one, just as it is for the artists of whom Kermode speaks,
whose belief "in the Image as a radiant truth out of space
and time" is combined with a belief "in the necessary isolation or estrangement of [those] who can perceive it" (p. 2).
For Maggie, however, the issue has an added complexity in
that she does succeed in winning over the Prince. Yet when

we speak of Maggie's "victory" we must do so with the understanding that it is tempered by the sacrifice she makes to gain it: never to see her father again. In this sense her freedom and her restriction are one, and they are contained within the image of the caged beast released. She has her radiant truth but pays the price of a necessary isolation from her father.

"Of a sudden somehow . . . an extraordinary fact came up," the narrator tells us. This kind of immediate apprehension characterizes Maggie's experience throughout *The Golden Bowl,* and it is another way, besides the use of symbolism, in which this novel, so traditional in some respects, can be said to have Romantic characteristics. Maggie is like a Romanticist in the manner in which she knows things. Her manner contrasts sharply with that of some of the other characters. Throughout much of James's fiction we meet two kinds of Americans: the "experienced" ones, like Mme Merle and Gilbert Osmond, like Maria Gostrey and the mature Chad, like Charlotte Stant; and the "innocent" ones, like Christopher Newman, Isabel Archer, Lambert Strether, Milly Theale, and Maggie Verver. What distinguishes the experienced from the innocent is, obviously, knowledge, and in James's world it is linguistic knowledge, what David Lodge calls "linguistic virtuosity," that counts. One of Strether's problems is accurately interpreting little Bilham's assessment of Chad and Mme de Vionnet's relationship as "virtuous"; in *The Golden Bowl* much is made of "lies," both those stated outright and those committed by omission, by a character's simply remaining silent. Charlotte and the Prince, for instance, agree not to tell Maggie of their former relationship or of their visit to Bloomsbury shortly before the wedding in which Charlotte offers the golden bowl to Amerigo; later, the Prince's silence to Charlotte about Maggie's new knowledge is a necessary step in Charlotte's undoing, just as Maggie's refusal to tell Amerigo exactly how much she knows plays an important role in saving their marriage.

Learning to control and thus to use the lie, both the stated and the concealed kind, is precisely Maggie's task. One version of the concealed lie is to allow someone else to assume you know more (or less) than you do. Maggie uses this in her encounter with Amerigo over the shattered pieces of the golden bowl:

> More strangely even than anything else her husband seemed to speak now but to help her in this. "I know nothing but what you tell me."
> "Then I've told you all I intended. Find out the rest—!"
> "Find it out—?" He waited.
> She stood before him a moment—it took that time to go on. Depth upon depth of her situation as she met his face surged and sank within her; but with the effect somehow once more that they rather lifted her than let her drop. She had her feet somewhere through it all—it was her companion absolutely who was at sea. . . . But she had to insist. "Find out for yourself!"
>
> (II, 201; ch. 34)

We have looked already at Maggie's successful use of outright lie—to Charlotte in the drawing room at Fawns. What Maggie learns, simply put, is how to lie, which is another way of saying that she learns how to operate in the Jamesian social world. What is particularly interesting for our purposes is the *way* Maggie learns to become a "successful" member of this society.

Maggie's characteristic way of perceiving the world is unlike that of the other "successful" characters, the full-fledged members of the Jamesian club. Charlotte and Fanny Assingham, for example, thrive on their subtle discriminations and analyses, on analytic reflection. For Maggie, however, the immediate apprehension of an experience is what is certain. Her reality is structured on a "disequilibrium between experience and idea" (these are Robert Langbaum's words in reference to Romantic literature). She suddenly senses, for instance, from the expression on Amerigo's face that his and Charlotte's relationship is not what it has appeared to be these many months (ch. 25; the first chapter of part 4). Similarly, when the Bloomsbury merchant recognizes the portraits of her husband and stepmother and relates their visit to his shop, Maggie apprehends immediately that their relationship before her marriage to the Prince was more significant than one might suspect from learning of a single meeting between them. Once altered by her immediate apprehension, Maggie becomes increasingly aware of a disequilibrium between her original idea—that Charlotte and Amerigo are perfect, innocent companions—and her experience—that their relationship is not innocent at all. Similarly, in her encounters with the two lovers, Maggie uses her intuition, her apprehension of the situation, to guide her, rather than a preanalyzed plan of action (although her resolve to follow out the consequences of her perceptions remains constant throughout). We are most strongly given a sense of this in the chapter I referred to just above, chapter 34, in which Maggie confronts Amerigo with the now shattered bowl. It is primarily through the narrator's assessments that we feel Maggie to be working out the consequences of her perceptions; take for example these three narrational comments (all from chapter 34):

Then it was that she knew how hugely expert she had been made—made for judging it quickly—by the vision of it, indelibly registered for reference, that had flashed a light into her troubled soul the night of his late return from Matcham. (II, 181)

It had operated within her now to the last intensity, her glimpse of the precious truth that by her helping him, helping him to help himself, as it were, she should help him to help *her*. (II, 187)

Something in the tone of it gave it a sense, or an ambiguity, almost foolish—leaving Maggie to feel as in a flash how such a consequence . . . might be of the very essence of the penalty of wrong-doing.   (II, 190)

Remarks like these tend to give us the sense that Maggie responds to the world in a manner similar to that of many personas of Romantic poems. And since it is Maggie's consciousness on which we center throughout most of the second half of the novel, our participation as readers takes on a characteristically Romantic nature. In this respect, *The Golden Bowl* resembles *The Ambassadors:* Maggie is very much "encaged and provided for" in the former novel the way that Strether is in the latter. The encagement symbols are thus endorsed and reinforced by James's treatment of his heroine: a traditional narrative structure is welded with a treatment of character that is Romantic in nature; the restriction of the "mere muffled majesty" of traditional narration is combined with the freedom of the new (Romantic) presentation of character, as well as with the use of symbols which closely resemble Romantic Images.

The Romantic Structure of *The Wings of the Dove*

One of the most important scenes in *The Wings of the Dove* occurs late in the novel when Milly Theale, having invited guests for the evening at the Palazzo Leporelli, appears wearing a white gown and a double strand of pearls. The effect she makes is startling, since she customarily dresses in simple, unornamented black. Both Kate Croy and Merton Densher, the two conspirators after Milly's fortune, are immediately struck by the pearls. Merton suggests that the jewels would "uncommonly suit" Kate, and she agrees. He has then a kind of Joycean epiphany or Woolfian moment: "As she saw herself, suddenly, he saw her—she would have been splendid; and with it he felt more what she was thinking of. Milly's royal ornament had—under pressure now not wholly occult—taken on the character of a symbol of differences, differences of which the vision was actually in Kate's face."[37] Milly's pearls, in other words, take on the character of a Romantic Image, which can be defined, in the very words of this passage, as "a symbol of differences." This image, as well as the central image of the novel which constitutes its title, suggests that *The Wings of the Dove,* like the two other novels of James's major phase, is inherently Romantic. But we can go further: *The Wings of the Dove,* I suggest, is James's most pervasively and insistently Romantic novel.

The Romantic features we saw in *The Ambassadors* and *The Golden Bowl* appear in this novel in an intensified, more integral way. They are more thoroughly woven into the texture of *The Wings* than is the case for the other two novels. If *The Golden Bowl* offers Romantic elements as a counterpoint to its traditional narrative structure, *The Wings* presents a wholly synthesized form which enacts its subject matter in as complete a way as, say, "Ode on a Grecian Urn."[38] If *The Ambassadors* induces us to participate in the characters' internal concern for freedom by tying us to Strether's consciousness, *The Wings* embodies a thoroughgoing thematic concern for freedom in the imagery and symbols of its author, narrator, and characters. Unlike the other two novels, however, *The Wings* also fully explores the structural possibilities of Romantic form in the novel.

Let us look first at the question of freedom. Freedom is as explicitly a concern in this novel as it is in James's other works; the words *freedom, freely,* and *free* appear more times in *The Wings* than in either *The Ambassadors* or *The Golden Bowl*—there are in fact only seven chapters out of thirty-eight in *The Wings* in which these words do not occur.[39] Their repetition, sometimes in seemingly unimportant phrases like "she spoke freely" or "he freely admitted," helps for one thing to unify the novel, but it also helps to keep the issue of freedom in the reader's consciousness. Freedom is, moreover, the stated goal of the major characters of *The Wings*.

Milly Theale has come to Europe to escape the restrictive social world she must inhabit in New York. She seeks to make a new life for herself; even when her suspicions about her frail health are confirmed by Sir Luke Strett, she clutches desperately at his Strether-like advice to "live," to escape from this new doom by living as intensely as she can in the time remaining to her. She seeks also to escape the role determined for her by her fortune. When she embraces the role of dove it is an ironic acceptance typically Jamesian in its proportions: Milly wishes to be as daring as Kate Croy and as independent, to escape the sheltering wings of protective friends and relatives—she wants to test her wings, to fly on her own—yet she succeeds only symbolically by giving up her flight. It is only after Lord Mark tells her of Kate and Merton's engagement that Milly finds the means to act out the role she had earlier resolved to embrace.

In the party scene Milly arrives dressed in white, like a dove, but wearing also the symbols of her wealth, a double strand of pearls. Kate notes that there is something both odd and proper about Milly's jewels: " 'She's a dove,' Kate went on, 'and one somehow does n't think of doves as bejewelled. Yet they suit her down to the ground.' " Kate's remark prompts Merton to a further perception of his own that also gives us the key to Milly's sacrifice:

> Densher saw now how they suited her, but was perhaps still more aware of something intense in his companion's feelings about them. Milly was indeed a dove; this was the figure, though it most applied to her spirit. Yet he knew in a moment that Kate was just now, for reasons hidden from him exceptionally under the impression of that element of wealth in her which was a power, which was a great power, and which was dove-like only so far as one re-

membered that doves have wings and wondrous flights, have them as well as tender tints and soft sounds. It even came to him dimly that such wings could in a given case— *had,* truly, in the case with which he was concerned— spread themselves for protection.   (II, 218; ch. 28)

If Milly's jewels "suit her down to the ground," they also *weigh* her down to the ground and prevent that flight which she seeks. Yet as dove she has another path open to her: she may spread her wings for protection, converting the liability of wealth, which ironically restricts her instead of freeing her (as both Milly and the novel point out on several occasions), into an asset: she will prosper in giving up her wealth, giving it up, moreover, in the face of the knowledge that Merton and Kate have been trying to "swindle" her out of it. Ironically, Kate and Merton unwittingly do Milly a favor by providing her the means to divest herself of a liability; Milly's "favor" to them, on the other hand, is deeply imbued in Jamesian irony since, instead of offering protection under a mutual wing, it drives them apart.

If Milly seeks to escape a kind of doom, so does Kate Croy: Kate may have either freedom from financial struggles or the man she loves. She devises the plan to defraud Milly to escape choosing between them, but in the pursuit of the former she loses the latter. There are no simple moral lessons in James, however. Merton as much proves himself unworthy of Kate as she does of him. Kate's attraction to him in the first place is only sketchily analyzed by the narrator, who seems to dodge the issue ("Of the strength of the tie that held them we shall sufficiently take the measure; but it was meanwhile almost obvious that if the great possibility had come up for them it had done so, to an exceptional degree, under the protection of the famous law of contraries" [I, 50; ch. 3]). Notwithstanding a certain calculated reticence on the narrator's part, we gather that Kate's attraction to Merton is based on three things: physical appearance (he is a sexually attractive man, as both Milly and Aunt Maud acknowledge, if only implicitly); her realization that marriage to Merton would allow her to assert her freedom from both her past life and her aunt's plans for her *if* she can also secure financial independence; and what she takes to be Merton's liberating intellect:

> Any deep harmony that might eventually govern them would not be the result of their having much in common—having anything in fact but their affection. . . . He represented what her life had never given her and certainly, without some such aid as his, never would give her; all the high dim things she lumped together as of the mind. It was on the side of the mind that Densher was rich for her and mysterious and strong; and he had rendered her in especial the sovereign service of making that element real. She had had all her days to take it terribly on trust, no creature she had ever encountered having been able to testify for it directly. (I, 50–51; ch. 3)

One way of looking at their relationship would be to say that Merton gives Kate a sense of her own intellectual power. And indeed as the novel progresses, Kate gains assurance in her intellectual capacities, outstrips Merton, and begins to delight in that power. She lives up to the expectations of her father, sister, and aunt, but she also pays the Jamesian penalty for the power she discovers within herself. At the end of the novel when both she and we take the measure of the strength of her tie to Merton, we see that the penalty has been great. Merton offers to marry Kate if she will renounce Milly's inheritance, but Kate perceives that Merton has changed, that he is now half in love with Milly's memory, and that the three causes of her original love for Merton have been drastically weakened or obliterated altogether. His physical desire for her is now tempered by his spiritual love for Milly; marriage to him without Milly's fortune offers no escape at all from the conditions of Kate's former life, from the life her sister in fact is living; and Merton proves Kate's intellectual inferior in his inability to live up to the consequences of the scheme to defraud Milly, having succumbed instead to Milly's dovelike acceptance of weakness and rejected Kate's strength. For Kate, Merton's failure is nothing short of a failure of imagination. She has no choice but to abandon him with the acknowledgment that " 'we shall never be again as we were!' "

For Merton the question of freedom is also important, although it scarcely seems to arise for him consciously until late in the novel when he must choose between his integrity and his lust. Merton's fate is to fail to strive for freedom. He is characterized from the beginning as a young man of limited achievement; he has never developed the strength or skill to be successfully self-assertive. His participation in Kate's scheme is a test of his willingness to engage himself in the effort to dominate his fate rather than merely to accept it, a test he fails. He first allows himself passively to be drawn into Kate's scheme; when he realizes how much he is committed, he makes his abortive play for dominance and control by compelling Kate to sleep with him. But when he misjudges both the situation and his own resources, pulls back from Kate's scheme, and permits himself to be drawn by Milly into her scheme to become a dove, he discovers himself wholly entwined in a web of someone else's design. Merton finds himself overwhelmed. He realizes too late that he had not the talent or the willingness to participate successfully in Kate's scheme; his experience of Milly as "prodigious" retires him to an acceptance of his fate, of his limited resources in dealing with people like Kate on their own grounds. In short, he ceases to compete.

In a sense, Merton is the most pitiful character in the novel. The loss of freedom, of control over one's life and actions, is the penalty most to be dreaded in the Jamesian world. Merton never succeeds at being an agent in any of the actions that determine his fate. He is first slave to his physical passion for Kate, then slave to his spiritual love for Milly. His one gesture toward control—his demand that Kate sleep with him—is ill-conceived: Kate spends one night with him before she departs Venice for London, and Merton is for days haunted by the memory of her physical presence. His "domination" of her is hollow not only because she is quite willing to sleep with him, but also because his part of the agreement is merely to comply with her wishes (if he refused to go through with her plan he would only be thwarting his own physical desire further). When he is ultimately "converted" to Milly's dovelike acceptance of sacrifice, he merely exchanges one kind of domination for another: he submits to Milly's spiritual instead of Kate's intellectual domination. In no way does Merton gain by the exchange. His moral victory in refusing to accept Milly's fortune is Pyrrhic; his offer of marriage to Kate is an offer for her to join him in defeat, to accept the enslavement of financial, emotional, and intellectual paucity. For Milly, acceptance of the sacrificial role of dove can provide a kind of salvation; Merton's acceptance of such a role is, on the other hand, a pale copy of Milly's and seems to me to signal defeat.

Freedom, we can conclude, is as important a thematic concern of *The Wings of the Dove* as it is of *The Ambassadors* or *The Golden Bowl*. Like the latter novel, *The Wings* also embodies this concern for freedom symbolically. And like the symbol of the golden bowl, the images and symbols of this novel work in the manner of a Romantic Image; that is, they embody contraries, join opposites together—they are "symbols of differences." The most prominent of these have already been mentioned: Milly as dove, the wings of the dove, the pearls that Milly wears. Each offers, like the cage imagery of *The Golden Bowl*, an ironic reconciliation of opposites. But there is another important image in *The Wings of the Dove*—one that has received less critical attention—

that also works as a Romantic Image. It is the image of the abyss. Jean Kimball notes that with Milly "enters the dominating, portentous image of the abyss."[40] At our first encounter with them, Milly Theale and her companion, Susan Stringham, are traveling in the Swiss Alps; through Susan's consciousness, James strikes the keynote of Milly's characterization—her ironically great potential for freedom coupled with her inability to achieve it. Susan has taken Milly in hand after discovering how sheltered her life has been (she "had been starved for culture," for one thing). Although Susan is momentarily concerned about her own qualifications to undertake such a task as giving Milly culture, she is struck by something that resolves her to go ahead—a "sense of harrowing pathos."

> That, primarily, was what appealed to her, what seemed to open the door of romance for her still wider than any, than a still more reckless, connexion with the 'picture-papers.' For such was essentially the point: it was rich, romantic, abysmal, to have, as was evident, thousands and thousands a year, to have youth and intelligence and, if not beauty, at least in equal measure a high dim charming ambiguous oddity, which was even better, and then on top of all to enjoy boundless freedom, the freedom of the wind in the desert—it was unspeakably touching to be so equipped and yet to have been reduced by fortune to little humble-minded mistakes.
>
> (I, 110; ch. 5)

Milly's situation is in fact "abysmal," although in less "romantic" a sense than Susan here intends. By the end of the novel we take a measure of the depth of Milly's misfortune, and the outcome is shaped by the reverberations of the word *abysmal*.

It first appears in the novel barely ten pages before—in the last sentence of the previous chapter—when Kate exclaims to

Merton: " 'Then that's exactly why we've such an abysmal need of you!' " (I, 99; ch. 4). Milly's need of Merton also turns out to be "abysmal" (i.e., bottomless). Yet for both Kate and Milly the pejorative sense (i.e., immeasurably bad) applies as well. Kate's plan fails abysmally, as does Milly's attempted flight, in that she renounces her chance for "life" with Merton. Yet Milly's plan succeeds in that she becomes a dove for whom Merton's admiration and love are bottomless and unfathomable. The pejorative and nonpejorative senses of the word seem to apply equally well to Milly's situation depending on the angle from which it is viewed.

Associated with *abysmal* is its root, *abyss*, both the word and the idea. Shortly after our first meeting with Milly, we are indirectly given the suggestion that Milly might wish to commit suicide by jumping from a precipice, metaphorically leaping into the abyss; that is Susan's initial thought, although she immediately rejects it. The idea, however, remains in the reader's mind and cannot but color the later conversation in which Milly says to her companion, " 'Don't tell me that—in this for instance—there are not abysses. I want abysses' " (I, 186; ch. 9). Again, two contrary meanings exist simultaneously. Milly wishes for some tremendous experience—of which she feels herself to be just on the brink—and in successfully taking on the role of sacrificial dove she has that experience. Viewed another way, the remark to Susan is ironic: Milly gets an abyss—death—she tries for most of the novel to avoid (death is literally the experience of which she is at the edge for the whole novel). To add yet another complication: a third meaning to Milly's "I want abysses" is relevant, for in a way we might say that Milly does commit suicide (metaphorically), does jump off that precipice, when, in Susan's phrase, she "turns her face to the wall."[41] Milly herself thus resembles a Romantic Image (like Robert Gregory in Yeats's poem) in that she embodies contraries: she both flies over the abyss and plunges into it.

Another area in which *The Wings of the Dove* is pervasively

Romantic is the area I have called "perspective." The questions of freedom as theme and of Romantic Images are really functions of the narration, functions of the creation and manipulation of various perspectives. James uses narrative perspective to give *The Wings* its Romantic form through point of view. Contending that "the psychological center of the drama in James's late novels is in the narrator's mind," Leo Bersani has this to say about point of view and *The Wings of the Dove:*

> One has the impression in reading the novel that the course the action takes is being determined by the demand of the point of view James wishes to develop. There is a curious reversal of the relationship one would expect between point of view and situation. One does not have the illusion that the latter is the given basis of human experience toward which a human perspective must be created, developed. Rather, the subject of the novel is so entirely the growth of a certain point of view, an inner choice, that the plot seems to be created step by step by the stage of inner recognition and choice to which James wants his center to proceed.[42]

Now Bersani has in effect described one of the major characteristics of Romantic literature in this assessment of *The Wings.* One might easily depict *The Prelude* or "Hyperion" or "Prometheus Unbound" or even "Don Juan"[43] in the very words Bersani uses here: each of these poems could be said to be "so entirely the growth of a certain point of view, an inner choice, that the plot [i.e., the unfolding experience of the subject matter] seems to be created step by step by the stage of inner recognition and choice to which James [or Wordsworth or Keats or Shelley or Byron] wants his center [i.e., his persona] to proceed." Indeed, this is precisely the point I made about "Ode to a Nightingale" in chapter two, although I used other words to describe it.

There are these three areas, then, in which *The Wings of the Dove* can be called Romantic: in its use of freedom as theme, in its Romantic Images, and in its narrational form. But I suggested at the outset of our discussion that there was another area in which *The Wings* is Romantic: in its structure. More so than either *The Ambassadors* or *The Golden Bowl*, *The Wings* explores the possibilities for structuring the form of the novel in such a way as to reinforce its other Romantic characteristics. In this sense, *The Wings* is more fully Romantic than its two companion novels of James's late phase.

James's structural discussion in his preface to *The Wings* offers our best starting point. He suggests that the novel is constructed in what he calls narrative "blocks," and notes that "my registers or 'reflectors' . . . work . . . in arranged alternation" (pp. 300–01). Thus in books 1 and 2 (chs. 1–4), the center of consciousness is shared by Kate and Merton (James calls the center of these books the "subjective community of my young pair" [p. 304], while Susan Stringham ("a supplementary reflector") is center for books 3 and 4 (chs. 5–9) and Milly for book 5 (chs. 10–16). This accounts for volume one of the New York edition. James offers no such paradigm for volume two, however, which he brands "the false and deformed half" of the novel (p. 302). I suspect that James labels this second half false and deformed in part because it cannot be broken down into alternating blocks in which separate registers or reflectors are employed. Instead, in the last half of the novel, as Leo Bersani demonstrates, the narrator becomes the real center; he has been so all along, of course, but it is in the second half of the novel that his assumption of the role of center can be most fully recognized.

Usually one of his most perceptive critics, James has been misled here, I suggest, by his concern over what he thinks is the "make-shift middle" of *The Wings*. (James worries in his preface to *The Tragic Muse* that he has not always succeeded in getting the "organic centre" of many of his works "into proper position" [p. 85]; indeed the idea of centricity is one that concerns him in several forms throughout the prefaces.)[44] Viewed as the narrator's drama, the novel no longer seems to have a makeshift middle or to be imbalanced; James was considering it from Milly's viewpoint when he pronounced the novel to have such a flaw.

If James's concern for the proper "center" for the novel leads him to underrate *The Wings of the Dove* somewhat—or to complain of a nonexistent or at least irrelevant fault—that concern also leads him to offer an illuminating and appropriate image for the experience the structure of the novel embodies, an image we encountered in our discussion of another Romantic novel, *Frankenstein*. The image is that of the whirlpool. James suggests that the persons around Milly would be "drawn in as by some pool of a Lorelei." Later he adds this qualifying remark: "I have named the Rhine-maiden, but our young friend's existence would create rather, all round her, very much that whirlpool movement of waters produced by the sinking of a big vessel or the failure of a great business; when we figure to ourselves the strong narrowing eddies, the immense force of suction, the general engulfment that, for any neighbouring object, makes immersion inevitable" (p. 291–93). I think that this image applies to the novel in several ways, some of which James did not seem consciously to intend. What he does intend is perfectly appropriate—Milly does, like a siren, draw the other characters to her and many of them can be said to be "immersed" in the process; this immersion, moreover, can be either a positive or a negative thing (we have once more a Romantic Image).

In another sense, however, the image of the whirlpool is an apt way to describe both the novel's structure and the nature of its aesthetic experience. To consider this latter point first: many of the events of the novel strike us with great emotional force, they seem to appear from a calm sea, just as whirlpools are often unexpectedly encountered in otherwise undisturbed waters. The naming of Milly as dove works this way, as Ernest Sandeen notes: "The first time Kate calls Milly a dove, she does so with dramatic suddenness, and yet the metaphor bursts out of the context of their conversation logically enough."[45] Similarly Kate's agreeing to sleep with Merton and Milly's decision to "turn her face to the wall" seem to strike us with the same kind of force of the unexpected. Richard Chartier calls our attention to the use of the whirlpool image in *The Ambassadors* ("Strether considers how his relation to Chad and Mme de Vionnet 'could still draw him down like a whirlpool' ") and concludes: "The whirlpool image suggests the unpredictability of life; the waters suck one in, confuse, alter perspective, and effect a sea change."[46] This is true for the characters in *The Wings,* and it is true for the reader too. The actions of sucking one in, confusing one, altering one's perspective, and bringing about a sea change are all appropriate ways to speak of the aesthetic experience of James's novels, especially of *The Wings.* It is just this kind of effect that Romantic literature in general seeks.

The whirlpool image is applicable to the structure of *The Wings of the Dove* in a way distinct from James's use of it in his preface. The novel begins and ends with scenes concerning Kate and Merton, while Milly appears only in the central chapters of the book, so that the novel as a whole can be said to be constructed like a whirlpool. (The vortical structure here is somewhat similar to that of *Frankenstein*—Milly's physical presence in the novel works in a manner like the monster's narrative—except that there are no formal rings of narration in *The Wings* to call special attention to the "vortex" itself.) So much James himself acknowledges in the preface:

> Yet it was none the less visibly my "key," as I have
> said, that though my regenerate young New Yorker, and
> what might depend on her, should form my centre, my
> circumference was every whit as treatable. Therefore I
> must trust myself to know when to proceed from the

one and when from the other. Preparatively, and as it were, yearningly—given the whole ground—one began, in the event, with the outer ring, approaching the centre thus by narrowing circumvallations. There, full-blown, accordingly, from one hour to the other, rose one's process—for which there remained all the while so many amusing formulae. (Pp. 294–95)

At the same time James suggests another, different image—that of a medal with two sides, hanging freely—to describe the book. He proposes this second image, I believe, in order to account for the progressive nature of the plot: if it is true to say that both Kate and Merton are sucked into Milly's whirlpool, their experiences thereafter are not identical. In the first half of the novel Kate and Merton constitute "the subjective community of my young pair" (p. 304), but by the end of it they can no longer be thought of as a "pair," and if anyone shares a "subjective community," it is now Milly and Merton who do so. James thus invents his image of a freely hanging medal to account for the change in Merton's allegiance; I suggest, however, that the whirlpool image will work just as well to emblemize Merton's experience, if we consider all of its ramifications.

If the whirlpool offers the possibility of being drawn in suddenly and violently, it equally provides a means to be driven clear. In his encounter with Charybdis at the end of book 12 of *The Odyssey*, Odysseus draws on the nature of the whirlpool itself to escape its destructive power. His ship has been destroyed and his crew lost because they disobeyed Odysseus's instructions and slaughtered the Oxen of the Sun; Odysseus saves himself by clinging to a broken mast, but it drifts toward the twin dangers of Scylla and Charybdis. He is blown by the winds toward the whirlpool; just as the mast is sucked under he leaps up and grasps the fig tree which overhangs the whirlpool. He hangs on until the mast is spewed back up, jumps down onto it, and is propelled by the force of the whirlpool itself to safety. In reference to *The Wings of the Dove,* we might say that, like Odysseus, Merton avoids being sucked into the whirlpool that Milly and her fortune create and escapes the moral annihilation that acceptance of her money would bring him. Yet since we are dealing here with a Romantic Image, one which reconciles or includes opposites, we might also alternatively say that since Milly's acceptance of the role of dove signals her salvation, Merton is drawn in and is thus saved, while Kate is thrown free of the effects of Milly's beneficial whirlpool and is thus doomed.

So would run a standard reading of Merton—such as Bersani's in "The Narrator as Center in 'The Wings of the Dove' "—but I have suggested above that his "salvation" through Milly is an acceptance of a kind of defeat. There is no inconsistency here as far as the image of the whirlpool goes. What is at stake is the value assigned to the whirlpool that Milly creates, and James is less than precise and unequivocal in making an such assignation. If she is innocent, the waves she creates around herself are perilous and taint her innocence. There is more than a hint that Milly must share responsibility for the attempts of others to exploit her for their own goals, hints both in the novel itself and in the preface (where in addition to calling her a "lorelei," James says that her own hands are "imbrued too, after all, in the measure of their never not being in some direction, generous and extravagant, and thereby provoking" [p. 293]). Similarly, James's attitude toward Merton suggests, to me at any rate, that while he certainly gains a measure of personal moral salvation, it is a somewhat diminished thing he has at the end of the novel. As Sallie Sears notes: "A paradoxical sense of things, antithetical modes of structuring and comprehending reality without granting authority to any one mode, is a fundamental characteristic of James's imagination."[47] I would not go as far as Sears does when she later condemns Merton Densher, but neither am I willing to accept the traditional view that Merton is somehow "saved" by his encounter with Milly. Regardless of which interpretation of Merton you favor, my point here is that the novel is structured to offer the contrasting experiences of Kate and Merton in regard to the whirlpool Milly sets up around herself; and the attempt to create such a fictional structure is an endeavor to give the novel a Romantic form.

FIVE

Joseph Conrad

If James moves toward Romantic form in his fiction, in the novels of Joseph Conrad we find a complex, fully Romantic vision of the world. In two of his novels in particular— *Heart of Darkness* and *Lord Jim*, perhaps Conrad's most widely read fiction—he explores this Romantic vision, not as James does through subtle shifts and evaluations *within* a consistent point-of-view narration, but as Mary Shelley and Emily Brontë do through complicated manipulation of narrative structure and through the use of several narrators. We shall concentrate our attention in this chapter primarily on those two works, *Heart of Darkness* and *Lord Jim*, both because they are, I believe, Conrad's most significant attempts to explore the mystery of human experience and because they are representative of the kinds of innovative and experimental literary endeavors characteristic of modern fiction in general.

My efforts in this chapter are made considerably easier by a study of Conrad that appeared in 1974, *Conrad's Romanticism* by David Thorburn. Thorburn presents a powerful case for precisely the thesis I am pursuing here, that we ought to judge Conrad's art as inherently Romantic in nature, although he approaches the subject from a perspective different from mine. He contrasts Conrad's exotic adventure stories with those of Haggard, Marryat, and Stevenson, suggesting that Conrad transformed the adventure story into serious literature that dealt with the same kinds of subjects to which the Romantics addressed themselves. The specifics of Thorburn's remarks on Conrad's handling of the characteristics of the adventure story—exotic setting, melo-dramatic action, etc.—need not delay us here. Thorburn does make two points that have a direct bearing on our discussion. First, he suggests that Conrad's narrative experimentation is one of the factors that set him apart from writers like Rider Haggard and tie him to the Romantics:

> But in both versions the narrating voice is explicitly separated temporally and ontologically from the protagonist of the story, and separation—which often determines both the shape and the meaning of Conrad's fiction—links the author of *Lord Jim* to the Romantic poets even more decisively than his fondness for exotic settings or his frequent reliance on variations of quest romance. It is striking, in fact, how closely Conrad's most characteristic works resemble what M. H. Abrams has identified as the greater Romantic lyric, a poetic form whose defining features are the play of memory across time and the juxtaposing of an older poet with his younger self.[1]

Second, Thorburn remarks Conrad's "abiding preoccupation with the gulf between art and life" and goes on to suggest that "that preoccupation pressed upon Conrad the potentially disabling suspicion that the complexities of life lie beyond the reach of language" (p. 111).

These two areas of Thorburn's discussion, then—experiments in narration and the distrust of language—mark a juncture between his treatment of Conrad and mine. I shall spend the bulk of this chapter considering the Romantic nature of *Lord Jim* and *Heart of Darkness* as specifically a function of their narrative modes; the different perspective I bring to this subject will augment and, I hope, enrich Thorburn's examination of Conrad. As for the second area, we need only glance at Thorburn's discussion of Conrad's attitudes toward language to see how it supports my thesis.

"This doubt about the usefulness of language," Thorburn says, "is not for Conrad merely an easy commonplace or an unexamined assumption. It is a tested if melancholy aesthetic principle" (p. 112). In *The Nature of Narrative*, Robert Scholes and Robert Kellogg trace the source of the distrust of language to Rousseau's *Confessions*, summarizing one response an artist might make this way: "The new and the typical can be sought at deeper and deeper levels of man's inarticulate nature, with a consequently greater and greater strain on the ability of language to serve as a vehicle for communicating the vision."[2] One might easily use these words to describe Marlow's position in *Lord Jim* and *Heart of Darkness* as well as Conrad's position as artist. Moreover, as Scholes and Kellogg point out, Rousseau's distrust of language partially helps to account for the narrative form of the *Confessions;* "time and again," they remark, "it is the task of the old narrator of the *Confessions* . . . to say what had been in the heart of his young hero that lay too deep for him to know with his head and formulate into speech."[3] Here is a fairly accurate characterization of the relationship between Marlow and his younger self in *Heart of Darkness* and, especially, between Marlow and Jim in *Lord Jim*, although in both cases Marlow does not successfully fulfill the outlined task.

Before we move on to the specific examination of the two novels, we need to consider the several varieties of the Romantic outlook that Conrad employs. Both works gain their characteristic effects from the interplay of the divergent attitudes embodied within them. There is the implied author's attitude, which is usually very carefully concealed, that is, almost always implicit; there is the attitude of the nominal narrator, the "I" of *Heart of Darkness*, who is one of Marlow's listeners, or the "omniscient" narrator of *Lord Jim;* there is Marlow's viewpoint, against which the others' attitudes are most often measured or compared; and there is the attitude of the object of Marlow's ruminations, Kurtz or

Jim. Conrad exploits perspective in these two works by forcing his readers to work their way through their own narrative difficulties just as his characters, especially and primarily Marlow, must.

The most obvious result of this kind of fictional structure is the active participation of the reader. The comparison that springs to mind immediately is to *Frankenstein*. What we might call the "Ancient Mariner" syndrome is at work in both Shelley's novel and Conrad's two works.[4] The oral aspects of narration carry great weight for both writers: in Shelley's novel, Frankenstein relates his story to Walton and the monster tells his to Frankenstein; in *Heart of Darkness* Marlow narrates aloud his tale to those gathered aboard the *Nellie*, and in *Lord Jim* he speaks to those gathered round a table on a hotel veranda, a situation which parallels Jim's narrative on the veranda to Marlow. *Lord Jim*, moreover, is crowded with similar oral narrations: in the courtroom, there are Jim's and the Malay helmsman's, and there are several to Marlow—Jim's, the French Lieutenant's, Chester's about Robinson, the "half-caste's," Stein's, Jewel's about her mother's death, Gentleman Brown's on his deathbed, and Tamb' Itam's about Jim's death. Conrad uses other devices that disturb the flow of the narrative as well, and they too demand the reader's active participation. As Guerard says in *Conrad the Novelist*: "The interposed narrator or interposed reporting witness, the careful manipulations of chronology, the vivid interruptive digressions, the sudden movements from the abstract to the concrete and back, the ebb and flow of a meditative wandering intellect, the constant narrowing and opening of the lens—all these are means of controlling the author's or narrator's distance from his subject. But also . . . they became the conscious and deliberate means of controlling the reader's responses, of manipulating his feelings" (p. 59).[5]

Guerard goes on immediately to suggest that Conrad's "creation of conflict in the reader, and his fine control of that conflict" set him apart from "any earlier English novelist." This claim is somewhat inflated, since we have already seen that Henry James creates and controls conflict in his readers, as do Mary Shelley and Emily Brontë. Guerard in fact reaches a conclusion about the reader's role in *Lord Jim* similar to my conclusion about that role in *Frankenstein*. He says: "The reader in a sense . . . turns out to be the hero of the novel, either succeeding or failing in his human task of achieving a balanced view" (p. 142).[6] The word "hero" could mislead us, but the source of the fictional experience Guerard isolates is the same for my point about *Frankenstein*—that the reader assumes the role of a narrator. Readers of both Shelley and Conrad must piece together a coherent story for themselves. There is not time nor is there opportunity, as there is in a George Eliot novel, for contemplation; one must participate along with the central consciousness, which in the two cases at hand is Marlow's. For readers, like the auditors aboard the *Nellie*, who become inattentive or nod off, Marlow's tales are bound to be pointless as well as inconclusive. But for those readers, like the committed readers of James, who attend fully, piece things together, create an order and a meaning, the question of Marlow's inconclusiveness is irrelevant. The meaning consists in the experience of searching for it; "the revelation is not a formulated idea that dispels mystery, but a perception that advances in intensity to a deeper and wider, a more inclusive, mystery."[7]

Although the narrative structure of *Heart of Darkness* and *Lord Jim* forces the reader's participation, one primary and necessary aspect of Romantic literature in general, the Romantic nature of these works is made immensely richer by Conrad's handling of characterization. Marlow, his major narrative agent, is himself a Romanticist (or a would-be Romanticist at any rate), and the other important character he encounters in each work, Kurtz or Jim, is a kind of Romantic hero. The resulting clash of three kinds of Romantic perspective—the implied author's, Marlow's, and Kurtz's or Jim's—confirms the status of these works as Romantic masterpieces. It adds a depth and a complexity, a mystery, to the fictional experience Conrad tries to create. Let us first consider Marlow, one of the most striking and compelling narrative figures in literature.

There are obviously many ways to approach Marlow. He is a rich, subtle, complicated creation. I shall not attempt to summarize critical assessments of him; rather, I shall emphasize those aspects of his character that are most useful for the study of Conrad's Romantic fiction. The Marlow who appears in "Youth" and *Chance* has thus relatively little interest for us.[8] Perhaps the best place to begin is Ian Watt's proposal that "it was through Marlow that Conrad achieved his version of James's registering consciousness. Conrad's version is, of course, very different from that of James. In a sense it is technically more extreme, since where Marlow occurs, Conrad largely gives up the use of direct authorial narrative, which James usually retained; on the other hand Conrad's method is more expandable—there can be several narrators—and more suited to concrete visualization—Marlow tells us what he saw and heard, and we can see him doing it."[9] If Marlow is Conrad's version of a registering consciousness, he is more like the narrators of several of James's stories (like "The Aspern Papers" or "The Figure in the Carpet") than the central consciousnesses (like Strether) of the Jamesian novels examined in the previous chapter, since Marlow always appears as a first-person narrator. James criticized such a narration in a long work like a novel for its "looseness" and its fostering of "the terrible fluidity of self-revelation."[10] James used this kind of narration to good effect, however, in his own short stories—where presumably the danger of looseness was minimized by the strict demands for conciseness—because self-revelation was often exactly the fictional point he sought to explore. "The fluidity of self-revelation" (I shall omit the adjective) was also an effect on which Conrad sought to capitalize. As Watt says, it is important that we "see" Marlow telling us what he saw or heard; Marlow needs to engage us directly if *Heart of Darkness* or *Lord Jim* is to succeed.[11]

Marlow is, then, the prime agent in Conrad's compelling of reader participation. The nature of Marlow's narrative also clearly sets the tone for the novel: if Marlow can be shown to be a Romanticist, then the book as a whole can be shown to be Romantic. Marlow is similar, I suggest, to the persona of a Keats poem. We need only recall Robert Langbaum's discussion in *The Poetry of Experience* to demonstrate the point: "The process of experience is for the romanticist a process of self-realization, of a constantly expanding discovery of the self through discoveries of its imprint on the external world" (p. 25). Marlow's account of his experiences in the Congo is exactly this—a process of self-realization, a constantly expanding discovery of the self; so too is his account of his relationship with Jim. In both cases Marlow discovers the imprint of his self on the external world through his identification with the protagonist of his narrative, Kurtz or Jim. This perception goes a long way toward explaining Marlow's otherwise poorly motivated attraction to Kurtz and his insistence that Jim is "one of us."

Furthermore, according to Langbaum, "the romanticist discovers through experience the empiric ground for values" (p. 26). Such an endeavor is congenial to a gregarious sailor like Marlow. We can see this process beginning in "Youth," where he discovers through experience the practical values that govern the real lives of sailors; these values run counter to the ingenuous and adventurous ones (the "romantic" ones) he has learned from legend and literature. If Marlow is inexperienced when he ships out on the *Judea*, he is also less experienced as a teller of tales when he relates the experience of his first voyage as second mate.[12] A much more complex and serious discovery of the self through experience is made in *Heart of Darkness* because of his identification with Kurtz. The rest of Langbaum's explanation is now relevant: the Romanticist discovers the empiric grounds for values

> by giving himself so completely to each object that the object is allowed to generate its own laws, creating the values compatible with its fullest existence. But since the romanticist finds in the object the values he puts there, he finds also the objectification of at least one aspect of the values compatible with his own fullest existence. The romanticist's sympathy with the object leads to an illumination of beauty and truth in the object—an illumination which involves at the same time an experience of recognition, recognition of this beauty and truth as values he has known potentially all along in himself. As an experience, the illumination is undeniably valid. But once the perception of value is abstracted from the immediate experience and formulated for application elsewhere, it becomes mere theory and therefore problematical. The formulation remains useful, however, as long as we can earn it, to paraphrase Faust, every day anew.
>
> (P. 26)

The process Langbaum here summarizes could be used as a paradigm for Marlow's experience in *Heart of Darkness*. Just as Robert Browning chose unsavory characters like the Duke of "My Last Duchess" in which to see beauty and truth, so Marlow chooses Kurtz, whose own self-evaluation—"The horror! The horror!"—serves to deepen the mystery of Marlow's illumination of beauty and truth in him. Marlow allows Kurtz to "generate [his] own laws, creating the values compatible with [his] fullest existence," and his recognition that Kurtz's values are compatible with his own leaves him shaken. His perception of beauty and truth in Kurtz is "undeniably valid," but Marlow—and this is where he differs from the complete Romanticist—is enough of a "consequitive" thinker (in Keats's words) to be troubled by the recognition of Kurtz's values as the "values he has known potentially all along in himself." In other words, where Browning goes all the way and accepts the beauty and truth of such a character as the Duke, a part of Marlow wants to cling to old, moralistic values; he tries to formulate his experience "for application elsewhere" (i.e., in the sphere of moral judgments) and it therefore becomes problematical. Most of the narrative difficulty that Marlow has in *Heart of Darkness* can be traced to the problematical nature of his abstracted formulation of his perception of Kurtz's values and his recognition of those values as potentially his own.

Another way to approach Marlow's experience in both the works at hand is to consider the "effect created by the tension between sympathy and moral judgment" (these are Langbaum's words in reference to "My Last Duchess" [p. 85]). For Browning's poem, Langbaum contends, "we suspend moral judgment because we prefer to participate in the duke's power and freedom, in his hard core of character fiercely loyal to itself. Moral judgment is in fact important as the thing to be suspended, as a measure of the price we pay for the privilege of appreciating to the full this extraordinary man" (p. 83). The same price—suspension of moral judgment—needs to be paid to appreciate Kurtz fully, but Marlow is reluctant to pay it. Similarly, with Jim, as Guerard says, "Marlow must resist an excessive identification . . . ; he must maintain a satisfactory balance of sympathy and judgment."[13] Marlow is torn between two positions: on the one hand he seeks to maintain an allegiance to the traditional moral ethic—what Daiches calls a commonly agreed-upon sense of public significance—while on the other hand he finds himself responding as the Romanticist does by suspending moral judgment to allow sympathy to be his way of knowing. Following Northrop Frye's distinction between "conservative" and "revolutionary" Romantics, we might call Marlow a conservative Romantic; "the conservative Romantics," says Frye, "who accept the structure of civilization, as something to be imaginatively trusted, tend to stress the traditional elements in it . . . and lament their decline or hope for their renewal."[14] So Marlow, as a member of a basically conservative profession, feels the need to stress the traditional elements of civilization as he knows it and to lament, especially in *Heart of Darkness,* their decline.

"For many Romantics," Frye goes on to say, "especially the more conservative ones, a world which by definition cannot be known by ordinary experience becomes sinister as soon as it is translated from the language of concern. At best it encourages a greater reliance on forms of consciousness which seem to evade or by-pass ordinary experience" (p. 112).[15] So the world of the Congo, the world Kurtz inhabits, becomes both sinister and mysterious for Marlow once he encounters Kurtz, once he translates his initial interest in Kurtz from the language of concept into the language of concern. All Marlow's troubles begin at that moment of translation: the traditional values must be suspended—Kurtz ought not to be judged, as the Russian sailor knows—and sympathy ought to rule, but Marlow is unable to bring himself to surrender his old values. He still wants to find meaning in his experience while he rejects the ultimate step necessary for the full discovery of meaning: he does not want to give up the old system of knowing for the new.[16]

One of the ways Marlow attempts to find meaning is typically Romantic: he tries to use narrative itself to impose meaning. We saw the same thing in *Frankenstein:* Marlow, like Walton, Frankenstein, and the monster, tries to pretend (in Karl Kroeber's words), "if I tell you what occurred you will know what happened to me."[17] The Mariner's narration in Coleridge's poem gives the same effect. Moreover, Marlow's narratives in both *Heart of Darkness* and *Lord Jim* seem at times disjointed and fragmentary, like some of the fragmentary lyrics of the Romantic poets. Kroeber's description of these kinds of Romantic lyrics fits Marlow's efforts as well: "Narrative as it appears in these lyrics is an element of logical and rational organization; it implies a conception of experience as objectively apprehendable." In the great odes of Wordsworth, Shelley, and Keats, however, the narrative elements are "fully transmuted into the discontinuous structure demanded by the poets' efforts to express that which is not objective" (p. 58). Marlow's narratives approach such a transmutation, but it is Conrad through the implied author who effects it. That is, Marlow's narratives alone are in a sense inconclusive; the structure in which they are set creates, however, "a self-satisfying inner order, a non-logical continuity" (Kroeber, p. 58). What Marlow struggles toward—but Conrad achieves—is what, according to Kroeber, "the Romantics found in the poetic tale": they discovered "an effective means for asserting that the truths of intuitive art surpass anything that can be achieved by the methods of rationalistic science." Kroeber continues:

> At any rate, we see all the Romantic poets working against the methods of the eighteenth-century philosophers in treating of moral experience. They insist on the unified indivisibility of moral action and demand that it be judged in terms of its own entirety, as a total process. And they deny the ultimate utility of analysis, rejecting any suggestion of a moral calculus. To them good and evil, innocence and experience, sensual passion and spiritual passion are definite, irreducible components out of whose interactions the processes of human experience arise. Once these elements have been isolated, analysis cannot be carried further, and it becomes the poet's task to synthesize.   (P. 69)

That is the task Marlow faces, but because he cannot release his hold on the traditional ethic, on a commonly agreed-upon public standard of morality, he falls short of a true synthesis both in his tale of his Congo experiences with Kurtz and in his history of Tuan Jim. Marlow approaches the role of artist, of poet; but the completion of the poet's task is left to the implied author. Although it is always important not to confuse the narrator with the implied author, it is especially important that we keep Marlow separate from both the implied author and Conrad himself if we are clearly to assess works as complex as *Heart of Darkness* and *Lord Jim*.

Marlow, we can say in summary, is a Romanticist, a conservative one perhaps and a reluctant one, but a Romanticist nevertheless. So too, as we shall see in greater detail later, is the implied author of *Lord Jim* and *Heart of Darkness*. Yet another dimension to the Romanticism of Conrad's fiction is made visible when we consider the protagonists of Marlow's two tales. Jim of course is called a Romantic within the novel itself; we can add to Stein's assessment by making more specific the kind of Romantic Jim is. Both Jim and Kurtz are types of the Byronic hero. Neither completely fits this description by Northrop Frye, but both are obviously related to the figure he sketches:

> The so-called Byronic hero is often a Romantic version of the natural man, who, like Esau or Ishmael, is an outcast, a solitary much given to communing with untamed nature, and who thus represents the potentially expanding and liberating elements in that nature. He has great energy, often great powers of leadership, and even his vices are dignified enough to have some aesthetic attraction. . . . The greatest of all his incarnations in English literature, Emily Brontë's Heathcliff, has in full the sense of a natural man who eludes all moral categories just as nature itself does, and who cannot be simply condemned or accepted. (Pp. 30–31)

The aspect of the Byronic hero as "natural man" is more subdued in Kurtz and Jim than in Heathcliff certainly, but both of the former become outcasts; both have great energy and great powers of leadership; both have some vices that are "dignified enough to have some aesthetic attraction"; both elude moral categories; and both can be neither simply condemned nor simply accepted. Frye also tells us that "the great Romantic theme is the attaining of an apocalyptic vision by a fallen but potentially regenerate mind" (pp. 37–38); both Marlow's narrations—about Kurtz and about Jim—embody this "great Romantic theme" since we can say that in their own ways the stories of Jim and Kurtz are the stories of fallen but potentially regenerate minds which attain an apocalyptic vision.

Even more striking is the similarity between Kurtz's and Jim's visions of their roles in society and Frye's assessment of the Romantic poet's conception of his role: "He sees society as held together by its creative power, incarnate in himself, rather than by its leaders of action. Thus he himself steps into the role of hero, not as personally heroic but simply as the focus of society. For him, therefore, the real event is no longer even the universal or typical historical event, but the psychological or mental event; the event in his own consciousness of which the historical event is the outward sign or allegory" (p. 36). Kurtz, who starts out as a poet, as a well-rounded artist in general, enacts a perverse and macabre parody of the Romantic poet's role once he is ensconced in the jungle. Once in Patusan, Jim enacts this role seriously: he steps into the role of hero, as "the focus of society." Real events become his psychological or mental events so that he becomes the "romantic" hero of his boyhood dreams, and his death becomes the "historical event" which is the outward sign of his need to fulfill those dreams.

In fine, Kurtz and Jim are Romantics, Marlow is a reluctant Romanticist, and the implied authors of *Heart of Darkness* and *Lord Jim* are Romanticists who work to offset Marlow's reluctance and conservatism. The result is an interaction of three kinds of Romanticism that accounts for the compelling nature of the works.

Heart of Darkness

Conrad stopped work on *Lord Jim* in order to write *Heart of Darkness.* There are many points of similarity between them, the presence of Marlow not the least of them, but *Heart of Darkness* does not share, as Albert Guerard puts it, "the radical obfuscations and sudden wrenchings and violent ambiguities of *Lord Jim*" (p. 44). It is perhaps not merely idle speculation to suggest that Conrad put aside the novel in order to work out a less complex version in the short story of his (Romantic) vision. It would almost seem that he needed to sharpen his focus on Marlow by writing *Heart of Darkness* before he was able to make work the complex narrative experience of *Lord Jim,* that he needed to establish more clearly for himself Marlow's limitations and idiosyncratic grasp of reality. If *Heart of Darkness* is a more advanced experiment in the use of a narrative frame than "Youth," *Lord Jim* is a further step. Moreover, although Kurtz and Jim share a number of traits, it would seem that Conrad put into Kurtz many of the characteristics that would have been inappropriate for Jim or that would have changed significantly the aesthetic effect at which he was aiming in the novel. Although this is just guesswork, it is founded on aesthetic experience: I should like in this section to examine *Heart of Darkness* as one version of Conrad's Romantic fictional outlook, an outlook that was expanded and modified in *Lord Jim.*

The mysterious nature of human relations and of human experience in general is axiomatic in the fiction of Joseph Conrad. His insistence on mystery and his need to confront it wherever possible are the source of considerable critical controversy. The remarks of E. M. Forster and F. R. Leavis about Conrad's "obscurity" are perhaps the most well known; the whole issue is familiar enough, I suspect, to require no elaboration here. Where Leavis sees weakness, I see strength: Conrad's grappling with mystery is profound, although not in the way to which Leavis objects. Conrad is not merely trying to "inject 'significance' into his narrative," as Leavis suggests, when he has Marlow speak of an incomprehensible mystery.[18] The mystery is the central focus of Conrad's aesthetic endeavor in *Heart of Darkness*. One critic has even gone so far as to try to demystify Kurtz, to release him "from the romantic double-talk with which Marlow shrouds his phantom," seeking ordinary and "logical" explanations for his behavior.[19] Some of what this critic says seems plausible; much does not. In any case, when he finishes demystifying Kurtz, the story and its aesthetic power and value have eluded him; we see the endeavor for what it is—misguided. We clearly need some other approach to the mystery in Conrad.

That approach, I suggest, is to read the story as we would read a Romantic poem. Guerard calls the method of *Heart of Darkness* impressionistic—this is Keats's method in "Ode to a Nightingale" as well—and comments: "The random movement of the nightmare is also the controlled movement of a poem, in which a quality of feeling may be stated or suggested and only much later justified" (p. 44). The most obvious means of control here are narrative ones: narratives impose meaning; they impose a coherence on events and create an order for what was inchoate while it was happening or was being experienced. In this story, Marlow attempts to impose order and meaning on the past—his own as well as others'—by making narratives out of those pasts, by constructing a tale. Marlow thus assumes the function of the persona of a Romantic poem, although the narrative frame of the story adds a complexity that "Ode to a Nightingale" or

"Tintern Abbey" lacks. That complexity should caution us about simple interpretations, but Marlow's attempts at meaning ought nevertheless to be the focus of our attention. Marlow tries to confront the past through a narrative in "Youth," but he somehow never adequately approaches the real significance of his experiences aboard the *Judea*, beyond a general assessment of the idealism and naiveté of the young. As Edward Said says in *Conrad and the Fiction of Autobiography:* "Marlow's own captivity by the incredible is mitigated by his capacity in the present narrative recollection: as one tells a story of incredible happenings, one is forced to put the story in credible and familiar terms. That Marlow speaks in terms of the credible is a compromise both comforting and frustrating: because he has detached himself from the incredible, he cannot now totally command or convey the intensity of the past" (pp. 90–91). Marlow seeks to avoid that inability to command or convey the intensity of his past experience in *Heart of Darkness* partially by telling the story in incredible terms—for instance, by using the word *mysterious* or *mystery* so frequently (twenty-two times in the seventy-six pages of the Norton Critical Edition) or by his "adjectival insistence"—and partially by more confidently relying on the form of the narration, rather than its content alone, to supply a meaning, a credibility. Marlow's tale is rightly judged inconclusive by the standards of an ordinary narrative, since he uses narrative, as do some Romantic poets, as "an element of logical or rational organization," although the sources of his tale "are purely subjective and creative" and "cannot be told about" (Kroeber, p. 58). The meaning of his tale "is in all that has accrued since the original vision, in the gain in perception. But the gain is rather in the intensity of understanding than in what is understood" (Langbaum, p. 46). That "original vision" is for Marlow the moment in which he translates his experience of Kurtz from the language of concept into the language of concern, to use Northrop Frye's terms.

Marlow himself describes that moment of original vision as a "moral shock" (it corresponds to Coleridge's vision of the "secret ministry of frost" in "Frost at Midnight" [see Langbaum, pp. 45–46]). Marlow and the company officials have at last reached Kurtz's jungle hideaway and have brought him on board the ferry. At midnight Marlow is awakened: " 'I believe I dozed off leaning over the rail, till an abrupt burst of yells, an overwhelming outbreak of pent-up and mysterious frenzy, woke me up in a bewildered wonder.' " He looks into the cabin and discovers that Kurtz is gone: " 'I think I would have raised an outcry if I had believed my eyes. But I didn't believe them at first—the thing seemed so impossible. [Kurtz had been carried aboard too weak to walk.] The fact is, I was completely unnerved by a sheer blank fright, pure abstract terror, unconnected with any distinct shape of physical danger.' " The behavior of Kurtz's followers is unpredictable and unstable as far as the other Europeans are concerned, and at this point in the story simple physical fear for his safety is what we might logically expect of Marlow. But Marlow uses this logical element of his adventure narrative to try to get at something less easily defined or talked about:

> "What made this emotion so overpowering was—how shall I define it?—the moral shock I received, as if something altogether monstrous, intolerable to thought and odious to the soul, had been thrust upon me unexpectedly. This lasted of course the merest fraction of a second, and then the usual sense of commonplace, deadly danger, the possibility of a sudden onslaught and massacre, or something of the kind, which I saw impending, was positively welcome and composing. It pacified me, in fact, so much that I did not raise an alarm." (P. 65)

The remarks about the possible physical attack surround and conceal the comment about the other, metaphorical attack on his moral sense; they would seem thus to "explain" the moral shock. But they do not explain it because Marlow does not know why he is so emotionally affected. That a "sudden onslaught and massacre" could be "commonplace" is a measure of the force of that shock; and his failure to raise an alarm is hardly explained by the "welcome and composing" thought of physical violence.

Marlow succeeds in convincing us, I think, that there is no easy explanation of his moral shock—for instance, that he is merely appalled that Kurtz would choose to return to the savagery from which he has been "rescued"—by expressing his perception of it in so extraordinarly a manner. His claim to have been "pacified" by "deadly danger" is either nonsense or a serious attempt to convey the mystery of his experience. The story has very little to say to those who choose the first alternative; the rest of us may gain a better insight into its power by examining more closely Marlow's means of expression.

He goes on to say: " 'I did not betray Mr. Kurtz—it was ordered I should never betray him—it was written I should be loyal to the nightmare of my choice. I was anxious to deal with this shadow by myself alone—and to this day I don't know why I was so jealous of sharing with any one the peculiar blackness of that experience' " (pp. 65–66). It is in this moment that Marlow translates his experience of Kurtz from the language of concept to the language of concern; he does not know, however, why such a translation occurs. He knows that " 'it was ordered' " and " 'it was written,' " but the agency of these commands remains obscure: they stem from some deeper sense of identification with Kurtz that Marlow only then begins to apprehend. He is cut free from ordinary experience and everyday logic. At first this new sense of freedom makes him lightheaded: he thinks " 'imbecile thoughts' " and imagines himself doing " 'silly things,' " and he becomes reckless, heedless of physical danger in his pursuit of Kurtz (" 'I was strangely cocksure of everything that night' "). And most important, like Kurtz, he begins to feel himself part of the jungle life: " 'And I remember I confounded the beat of the drum with the beating of my heart, and was pleased at its calm regularity' " (p. 66).

Marlow traces the source of the change in Kurtz, which is by extension also the source of the change he feels in himself, to the mysterious power of the jungle: " 'I tried to break the spell—the heavy, mute spell of the wilderness— that seemed to draw him to its pitiless breast by the awakening of forgotten and brutal instincts, by the memory of gratified and monstrous passions. This alone, I was convinced, had driven him out to the edge of the forest, to the brush, towards the gleam of fires, the throb of drums, the drone of weird incantations; this alone had beguiled his unlawful soul beyond the bounds of permitted aspirations.' " But his use of the past tense (" 'I was convinced' "), as well as his insistence on a single, simple answer (" 'This alone' "), gives him away: here is the old, rationalist Marlow speaking, not the new Marlow who has felt some deeper, more compelling motivation in Kurtz's actions. Here is but the explanation of the moment, merely a description of what he felt at the time and not an explanation that will stand the scrutiny of hindsight. The mysterious power of the jungle, as important and relevant as it is, is too convenient a scapegoat to account fully for what has happened to Kurtz or to explain the consternation behind the assessment that immediately follows:

> "And, don't you see, the terror of the position was not in being knocked on the head—though I had a very lively sense of that danger too—but in this, that I had to deal with a being to whom I could not appeal in the name of anything high or low. I had, even like the niggers, to invoke him—himself—his own exalted and incredible degradation. There was nothing either above or below him, and I knew it. He had kicked himself loose

of the earth. Confound the man! he had kicked the very earth to pieces. He was alone, and I before him did not know whether I stood on the ground or floated in the air. . . . If anybody had ever struggled with a soul, I am the man. And I wasn't arguing with a lunatic either. Believe me or not, his intelligence was perfectly clear—concentrated, it is true, upon himself with horrible intensity, yet clear. . . . But his soul was mad. Being alone in the wilderness, it had looked within itself, and, by Heavens! I tell you, it had gone mad. . . . I saw the inconceivable mystery of a soul that knew no restraint, no faith, and no fear, yet struggling blindly with itself."

(Pp. 67–68)

This is a crucial passage, because Marlow here comes as close as he can to the real source of his fascination with and horror of Kurtz. His assessment of Kurtz is intimately tied to Romantic ideas. We can see Kurtz clearly here as Byronic hero. Like Heathcliff, he eludes moral categories and can be neither simply condemned nor simply accepted—he circumvents ordinary moral judgments which are based on some clearly defined hierarchy of values (" 'I had to deal with a being to whom I could not appeal in the name of anything high or low' "). Like Satan, one of the models for the Byronic hero, he has cut himself off from everyone and everything (" 'There was nothing either above or below him. . . . He was alone' "); he turns evil into his good; and he makes of his mind "its own place" and creates a heaven of hell and a hell of heaven.[20] Like Frankenstein, Kurtz must bear the complete moral burden of his world; since he has displaced traditional morality and its responsibilities, he must struggle by himself to control what he has wrought (" 'I saw the inconceivable mystery of a soul that knew no restraint, no faith, and no fear, yet struggling with itself' "). Like the Romantic poet, he sees himself as the focus of society, as the center of the universe; he concentrates his intelligence " 'upon himself with horrible intensity.' " Also like Romantic artists, Kurtz knows above all else freedom.

Freedom is precisely what is at stake for both Kurtz and Marlow: it is the bond between them. As Jerome Thale says: "And the discovery of the self is the discovery of one's freedom. Away from the grooves that society provides for keeping us safely in a state of subsisting, we can discover that we are free to be, to do anything, good or evil. For the mystic it means the freedom to love God. For Kurtz it means the freedom to become his own diabolical god. This radical freedom as it exists in Kurtz seems to Marlow both exalting and revolting."[21] The idea of radical freedom as the link between the two men helps to explain Marlow's endorsement of Kurtz's final words; here is Marlow on "the horror!":

"After all, this was the expression of some sort of belief; it had candour, it had conviction, it had a vibrating note of revolt in its whisper, it had the appalling face of a glimpsed truth—the strange commingling of desire and hate. And it is not my own extremity I remember best. . . . No! It is his extremity that I seem to have lived through. True, he had made that last stride, he had stepped over the edge, while I had been permitted to draw back my hesitating foot. And perhaps in this is the whole difference; perhaps all the wisdom, and all truth, and all sincerity, are just compressed into that inappreciable moment of time in which we step over the threshold of the invisible. Perhaps! I like to think my summing-up would not have been a word of careless contempt. Better his cry—much better. It was an affirmation, a moral victory paid for by innumerable satisfactions. But it was a victory! That is why I have remained loyal to Kurtz to the last, and even beyond." (P. 72)

Kurtz is like Frankenstein here in that he confronts the horror of his actions as Frankenstein confronts the horror of his (in the tangible form of the monster). Both men are entranced and repulsed by what they have done. Neither ever admits, however, that he was wrong to have tried to do what he did: both admit only that they failed to realize their dreams. Both ultimately accept responsibility for the consequences of their (Romantic) endeavors, but Kurtz, unlike Frankenstein who remains prisoner to his creation until death relieves him of the pursuit, attains a kind of affirmation of his freedom by fully accepting his failure. Thus can Marlow speak of Kurtz's moral victory.

Kurtz's assessment—"The horror! The horror!"—happens to coincide with what the traditional moralist would say about his behavior, but Marlow knows that that judgment is autonomous. It is made on the basis of Kurtz's own internal, private, idiosyncratic standards rather than on the basis of a publicly agreed-upon standard. Marlow is uncertain, in his own words, " 'whether I stood on the ground or floated in the air' " (p. 67) exactly because he knows that Kurtz's self-judgment is rendered totally independent of ordinary morality: Kurtz is remarkable partially because his own judgment is all that matters—he supplants the Christian God of Europe even in his death.[22] He is the complete Romantic hero, an amalgam of Satan, Frankenstein, and Prometheus: he successfully dismisses God and lives and dies in a universe of his own making. Even though by his own and conventional standards Kurtz is a failure, he still challenges the traditional morality that Marlow has grown up with: thus it is that Marlow calls his encounter with Kurtz a moral shock.

If for Marlow, as for the Romanticist, "the process of experience is . . . a process of self-realization" (Langbaum, p. 25), then we can better understand how overwhelming a shock his encounter with Kurtz is. Kurtz challenges Marlow's conception of himself and of the moral nature of the universe, and Marlow discovers that the values he has found through his experience with Kurtz do not correspond to those he held previously. Moreover, although Marlow finds himself, like the Romanticist, always in the process of formulating values without ever reaching a final formulation, he does not fully achieve, as the Romanticist does, the "positive accomplishment" of "an expanding potentiality for formulating values, an expanding area of sympathy and insight out of which values of increasing refinement can emerge and to which they can return" (Langbaum, p. 26). Marlow cannot fully achieve this "positive accomplishment" in *Heart of Darkness* because, as I have already said, he is unable wholeheartedly to embrace the Romanticist's position; he is rather like the narrator of Wordsworth's "The Thorn," an old sea captain, who encounters a mysterious event which his rationality rejects yet which haunts him nonetheless. As Said remarks: "Even though he had never seen Kurtz as he really is . . . Marlow finds that he is attracted to him because Kurtz is a *point d'appui* of Marlow's own making, a kind of secret dream, a companion of his enforced idleness. To the young and inexperienced Marlow, whose character . . . seems formed of orderly routines until, under the influence of disaster, he is thrust into a new realm of experience, Kurtz is what Marlow would like most to find" (pp. 186–87).

If Kurtz is a *point d'appui* for Marlow, and if Marlow is a reluctant Romanticist, we might expect to find a dialectic at the heart of Marlow's narrative. What we do find is an attempted dialectic, a vacillation really, between the Romanticist's insight and the position of the traditional moralist. Consider, for example, these two judgments: one comes relatively early in the story and is, I suggest, informed by the attitudes and outlook instilled in Marlow by his experience with Kurtz; the other is made later in his narration and is an attempted reversion to traditional moral values. The first is Marlow's musings prompted by the behavior of the natives along the banks of the river:

"The earth seemed unearthly. We are accustomed to
look upon the shackled form of a conquered monster,
but there—there you could look at a thing monstrous
and free. It was unearthly, and that was the worst of
it—this suspicion of their not being inhuman. It would
come slowly to one. They howled and leaped, and spun,
and made horrid faces; but what thrilled you was just
the thought of their humanity—like yours—the thought
of your remote kinship with this wild and passionate
uproar. Ugly. Yes, it was ugly enough; but if you were
man enough you would admit to yourself that there was
in you just the faintest trace of a response to the terrible
frankness of that noise, a dim suspicion of there being a
meaning in it which you—you so remote from the night
of first ages—would comprehend. And why not? Joy,
fear, sorrow, devotion, valour, rage—who can tell?—but
truth—truth stripped of its cloak of time. Let the fool
gape and shudder—the man knows. . . . He must meet
that truth with his own true stuff—with his own inborn
strength. Principles? Principles won't do. Acquisitions,
clothes, pretty rags—rags that would fly off at the first
good shake. No; you want a deliberate belief. An appeal
to me in this fiendish row—is there? Very well; I hear; I
admit, but I have a voice too, and for good or evil mine
is the speech that cannot be silenced."   (Pp. 36–37)

The second is this well-known evaluation of Kurtz:

"Mr. Kurtz lacked restraint in the gratification of his
various lusts, . . . there was something wanting in
him—some small matter which, when the pressing
need arose, could not be found under his magnificent
eloquence. Whether he knew of this deficiency himself I
can't say. I think the knowledge of it came to him at
last—only at the very last. But the wilderness had
found him out early, and had taken on him a terrible

vengeance for the fantastic invasion. I think it had
whispered to him things about himself which he did
not know, things of which he had no conception till he
took counsel with this great solitude—and the whisper
had proved irresistibly fascinating. It echoed loudly
within him because he was hollow at the core." (Pp. 58–59)

At first glance there seems to be a consistency here: the
jungle threatens to corrode one's moral character if one does
not keep one's "voice" and speak out against it; Kurtz suc-
cumbs to the appeal of the "fiendish row" of the jungle
because he is "hollow at the core," that is, he lacks inborn
strength. Indeed, this is a common reading of the story; it
leaves a number of questions unanswered, however, the
most important of which is: how do we account for the
intensity of Marlow's identification with Kurtz? The usual
answer is that Marlow sees the potential in himself to be as
completely corrupted as Kurtz, but the story offers very
little concrete evidence that Marlow is fundamentally similar enough to Kurtz to follow an identical path to self-
destruction: we are left instead with some kind of abstract
and mysterious bond between the men. Yet this mystery is
of a different order from the mystery that Conrad tries to
penetrate; its sources are confusion and inadequate information—we are not told enough of the right kinds of
things to justify reading the relationship between Marlow
and Kurtz in the way that we have to in order to make
Marlow's remarks in the two passages above consistent.

Considering the analysis I have offered above of the bond
between Kurtz and Marlow, I would argue instead that the
consistency between the passages is only superficial and
illusory. When Marlow says in the first passage that principles will not do and that what is needed is a " 'deliberate
belief,' " he is implicitly denying the validity of the traditional European moral code (a permutation of Daiches' commonly agreed-upon sense of what is significant in human

behavior).[23] Marlow argues that a person must meet the truth of the jungle, of the earth itself, with his or her " 'own true stuff' " and must have a voice that " 'for good or evil' " cannot be silenced. That is exactly Kurtz's position. By contrast, Marlow tries in the second passage to reassert traditional moral grounds for judgment: Kurtz lacks "restraint" in the gratification of lusts and is destroyed by his own moral emptiness, his inability to resist the whisperings of the jungle. The ease with which Marlow arrives at so neat and facile a summation of Kurtz tips his hand: although by traditional standards Kurtz is undoubtedly empty at the core, this kind of moral judgment, as the rest of the tale itself and Marlow's need to tell it demonstrate, is almost useless in helping us to understand Kurtz and his power. Just as Frankenstein pretends to Walton that the latter may be able to "deduce an apt moral" from his tale, yet offers not a real moral but only a statement that gives the illusion of one, so Marlow offers this moral to his listeners to create an illusion that Kurtz's behavior can be easily understood. Such an illusion is necessary for Marlow himself to keep a grasp on his experience; he needs to return to some common ground occasionally in order to maintain his ability to confront his experience at all.

Marlow faces a genuine dilemma, one inextricably bound to the Romantic dialectic between sympathy and judgment. His judgments tend to be based on traditional morality, while his sympathy for Kurtz renders irrelevant the grounds for his judgments. He intuitively recognizes the challenge that his sympathy poses to his judgment, and his narrative takes its shape and gains its energy from his response to this challenge. His encounter with Kurtz has threatened to make meaningless both his past knowledge and his way of knowing; he realizes that he must seek to emulate Kurtz if he is to make experience fully meaningful, but the consequences of failure, as Kurtz's example shows, are too frightening for Marlow. He withdraws his hesitating foot and seeks a compromise between his former reliance on traditional morality and Kurtz's way of knowing; that compromise is immediately put to the test when Marlow encounters Kurtz's Intended—and it is found wanting. Conrad himself insisted on the importance of the last scene, saying that the interview between Marlow and the Intended "locks in—as it were—the whole 30,000 words of narrative description into one suggestive view of a whole phase of life, and makes of that story something quite on another plane than an anecdote of a man who went mad in the Centre of Africa."[24] I suggest that the last scene is important because it is a clear refutation of Marlow's attempted compromise, and he knows it: the blackness at the end is his blackness, not Kurtz's. If in the wilderness Marlow affirmed that he had a voice and that his is " 'the speech that cannot be silenced,' " once he is back in civilization he is no longer sure of that voice, his speech *is* silenced, at least insofar as he fails to " 'meet [the] truth with his own true stuff' " (p. 36) and lies to the woman about Kurtz's last words. This failure is one source of his need to tell his tale to the others aboard the *Nellie*.

Whereas Marlow seems doomed to shuttled from one pole to another, never successfully to impose the kind of meaning that Kurtz manages to impose on his experience, the reader is in a different position. Here is where the implied author plays an important role: because of the narrative frame we are able to step back from Marlow and to assess his narration with the assurance that this is precisely what the implied author intends us to do. In other words, although Marlow engages our participation in his narrative in the same way that the persona of a Romantic poem engages our participation, the narrative frame gives us just the extra perspective that we need to read this story as a Romantic tale of a character (Marlow) who is himself struggling to accept a Romantic view point. Conrad is attempting an aesthetic project here somewhat more ambitious than anything Keats approached in his odes. Our quest as readers, then, takes on a characteristically Romantic air: we pick up meaning organically through Marlow's journey, his adventure, and we learn something about what a person goes through to create meaning for himself or herself in an alien universe.[25] In other words, *Heart of Darkness* is like "Tintern Abbey" in that its purpose, "its way of meaning, [is] to give just this apprehension of life [a sense of movement, of the moving, stirring life of the mystery], to transform knowledge into experience" (Langbaum, p. 46). We might at first be tempted to say that the reverse holds true, that *Heart of Darkness* turns experience into knowledge, but to accept this as the story's goal will probably lead one ultimately to agree with Leavis about Conrad's "obscurity." To transform experience into knowledge is a goal consistent with Marlow's endeavor as a traditional moralist; *Heart of Darkness* does what Marlow ought more fully to be doing as a Romanticist: it tries to transform knowledge into experience.

Lord Jim

Although Marlow is unable fully to achieve the "positive accomplishment" of the Romanticist in *Heart of Darkness*—the accomplishment of "an expanding potentiality for formulating values, an expanding area of sympathy and insight out of which values of increasing refinement can emerge and to which they can return" (Langbaum, p. 26)—he is given another opportunity to formulate values and expand his sympathy and insight in *Lord Jim*. In this novel he again meets a Byronic figure, one who lacks the perversity and seems to him to lack the hollowness of Kurtz, but who engages Marlow's interest more completely than Kurtz. While Kurtz is exceptional—a poet, a painter, and a musician; a gifted orator; the most successful ivory agent the company has; in short, the best that Europe has produced—Jim is in many ways ordinary, a common sailor with great dreams and little to sustain them. While Marlow was young and relatively impressionable when he encountered Kurtz, he is older and wiser (and perhaps, like the Wedding Guest of "The Ancient Mariner," sadder) when he meets Jim. These differences would seem to argue against any repetition of Marlow's experiences in the Congo; we should expect him to be less intrigued by Jim than by Kurtz, but instead his involvement with Jim is more direct and more prolonged. The mystery deepens: Marlow undertakes a deeper, more searching quest into human nature in choosing a subject who might otherwise be simply and easily dismissed as a second-rate young man with illusions of heroism.

The central focus of the novel is Marlow's identification with Jim. Most of the other people in the novel find Jim a curiosity, essentially unworthy of more than passing or idle interest, but Marlow thinks of Jim as "one of us." Those who believe in or pay lip service to traditional moral standards easily dismiss Jim as a failure, while Marlow is haunted by him and by his fate. Part of Jim's fascination for Marlow is the challenge Jim's existence implicitly makes to his traditional moral code. J. Hillis Miller explains:

> The discrepancy between what Jim looks like and what he is puts in question for Marlow "the sovereign power enthroned in a fixed standard of conduct." He does not doubt the existence of the standard [but he] comes to question the power installed behind this standard and within it. . . . If there is no sovereign power enthroned in the fixed standard of conduct then the standard is without validity. It is an all-too-human fiction, an arbitrary code of behavior—"this precious notion of a convention," as Marlow says, "only one of the rules of the game, nothing more." . . . Marlow's aim (or Conrad's) seems clear: to find some explanation for Jim's action which will make it still possible to believe in the sovereign power.[26]

Just as Kurtz undermines Marlow's conservative reliance on a traditional moral code of behavior by operating in a world outside of that code's power, by generating his own grounds for judgment and sympathy, so too does Jim exist beyond and outside that power.[27] Marlow discovers that his sympathy for Jim forces him to suspend his moral judgment. That suspension makes him uneasy, so he seeks a reconciliation between sympathy and judgment that will not compel him to surrender his belief in the old moral code. No such reconciliation is possible, but Marlow's gestures in that direction give shape and energy to the novel.

We noted at the outset of our discussion what David Thorburn calls Conrad's distrust of language, a trait characteristic of much Romantic literature. A conscious and deliberate concern for the verbal nature of reality lies at the center of both *Heart of Darkness* and *Lord Jim*, as many critics have noted. If Marlow focuses "on Kurtz's particular 'aloneness' or remoteness from the world of language" in *Heart of Darkness*,[28] in *Lord Jim* he focuses, more intensely if anything, on Jim's particular "aloneness," his remoteness from that world. *Lord Jim* in fact is pervasively structured around the various characters' attempts at articulation. The characters' experiences, emotional states, and relationships to each other are continually defined or redefined through their use of language, more specifically through the immediate degree of their articulateness or speechlessness, through the sound of their voices, through their (often temporary) ability to verbalize their thoughts, emotions, or experiences. Consider for example these incidents involving language or speech:

• At the inquest into the *Patna* affair the Malay helmsman loses control during his testimony " 'and, suddenly, with shaky excitement he poured upon our spellbound attention a lot of queer-sounding names, names of dead-and-gone skippers, names of forgotten country ships, names of familiar and distorted sound, as if the hand of dumb time had been at work on them for ages. They stopped him at last. A silence fell upon the court. . . . The episode was *the* sensation of the second day's proceedings.' "²⁹

• In the lifeboat after they jump ship, the members of the *Patna* crew must verbally convince themselves that the ship has indeed sunk: " 'they were suddenly and unanimously moved to make a noise over their escape. "I knew from the first she would go." "Not a minute too soon." "A narrow squeak, b'gosh!" . . . She was gone! She was gone! Not a doubt of it. Nobody could have helped. They repeated the same words over and over again as though they couldn't stop themselves' " (p. 70).

• Tamb' Itam is miraculously converted from a silent man mistrustful of language (" 'It was very difficult to make this faithful and grim retainer talk. Even Jim himself was answered in jerky, short sentences, under protest as it were. Talking, he seemed to imply, was no business of his' " [p. 173]) to Marlow's primary narrative source for the events surrounding Jim's death. Marlow's explanation for this conversion—that Jim's death " 'made the surly, taciturn Tamb' Itam almost loquacious' " (p. 214)—might be a simple narrative necessity, but it is consistent with the other kinds of linguistic behavior associated with the characters in this novel.

Incidents such as these, and others like them, form a background and context for the central relationship of the novel, that between Jim and Marlow. That relationship as well is defined by both participants' vacillations between moments of fluent and rapid articulation and stuttering, faltering inarticulateness. There are times, for instance, when Jim speaks compulsively:

"He could no more stop telling now than he could have stopped living by the mere exertion of his will." (P. 62)

"He ran on like this, forgetting his plate, with a knife and fork in hand . . . slightly flushed, and with his eyes

darkened by many shades, which was with him a sign
of excitement. . . . He impressed, almost frightened me
with his elated rattle." (P. 143)

Jim, like Kurtz, discovers the power of oratory; he becomes
eloquent when addressing the inhabitants of Patusan:

"Jim began to speak. Resolutely, coolly, and for some
time he enlarged upon the text that no man should be
prevented from getting his food and his children's food
honestly. . . . When Jim had done there was a great
stillness." (P. 155)

"Jim spent the day with the old *nakhoda*, preaching the
necessity of rigorous action. . . . He remembered with
pleasure how very eloquent and persuasive he had
been." (P. 179)

But there are other times when Jim is rendered virtually
speechless:

"He made an inarticulate noise in his throat like a man
imperfectly stunned by a blow on the head. It was
pitiful." (P. 46)

"He became another man altogether. 'And I had never
seen,' he shouted; then suddenly bit his lip and
frowned. 'What a bally ass I've been,' he said very slow
in an awed tone. . . . 'You are a brick!' he cried next in
a muffled voice. . . . 'Why! this is what I—you—I . . .'
he stammered, and then with a return of his old stolid, I
may say mulish, manner he began heavily, 'I would be
a brute now if I . . .' and then his voice seemed to
break." (P. 112, last two ellipses Conrad's)

It is through Marlow's consciousness that these two sides
of Jim are filtered; they are parts in the puzzle of Jim's

nature that Marlow attempts to piece together. As such, they are the focus of a great deal of musing on his part. Marlow is also a victim, however, of the same pattern of behavior. At one moment he ponders and analyzes Jim's motives in great detail or confidently lectures his auditors (see, for instance, his sermon on the virtues of going home, pp. 135 ff); at other moments he becomes inarticulate.[30] The most celebrated example of the latter is during his encounter with Jewel in Patusan; it is a scene reminiscent of his meeting with Kurtz's Intended. He lies to Jewel just as he lies to the Intended. Jewel has asked for assurances that Jim will not desert her. In so asking she narrates the death of her mother; Marlow describes the effect of her narration on him this way:

> "For a moment I had a view of a world that seemed to wear a vast and dismal aspect of disorder, while, in truth, thanks to our unwearied efforts, it is as sunny an arrangement of small conveniences as the mind of man can conceive. But still—it was only a moment: I went back into my shell directly. One *must*—don't you know? —though I seemed to have lost all my words in the chaos of dark thoughts I had contemplated for a second or two beyond the pale. These came back, too, very soon, for words also belong to the sheltering conception of light and order which is our refuge." (P. 190)

A few moments later, when she presses for his reassurance, he envisions himself exorcising a spectre, speaking to Jewel " 'with a heavy heart, with a sort of sullen anger in it, too' " (p. 192), because he suspects that Jim is not likely to remain faithful to her, at least not in the way in which she demands. He affirms to her what he does not really believe: " 'Nothing—I said, speaking in a distinct murmur—there could be nothing in that unknown world she fancied so eager to rob her of her happiness, there was nothing, neither living nor dead, there was no face, no voice, no power that could tear Jim from her side. I drew breath and she whispered softly, "He told me so." "He told you the truth," I said' " (pp. 192–93). But he is immediately distressed at what he has done in lying for Jim: " 'I felt I had done nothing. And what is it that I had wished to do? I am not sure now. . . . There are in all our lives such moments, such influences, coming from the outside, as it were, irresistible, incomprehensible—as if brought about by the mysterious conjunction of the planets' " (p. 193).

The point about language and Marlow's attitudes toward it is important because it shows us how he responds to verbal experience as a Romanticist. If, for example, the process of experience for him is the same as the Romanticist's, that is, a "process of self-realization, of a constantly expanding discovery of the self through discoveries of its imprint on the external world" (Langbaum, p. 25), then the means by which he conducts this discovery are first and foremost linguistic ones: his most important role is after all that of narrator. And as narrator, as teller of tales, he must inevitably become preoccupied with words. The function of language and the effect of words does in fact become the specific subject of his attention on a number of occasions. (A cursory check that I made for the noun *word*—or *words*—revealed that it appears 118 times in the novel, or slightly less than once every two pages in the Norton Critical Edition.) The full depth and breadth of Marlow's involvement with language is best assessed by David Thorburn:

> Marlow's characteristic diction, his persistent reliance on what might be called a vocabulary of uncertainty, is intimately related to these confessions of limitation and bafflement. In *Lord Jim*, as in *Heart of Darkness*, the famous adjectival insistence which has so disturbed Leavis and others is for the most part an essential aspect of the

novel's meaning. For Marlow's fondness for vague, abstract adjectives—one might call them Shelleyan adjectives—reinforces his stated conviction that his telling must fall short of perfect truth. The drama of Marlow's rhetoric is a drama of Romantic aspiration and failure, a drama in which vividly precise scenic details are juxtaposed against an abstract commentary which continually calls that scenic vividness into question or which insists on its radical incompleteness. . . . Marlow's eloquence, like Wordsworth's, is driven, tentative, self-doubting: a harsh, earned eloquence which registers, above all, a fundamental humility. (Pp. 117–18)

Let us focus our attention on one specific aspect of that "drama of Romantic aspiration and failure" which is Marlow's rhetoric. We will remember Karl Kroeber's suggestion that what the Romantics found in the poetic tale was "an effective means for asserting that the truths of intuitive art surpass anything that can be achieved by the methods of rationalistic science"; that the Romantic poets felt that once the "irreducible components out of whose interactions the processes of human experience arise" were isolated, analysis could not be carried further, and it became the poet's task to synthesize (p. 96). Marlow's task in *Lord Jim* is much the same as the task here outlined for the Romantic poet; he searches, unsuccessfully for the most part, for an effective means to assert that the truths of his brand of "intuitive art"—his inconclusive tales—surpass anything that the methods of rationality can achieve in understanding, sympathetically, Jim's experience. The drama is, according to Thorburn, one of aspiration and *failure,* however, and a major source of Marlow's failure is his refusal wholeheartedly to accept the Romanticist's role. He is doomed to draw back his hesitating foot just as he did in *Heart of Darkness,* although in this novel he goes further down the path to that successful synthesis which is the poet's task. The challenge to his way of knowing is thus a major determinant of his narrative; it is a significant aspect of the drama of his rhetoric.

One problem that Marlow faces is that although he realizes, to borrow Kroeber's language, that analysis cannot be taken further in isolating the specific components from whose interactions the processes of Jim's experience arise, he is reluctant to pursue any method of understanding other than analysis. He has several disturbing glances at the reality that lies beyond his analysis—an analysis based, as he tells us, on the notion of a " 'sovereign power enthroned in a fixed standard of conduct' " (p. 31)—and he is both attracted to and frightened by what he sees. His encounter with Jewel offers a good example. While she is speaking he has a momentary " 'view of a world that seemed to wear a vast and dismal aspect of disorder' " (p. 190)—that is, it threatens fixed standards of conduct and the power that lies behind them. He loses " 'all my words in the chaos of dark thoughts,' " but the words return, he lies to Jewel about Jim, and he is left to lament an opportunity lost; it was an " 'irresistible' " and " 'incomprehensible' " moment brought about perhaps by " 'the mysterious conjunction of the planets' " (p. 193). As Janet Burstein says about this incident, "Though his words return to him, they are as ineffective against Jewel's fear as Jim's words are at the *Patna* inquiry; discursive language fails in both instances to touch upon the truth of feeling."[31]

Burstein's analysis in general raises an issue relevant to our discussion here. She suggests that Jim's way of knowing is, in Ernst Cassirer's terms, mythic—it makes a "characteristic leap of thought from sensory fact to emotional conclusion"—while Marlow's thought processes are "more logical, analytical" (p. 459). The mythical thinker, according to Cassirer, lives "entirely by the presence of [the] object—by the intensity with which it seizes and takes possession of consciousness in a specific manner."[32] Jim, the Romantic, lives exactly this way; moreover, such a mode of apprehending reality lies at the heart of Stein's famous injunction at the center of *Lord Jim:* " ' "The way is to the destructive element submit yourself" ' " (p. 130). The destructive element is the Romantic vision of reality, a vision informed by the kind of involvement with the object that Cassirer delineates in *The Philosophy of Symbolic Forms.* To the rationalist, to the older Stein, such an involvement must seem dreamlike since, as Cassirer says, the nuances of significance and value that enable knowledge "to distinguish different spheres of objects and to draw a line between the world of truth and the world of appearance, are utterly lacking" for the mythical thinker (II, 35). Stein suggests that " ' "A man that is born falls into a dream like a man who falls into the sea" ' " (p. 130) because, I think, he intuitively recognizes that Romantics like himself when he was young and like Jim cannot draw the line between the world of truth and the world of appearance; from the viewpoint of the rationalist—Stein is talking to Marlow—such a situation must seem dreamlike, possessing the logic of the nightmare perhaps, like Marlow's experiences in the Congo.

But if Marlow is unable here completely to comprehend Jim's Romantic destiny, he still makes a greater effort at understanding than he did in *Heart of Darkness.* Marlow shares with Stein a sense of the pitfalls of the Romantic endeavor on which the two men have sent Jim, but he is more profoundly troubled than Stein by the consequences of Jim's Romanticism, that is, his death. Stein is aware from the beginning that not everyone will survive Romantic adventures to retire to a palatial estate and a collection of butterflies: " ' "He is romantic—romantic," he repeated. "And that is very bad—very bad. . . . Very good, too," he added' " (p. 132). After Jim's death, he sticks to his faith that submergence in the destructive element is the only way: he tells Jewel, when she has accused Jim of being false:

'' 'No! no! no! My poor child! . . .' He patted her hand lying passively on his sleeve. 'No! no! Not false! True! true! true!' He tried to look into her stony face. 'You don't understand. Ach! Why you do not understand? . . . Terrible,' he said to me. 'Some day she *shall* understand.' ''

(P. 213)

Right from the beginning, however, Marlow's response to Stein's evaluation of Jim as a Romantic is considerably more pessimistic; for him the dream turns sinister. Stein's pronouncement—'' ' ''That was the way. To follow the dream, and again to follow the dream—and so—*ewig—usque ad finem*'' ' '' (p. 131)—draws these equivocal musings from Marlow:

> ''The whisper of his conviction seemed to open before me a vast and uncertain expanse, as of a crepuscular horizon on a plain at dawn—or was it, perchance, at the coming of night? One had not the courage to decide; but it was a charming and deceptive light, throwing the impalpable poesy of its dimness over pitfalls—over graves. His life had begun in sacrifice, in enthusiasm for generous ideas; he had traveled very far, on various ways, on strange paths, and whatever he followed it had been without faltering, and therefore without shame and without regret. In so far he was right. That was the way, no doubt. Yet for all that, the great plain on which men wander amongst graves and pitfalls remained very desolate under the impalpable poesy of its crepuscular light, overshadowed in the centre, circled with a bright edge as if surrounded by an abyss full of flames.''   (P. 131)

Marlow's ambivalence and some of his imagery in this passage are very Wagnerian: Jim's experiences on Patusan in fact turn out to resemble a kind of *Götterdämmerung.*

Marlow's imagery here is also rather Keatsian: darkling

he listens to Stein's Romantic injunction and his thoughts echo a number of Keatsian ideas.[33] In general his mood is much the same as Keats's when the poet is despairing. But I was also reminded of the "Epistle to John Hamilton Reynolds," in which there comes to the persona "that wonted thread / Of shapes, and shadows, and remembrances, / That every other minute vex and please" (2–4). One section of this poem especially seems relevant to Marlow's position in *Lord Jim:*

> O that our dreamings all, of sleep or wake,
> Would all their colours from the sunset take:
>   .   .   .   .
>   Oh, never will the prize,
> High reason, and the love of good and ill,
> Be my award! Things cannot to the will
> Be settled, but they tease us out of thought;
> Or is it that imagination brought
> Beyond its proper bound, yet still confin'd,
> Lost in a sort of Purgatory blind,
> Cannot refer to any standard law
> Of either earth or heaven?   (67–68, 74–82)

We could almost be listening to Marlow here; so might we be a few lines later, when the persona says, "I have a mysterious tale, / And cannot speak it" (86–87).

It is especially appropriate that we compare Marlow as he appears in this novel with a Romantic poet, since Marlow, as Janet Burstein contends, "performs, to some extent, the poet's function" (p. 465). Marlow tries to do what the Romantic poets attempted: to approach, in Cassirer's terms, the mythic world; the poets did so through poetry which obeys its own laws, rather than through discursive reasoning. Their task was complex because many of them felt that they had first to dissociate the truly poetic from the kind of poetry written in the previous century, at least from that eighteenth-century poetry which tended to stress reason and rationality. The manner in which Marlow performs the poet's function is wholly tied to his narrative function in *Lord Jim*. Here is Burstein's explanation:

> To see Marlow's journey as a search for a way of knowing rather than as a quest for moral or philosophical certainty also explains the shift in narrative style which Conrad intended in the final chapters of *Lord Jim*. If the talkative half-caste and the journey by water to Patusan suggest a passage from discursive to mythic worlds, the fact that Marlow "begins to *write*" after he leaves Patusan may suggest a corresponding transition from the mode of myth to that of poetry. Actually, Marlow's medium in the last chapters *is* the written rather than the spoken word. . . . To some extent, Marlow does abandon his original narrative method, heavy with analysis, comparison and contrast; he turns instead to the language of facts, "so often more enigmatic than the craftiest arrangement of words." In the end he tries to allow the complex poetic fact to speak its own truth, unanalyzed and uninterpreted. (P. 466)

The general point of Burstein's analysis is accurate, but some of the specifics of her remarks need qualification. First, it is important to recognize that the "truth" of the "complex poetic fact" is unanalyzed and uninterpreted not because Marlow chooses not to analyze or interpret it but because he is *unable* to subject that truth to those processes. It is inaccessible to analysis. The best compromise Marlow can make is to "turn instead to the language of facts," even though he knows full well that the facts themselves cannot penetrate the mystery of the real Jim, just as facts at the inquiry do not express the truth of the *Patna* incident. The other half of the sentence which Burstein quotes adds an important element. Marlow turns to facts with a much more skeptical attitude than she suggests: " 'There will be no message,' " says Marlow, " 'unless such as each of us can interpret for himself from the language of facts, that are so often more enigmatic than the craftiest arrangement of words' " (p. 206). Thus, he is thrown back on the position he reiterates throughout—that he can only approach the reality of the experience with words but can never capture it. We have considered his doubts about language at some length; these complaints are obviously only half the story since words are the only means at his disposal, just as words are the only means that the poet has ("poet" here meaning any artist who uses language as his or her raw material).

Marlow's awareness of the inadequacies of language runs side by side throughout the novel with his awareness of his role as storyteller, with his recognition of the very real ways in which he is creating Jim and Jim's experiences for his listeners. This awareness confirms his function as poet; he acknowledges that his task is like Keats's task in re-creating for the reader his experiences with the nightingale's song or the Grecian urn: " 'Even Stein could say no more than that he was romantic. I only know he was one of us. And what business had he to be romantic? I am telling you so much about my own instinctive feelings and bemused reflections because there remains so little to be told of him. He existed for me, and after all it is only through me that he exists for you. I've led him out by the hand; I have paraded him before you' " (p. 137). He also explicitly acknowledges his creative function: he must synthesize, not merely report. He tells his unnamed correspondent to whom the final chapters are sent in their written form: " 'I put it down for you as though I had been an eye-witness. My information was fragmentary, but I've fitted the pieces together, and there is enough of them to make an intelligible picture' " (p. 208). But Marlow's preoccupations are circular: he cannot adequately parade Jim before his listeners or make an "intelli-

gible picture" unless he has the right words with which to
do so. Moreover, an important question lies just below the
surface of Marlow's preoccupations: why does he think it is
so important to parade Jim before his listeners at all? Early
in his narrative he answers exactly this question, and in the
process he most clearly allows us to see him confronting the
Romanticist's experience:

> "I can't explain to you who haven't seen him and who
> hear his words only at second hand the mixed nature of
> my feelings. It seemed to me I was being made to com-
> prehend the Inconceivable—and I know of nothing to
> compare with the discomfort of such a sensation. I was
> made to look at the convention that lurks in all truth
> and on the essential sincerity of falsehood. He appealed
> to all sides at once—to the side turned perpetually to the
> light of day, and to that side of us which, like the other
> hemisphere of the moon, exists stealthily in perpetual
> darkness, with only a fearful ashy light falling at times
> on the edge. He swayed me. I own to it, I own up. The
> occasion was obscure, insignificant—what you will: a
> lost youngster, one in a million—but then he was one of
> us; an incident as completely devoid of importance as
> the flooding of an ant-heap, and yet the mystery of his
> attitude got hold of me as though he had been an indi-
> vidual in the forefront of his kind, as if the obscure
> truth involved were momentous enough to affect man-
> kind's conception of itself." (P. 57)

Many of the points we have been analyzing about Marlow are crystalized in this passage. Marlow the rationalist,
the moralist, the believer in a fixed standard of conduct
here comes face to face with what for him *is* the "Inconceivable": he meets Jim and, despite everything he knows and
believes as a rationalist, he sympathizes and identifies with
him, knows him in the way that Romanticists know the

objects of their attention—through "sympathy or projective-ness, what the Germans call *Einfühlung*, [which] is the spe-cifically romantic way of knowing" (Langbaum, p. 79). Mar-low responds to Jim in the way that one responds to the characters in a Romantic drama like Wordsworth's *The Borderers:* "The difference [between characters of the nine-teenth-century romantic rebellion and characters of the eighteenth-century rationalist rebellion] depends not on what the characters *do* but on what they *are.* We sympathize with the hero because as a complete human being he is the counterpart of ourselves" (Langbaum, p. 63). Marlow clearly sees Jim as our counterpart—he is "one of us"—and he is obsessed with what Jim is as a person rather than what he has done. Others condemn or dismiss Jim for jumping from the *Patna*, but Marlow sees beyond Jim's momentary act of cowardice to something more important within him; the narrator of the frame, who for the first four chapters acts as an "omniscient" narrator, introduces Marlow to us with just this fact of his interest and sympathy in Jim:

> Jim's eyes, wandering in the intervals of his answers,
> rested upon a white man who sat apart from the others,
> with his face worn and clouded, but with his quiet eyes
> that glanced straight, interested, and clear. . . . He met
> the eyes of the white man. The glance directed at him
> was not the fascinated stare of the others. It was an act
> of intelligent volition. Jim between two questions forgot
> himself so far as to find leisure for a thought. This fel-
> low—ran the thought—looks at me as though he could
> see somebody or something past my shoulder. . . . That
> man there seemed to be aware of [Jim's] hopeless
> difficulty.   (P. 21)

Shortly after this Marlow and Jim meet for the first time. Their encounter results from a misunderstanding. An ac-quaintance casually remarks to Marlow about a mangy dog he sees in the street; Jim, whose back is turned, thinks Marlow has made the remark (" 'Look at that wretched cur' " [p. 43]) about him and comments to Marlow about it. An agreement to have dinner results from this encounter and during the dinner Jim begins his narrative of his experiences. Marlow's incipient interest in and sympathy for Jim grows stronger and stronger during the meal, which lasts late into the night; Marlow's sense of Jim as a mystery grows stronger as well. It is hard not to read Marlow's comments about Jim's relationship to the people of Patusan as an evaluation that also applies to his own relationship with Jim: " ' "My dear chap," I cried, "you shall always remain for them an insoluble mystery" ' " (p. 186). For Marlow at the end of the novel, Jim " 'passes away under a cloud, inscrutable at heart, forgotten, unforgiven, and excessively romantic' " (p. 253).

We have followed Marlow throughout this discussion, but this is as far as he can take us in understanding the novel. He remains fixed at one point, destined to go over and over the facts. Insofar as he is "always in the process of formulating values [from his experience with Jim and about it], although he never arrives at a final formulation" (Langbaum, p. 26), he implicitly asks us to read his narrative as we would read a Romantic poem. But he himself, as we have already noted, refuses to respond to his narrative in this way; he refuses to "derive meaning that is from the poetic material itself rather than from an external standard of judgment" (Langbaum, pp. 78–79) and he thus thwarts his only real way of knowing Jim—Romantically. Here is where the complex narrative frame of the novel becomes vitally important. Through it Conrad effects a double analogy: Jim is to Marlow what Marlow is to readers of the novel. In the first half of the novel Jim, we must remember, is an important narrator, an important observer of his own fate. Thus, Jim's narration functions as a kind of poetry of experience for Marlow, while Marlow's narration functions that way for readers; Jim is a "pole for sympathy" for Marlow and Marlow is a "pole for sympathy" for the reader. Seen in this light, *Lord Jim* can be said to work the way the poetry of experience does. As Langbaum comments: "For the poetry of experience is, in its meaning if not its events, autobiographical both for the writer and the reader. The observer is thus a character not in the Aristotelian sense of a moral force to be judged morally, but in the modern sense of a pole for sympathy—the means by which writer and reader project themselves into the poem, the one to communicate, the other to apprehend it as an experience" (p. 53). It is in the sense that Langbaum means it here that *Lord Jim* is autobiographical. Clearly, then, if Marlow is meant to be a pole for sympathy for the reader, just as Jim is for Marlow a pole for sympathy, then the reader is not expected to identify Marlow's moral judgments as the judgments of the novel itself. Such is the raison d'être of the novel's complex narration: to separate Marlow's musings and judgments from the implied author's intentions.

Let us look specifically at a crucial issue for the novel, an issue to which we as readers are expected to respond in a manner unlike Marlow; we are asked in fact to respond both to Marlow's response and to his *way* of responding. That issue is this: What is the meaning of Jim's death? How are we to interpret the significance of his death in relation to the meaning of the novel as a whole? We shall start with Marlow. We are immediately met with ambivalence. One side of Marlow admits that Jim's death is "successful" in that he lives up to his wildest Romantic dreams by dying an honorable death; that his act is perhaps gratuitous only makes it that much more a sacrifice, that much more heroic. " 'Not in the wildest days of his boyish visions,' " says Marlow, " 'could he have seen the alluring shape of such an extraordinary success!' " (p. 253). Marlow sees a frightening logic in Jim's death; he tells his unnamed correspondent:

"The story of the last events you will find in the few pages enclosed here. You must admit that it is romantic beyond the wildest dreams of boyhood, and yet there is to my mind a sort of profound and terrifying logic in it, as if it were our imagination alone that could set loose upon us the might of an overwhelming destiny. The imprudence of our thoughts recoils upon our heads; who toys with the sword shall perish by the sword. This astounding adventure, of which the most astounding part is that it is true, comes on as an unavoidable consequence. Something of the sort had to happen. You repeat this to yourself while you marvel that such a thing could happen in the year of grace before last. But it has happened—and there is no disputing its logic." (P. 208)

Marlow's astonishment at Jim's Romantic success is clearly mixed in this passage with an unfavorable judgment. His censure resembles the stern pronouncements of an Old Testament prophet: he who toys with the sword shall perish by it. But while Marlow's remarks assume the outward form of a judgment of Jim they are not overtly directed at Jim's behavior. What seems to disturb Marlow more than that Jim specifically acted the way he did is that anyone might act that way. The possibility of such behavior distresses Marlow and provokes his dismay. Marlow's doubts plague him right to the last page of the novel:

"Is he satisfied—quite, now, I wonder? We ought to know. He is one of us—and have I not stood up once, like an evoked ghost, to answer for his eternal constancy? Was I so very wrong after all? Now he is no more, there are days when the reality of his existence comes to me with an immense, with an overwhelming force; and yet upon my honour there are moments, too, when he passes from my eyes like a disembodied spirit astray amongst the passions of his earth ready to surrender himself faithfully to the claim of his own world of shades.

"Who knows? He is gone, inscrutable at heart, and the poor girl is leading a sort of soundless, inert life in Stein's house." (P. 253)

It is senseless to ask, "Is he satisfied?" of a dead man; the question must be one Marlow is implicitly asking himself. We know his answer: a resounding no. Moreover, one begins to suspect that his concern for Jewel is a disguised expression of his own reaction: he seems to feel as betrayed by Jim as Jewel does. The only answer we get from Marlow to our question about the significance of Jim's death is thus an ambiguous one.

Perhaps Conrad intended ambiguity as our only answer; let us reserve judgment on this possibility for a moment. What can we say about Jim's motivations? If they remain somewhat of a mystery for Marlow, are they equally mysterious for us as readers? I think not; our reaction is closer to Stein's than to Marlow's. Stein tells Jewel that Jim has been true, not false. So he has: in agreeing to give up his life for Dain Waris's, Jim is literally being true to his word as well as to the Romantic destiny he has imagined for himself. In living up to his word, he fulfills and simultaneously transcends his Romantic dreams, transcends that imagination which Marlow thinks has set loose on Jim an "overwhelming destiny," because Jim accepts the responsibility for and the finality of his words. Jim's dreams of heroism are translated from his imagination through language—the literal giving of his word to Doramin that no one would die because of Gentleman Brown's presence in Patusan—into reality: he becomes a hero by living up to his own definition of one. For once, Jim's actions are the result of his beliefs and are consistent with them; and what is more, his actions in this instance work an atonement for his past cowardice. The most horrifying thing in his life has been not the simple act of cowardice by itself, but also the recognition, because of his leap from the *Patna,* of the disparity between his inner world—his imagination—and the outer world. (Marlow notes: " 'From the way he narrated that part I was at liberty to infer he was partly stunned by the discovery he had made—the discovery about himself—and no doubt was at work trying to explain it away to the only man who was capable of appreciating all its tremendous magnitude' " [p. 50].) In Patusan, Jim effects an alignment between his inner vision of himself as hero and the judgment of the outside world (or at least of his idea of that judgment). He does not do so solely on the basis of the native populace's adoration of him, however, or on the basis of merely physical acts of courage, such as his storming of Sherif Ali's camp or his escape from the Rajah's courtyard (another leap; see pp. 153–54). Rather, Jim accepts himself as hero only after he has earned the right in his own eyes to be a hero: the price is fidelity to his word.

If Marlow's question—" 'Is he satisfied—quite, now, I wonder?' " (p. 253)—were sensible, and Jim could answer it, the response would be yes. Jewel's fate after Jim's death does not concern him at all; it plays almost no part in his "overwhelming destiny." Marlow is right when he describes Jim as " 'at the call of his exalted egoism' " (p. 253); since there is very little else in the novel to give substance to his relationship with Jewel—she explains her past and pleads her love for him, but there is only minimal reciprocation from Jim—it is difficult to assess the nature of his commitment to her. Because he easily ignores her desperate pleas to flee when news of Dain Waris's death reaches the village, I think we must assume that Jim's values are self-centered and inner-directed. Jim's act is thus not marred *for him* by any sense of responsibility to Jewel—in his own eyes he dies the hero, his only blemish his past leap from the *Patna* that his self-sacrifice in Patusan somehow redeems.

There is no ambiguity in Jim's own attitude, I think, but

his "exalted egoism" raises a problem for the reader: his brusque dismissal of Jewel's pleas certainly tarnishes his heroism. His death cannot be quite the "extraordinary success" for us that it is for him. Miller is correct when he says: "In *Lord Jim* no point of view is entirely trustworthy. The novel is a complex design of interrelated minds, no one of which can be taken as a reliable point of reference from which the others can be judged" (pp. 220–21). If neither Marlow nor Jim can offer an "entirely trustworthy" point of view, then we must look elsewhere in the novel for some clues to help us find a way to answer the question we posed earlier. The most obvious place to turn is the larger narrative structure into which Marlow's remarks are placed.

The novel opens with a narrator who seems to be the kind of "omniscient" narrator one finds in earlier fiction. In Wayne Booth's terminology from *The Rhetoric of Fiction*, we would call him an observer-narrator who is undramatized and isolated, that is, he does not appear as a character nor is he given support by any of the characters; he offers limited comments on the characters and on the action but does not speak self-consciously of his narrative function (as Marlow does of his, for instance); he is "privileged to know what could not be learned by strictly natural means" (Booth, p. 160); and he appears to be reliable. I say "appears" because in order to make a judgment about his reliability we need to see more of him than we do in the four brief chapters before he abdicates the narration to Marlow. Certainly nothing he says can be demonstrated to be unreliable by reference to anything else in the novel. His most salient characteristic is that, while he is privileged to know what could not be learned by strictly natural means, he refuses to exercise that privilege except to see into Jim's mind on a few occasions to explain his motivations. At one point, for example, he tells us about Jim: "At such times his thoughts would be full of valorous deeds: he loved these dreams and the success of his imaginary achievements. They were the best parts of his life, its secret truth, its hidden reality. They had a gorgeous virility, the charm of vagueness, they passed before him with an heroic tread; they carried his soul away with them and made it drunk with the divine philtre of an unbounded confidence itself. There was nothing he could not face. He was so pleased with the idea that he smiled, keeping perfunctorily his eyes ahead" (p. 13). A narrator who can enter a character's mind this way is also a narrator who can reliably interpret for the reader the meaning of the thoughts in relation to the character's function in the novel as a whole; this narrator will not do so. In the beginning we do not question his failure to give us the kind of evaluative statements we shall need later because we do not yet know that we shall require such assistance. We accept as conventional the narrator's entrance into Jim's consciousness in order more fully to expose that consciousness to us. At just the point we need him most, however, he turns us over to Marlow.

The first four chapters of *Lord Jim* briefly trace Jim's career from his childhood to the time of the inquiry into the *Patna* scandal. Jim's romantic nature is clearly sketched. He sets out to sea with high hopes and grand illusions, is injured and must spend time recuperating; he gets restless in the hospital and joins the *Patna* crew. Something strange happens on the passage to Jeddah, and the next time we see him Jim is testifying at the hearing by the Board of Inquiry. During the narration of these events, the narrator moves more and more inside Jim's consciousness; then, during the inquiry itself, when we need an authoritative outside perspective, he still stays within Jim's point of view. While speaking from that point of view, the narrator comments: "They wanted facts. Facts! they demanded facts from him as if facts could explain anything!" (p. 18). This statement turns out to be one of the most crucial statements of the novel. For, although we cannot know it at the time, Conrad here offers a serious challenge to the reader's willing participation and threatens to precipitate a fictional crisis. On the one hand, "facts" are precisely what we need at that point: we do not even know yet what has happened aboard the *Patna*, nor do we know anything substantial about Jim or his moral character. On the other hand, Jim is the character on whom the novel has exclusively concentrated up to this point and our sympathy is vested with him: if he has been accused of some crime or misdeed, we are willing to take his side to sympathize with his natural desire to express his reality in human, subjective terms rather than the cold, scientific, objective "language of facts"; we can sympathize with his inability to express himself precisely since that is a profoundly human trait, one which the novel insists on throughout. "He wanted to go on talking for truth's sake, perhaps for his own sake also; and while his utterance was deliberate, his mind positively flew round and round the serried circle of facts that had surged up all about him to cut him off from the rest of his kind" (p. 19). As readers we find ourselves in a bind: we are asked to accept Jim's view, which a seemingly omniscient and reliable narrator appears to be endorsing—his view that facts will not really explain anything—at exactly the moment we feel the most need to know, because of the nature of our participation in the novel, certain basic facts about the plot (e.g., what happened?). Conrad risks the reader's complete alienation, but he disguises the challenge of the narrator's statement and avoids the kind of confrontation that this early in the novel could easily prevent the reader from going on by introducing Marlow. It is not until much later that the reader realizes what has happened.

In retrospect, moreover, we can see another aspect of the initial narrator's remarks: he has himself given us only facts in his portion of the total narrative, when what we needed was also some evaluative perspective from which to assess Jim. He thus "proves" Jim's statement about facts—that they cannot explain anything, that they are not enough. The narrative form of *Lord Jim* thus works a kind of demonstration of what the novel says: just as facts miss the whole truth, so too does the narrative equivalent of a factual report—the initial narrator's quasi-omniscient narration. His narrative puts us as readers into the position of the Board of Inquiry and demonstrates by implication that "facts" are not enough to understand Lord Jim (or *Lord Jim*); discursive knowledge—Cassirer's "empirical thinking"— is inadequate by itself. It is during his testimony at the inquiry that Jim abandons faith in words alone to express the truth and the reality of his experience and of himself as a person; at precisely the same point the narrator, who has appeared to be omniscient, ceases speaking and relinquishes to Marlow the responsibility for continuing Jim's story. The narrator seems to dwindle to the status of one of Marlow's listeners, although he is brought back briefly near the end of the novel to smooth the transition from Marlow's oral narrative to his written one, a function he carries out in a simple, efficient manner.

Miller suggests that the narrator returns to remind the reader that Marlow's interpretation may not be the correct one; that is perhaps the primary reason he reappears.[34] But he also offers a short sketch of Marlow's unnamed correspondent, that "privileged man" who was the only one of the people listening to Marlow "to hear the last word of the story" (p. 205). This man, whose "wandering days were over," seems rather like Stein or even Marlow himself. As Marlow says in his letter, the unnamed listener " 'alone . . . showed an interest in [Jim] that survived the telling of his story' "; he also has had a romantic youth with adventures of his own and is perhaps for that reason more sympathetic to Jim than the others. This is what the initial narrator has to say about him: "No more horizons as boundless as hope, no more twilights within the forests as solemn as temples, in the hot quest of the Ever-undiscovered Country over the hill, across the stream, beyond the wave. The hour was striking! No more! No more!—but the opened packet under the lamp brought back the sounds, the visions, the very savour of the past—a multitude of fading faces, a tumult of low voices, dying away upon the shores of distant seas under a passionate and unconsoling sunshine. He sighed and sat down to read" (p. 205). The plot requires a sympathetic listener to whom Marlow can write—that is certainly one reason the listener is described this way. Perhaps another is that Conrad wants to give us the impression that we are part of a community, a small and select one but a community nevertheless. The sympathetic listener helps to validate Marlow's—and thus our—interest in Jim; his presence suggests that the effort to grapple with the significance of Jim's story is worth it.

Although the narrator's return in chapter 36 does give us this extra validation of Marlow's and our concern for Jim, we cannot turn to the initial narrator directly for help in answering our question about the meaning of Jim's death. Indirectly, however, he may be able to point us in the right direction. Marlow's written narrative at the end does the same thing that the initial narrator's narrative (also "written" of course) does at the beginning—with one significant and overwhelming difference. Both narratives give primarily just the facts; they explain, from Jim's point of view as much as possible, what happened. They both assert Karl Kroeber's proposal, "If I tell you what occurred you will know what happened." The major difference between them, however, is that Marlow's narration follows an "oral" narration in which a definite perspective is clearly established for the reader. What was wanting in the initial narrator's discussion was some evaluative focus, some perspective that would allow us to get a fix on Jim. We do not know how to respond in the beginning: the nature of his presence as protagonist says that we should sympathize with him, yet at the point at which he stands accused of a crime we have no reason other than his position as protagonist to extend such sympathy. But by the time of his written narrative, Marlow is able, as Janet Burstein says, to let it, as "complex poetic fact," speak "its own truth, unanalyzed and uninterpreted" (p. 466). He can do so and not risk the same kind of alienation that the initial narrator risks because we have already seen Marlow's numerous attempts to analyze Jim meet with failure and are ready now ourselves to begin our assessment.

If Conrad has been successful, we shall conduct that assessment as we would an evaluation of a Romantic poem. One of the first things that we shall conclude, I think, is that our question about the meaning of Jim's death is of relatively little importance to our evaluation as a whole, at least in its present form. That is, Jim's death is meaningful to us as readers only insofar as it is the culmination of the process by which Jim attains an apocalyptic vision (the attainment of which vision by "a fallen but potentially regenerate mind" Northrop Frye calls "the great Romantic theme" [pp. 37–38]). The significance of Jim's death for the novel as a whole is thus as a validating event in his struggle to become a Romantic hero. The kind of moral question Marlow wants it to be is irrelevant to our experience; what is relevant is the way of knowing to which Marlow implicitly directs us, even if he himself is unable to embrace it. The narrative frame, I think, makes it possible for us to take the step Marlow hesitates to take and thus to read the novel as a Romantic work of art.

If we do take that step one of the first things we discover is that Marlow's moral concerns for Jim and for Jim's behavior matter only as expressions of Marlow's struggle to understand, not as judgments of Jim. We find, I think, that whatever meaning this novel has lies not in analytical reflection, Marlow's or our own, which is problematical and secondary, but in all that has accrued since Marlow's original encounter with Jim at the *Patna* inquiry; what is primary and certain is the "imaginative apprehension gained through immediate experience"—Marlow's apprehension of Jim and our apprehension of Marlow grappling with his apprehension. I agree for the most part with J. Hillis Miller's conclusion: "From whatever angle it is approached *Lord Jim* reveals itself to be a work which raises questions rather than answering them. The fact that it contains its own interpretations does not make it easier to understand. The overabundance of possible explanations only inveigles the reader to share the self-sustaining motion of an unending process of interpretation. This weaving movement of advance and retreat constitutes and sustains the 'meaning' of the text, that evasive center which is everywhere and nowhere in the play of its language" (p. 227). Miller exaggerates, I think, when he speaks of an "unending" process of interpretation, at least as far as the reader is concerned, but his idea of a "weaving movement of advance and retreat" is, I think, an accurate description of what "constitutes and sustains the 'meaning' of the text." This description might easily be applied to "Ode to a Nightingale" or *Frankenstein* as well, however, so that the meaning of *Lord Jim* will be determined in much the same way that we determine meaning in a Romantic work of art: "Meaning is evolved and is itself only an incident in the evolution of a soul," because "each encounter with the external world gives us a chance to project ourselves sympathetically into the Other and, by identifying there another aspect of the spiritual Self, to evolve a soul or identity" (Langbaum, p. 50).

Lord Jim offers us the record of just such an encounter, just such an attempted evolution, in a rich and aesthetically satisfying form, one as rich as any Romantic poem. What Langbaum says of "Ode to a Nightingale" applies equally well to this novel: "The thing we are left with is the thing the observer is left with—a total movement of soul, a step forward in self-articulation" (p. 51). In this case, of course, that step is ambiguous. To return to a point I raised earlier, I think that Conrad did intend our question about Jim's death to be answered ambiguously, but as Langbaum goes on to say: "The ambiguity of circumstance tells us a great deal about how the poetry of experience communicates—that it communicates not as truth but experience, making its circumstance ambiguously objective in order to make it emphatically someone's experience" (pp. 51–52). *Lord Jim*, then, like *Heart of Darkness*, tries to turn knowledge into experience. Its revelation, to quote Langbaum yet again, "is not a formulated idea that dispels mystery, but a perception that advances in intensity to a deeper and wider, a more inclusive, mystery" (p. 46). Conrad attempts thus to deal with the mysteries of human experience in his fiction in very much the way that the Romantic poets did in their poetry; in the process he helped to alter the face of an art form.

SIX

Virginia Woolf

Although there is no full-length study of Virginia Woolf's Romanticism as there is of Conrad's, some critics have suggested a relationship between her work and that of the Romantics. The most sustained such examination of Woolf is the chapter Ralph Freedman devotes to her in *The Lyrical Novel;* there are also two articles concerned with Woolf and Romanticism, as well as scattered references elsewhere.[1] But none of these critics suggests that her novels have the kind of Romantic form we have been considering throughout this study. However, two other aspects of her fiction that have received more critical attention than her Romanticism have a direct bearing on our considerations. The first is a point Woolf herself raises, one which is endorsed by nearly all her critics: that her novels strive toward the status of poetry. The second aspect is her use of narration, especially in the three novels most widely commented on, *Mrs. Dalloway, To the Lighthouse,* and *The Waves.* I shall consider the first two of these novels in this chapter; let us first examine some general facets of Woolf's Romanticism and their relationship to the two areas I have mentioned.

In an entry in her diary written shortly after she completed *To the Lighthouse,* Virginia Woolf expresses a desire for "an escapade after these serious poetic experimental books whose form is so closely considered."[2] That escapade became *Orlando,* which was immediately succeeded, however, by yet another "poetic experimental book," *The Waves* (about which G. Lowes Dickinson exclaimed, "Your book is a poem, and as I think a great poem").[3] Taking their cue from her own remarks about fiction, most modern critics agree that Woolf's novels are "poetic"; there is a consensus, from David Daiches in 1943 to Morris Philipson in 1974, about the poetic nature of her fiction.[4] Perhaps the most extended such discussion is Ralph Freedman's in 1963. He contends that Woolf imposes poetic techniques on her novels "as a method to redefine rather than to supplant traditional concepts of fiction" and that she develops novels of a "new design [which] are composed of carefully distributed individual images or illustrative descriptions and motifs with *monologues* of particular characters." As poetry these monologues serve another purpose as well. "They are the *forms* in which moments—the meeting of association and memory with the facts of the external world—are caught to reflect content and coherence in lyrical narrative. They act as units, both lyrical and dramatic, to supply the instances of perceptions and recognition of which the novels are composed. These monologues deal with the matter of experience and infer the substance of speech and action from a postulated point of view behind the figure."[5] Woolf's efforts at making her fiction poetic thus involve at their root a rethinking of the narrative possibilities of novels. According to Freedman, she telescopes "the poet's 'lyrical self' and the novelist's omniscient point of view" (p. 202). I shall have more to say about omniscience in Woolf's novels later; for the moment I should like to suggest an addition to Freedman's discussion.

He is concerned to locate specifically lyrical effects in three modern writers of fiction (Hesse, Gide, and Woolf) and he proposes a severely limited fictional genre—the lyrical novel—as a result. His limited focus allows him to make valid and useful points about these novelists, but as I suggested above, the phenomenon he examines is more widespread than he thinks and can be more effectively assessed if we see its sources in Romantic poetry rather than in lyric poetry alone. Seen my way, Woolf's fictional experiments are central to the other contemporary fictional experiments of writers like James, Conrad, Lawrence, and Joyce, as E. M. Forster hinted in 1926. He says in his essay "The Novels of Virginia Woolf," after noting that she approaches "character construction in the Tolstoyan sense" in *Mrs. Dalloway:* "Any approach is significant, for it suggests that in future books she may solve the problem as a whole. She herself believes it can be done, and, with the exception of Joyce, she is the only writer of genius who is trying. All the other so-called innovators are (if not pretentious bunglers) merely innovators in subject matter and the praise we give them is of the kind we should accord to scientists. . . . But they do not advance the novelist's art. Virginia Woolf has already done that a little, and if she succeeds in her problem of rendering character, she will advance it enormously."[6] I propose that we turn (yet again) to modern theories of Romanticism, especially to the work of Robert Langbaum and Karl Kroeber, to illuminate Woolf's fictional experiments.

When Ralph Freedman speaks of Woolf's "lyrical narratives" we are reminded of Kroeber's discussion in *Romantic Narrative Art,* where he contends that one characteristic of the Romantic aesthetic endeavor at the beginning of the nineteenth century is "a new interest in and a new value for a narrative lyricism sybolical rather than rhetorical in structure and purpose."[7] One manifestation of this narrative lyricism is what Kroeber labels the "visionary lyric." These kinds of lyrics employ narrative "as an element of logical or rational organization" although "the sources of the poems' energy are purely subjective and creative; they cannot be told about." But in the great odes of the period, such as "Ode to a Nightingale," a transmutation of "rational, continuous narrative into a discontinuous structure" occurs; these odes thus create "a self-satisfying inner order, a nonlogical continuity" (pp. 57–59). As we saw earlier, both Mary Shelley and Joseph Conrad use narrative itself as an element of logical or rational organization in their novels and many of their characters pretend that "if I tell you what occurred you will know what happened to me" (Kroeber, p. 58). Shelley and Conrad thus reach in their novels for the status of the great Romantic odes. Virginia Woolf makes such an attempt as well, and of the novelists we have considered, her efforts are, I think, the most successful. Of all the modern novelists, although Joyce is a close second, it is she who most fully achieves "a narrative lyricism symbolical rather than rhetorical in structure and purpose." Woolf's great contribution to modern fiction is the successful imposition on the novel, a primarily narrative form, of a "self-satisfying inner order, a non-logical continuity" in order to penetrate and to express in a fictional mode the inner, subjective world of experience.

The incorporation of lyric effects into the novel involves, as I said, a rethinking of the narrative possibilities of the novel. In her *Diary,* Woolf confesses herself "bored by narrative"; she writes to Lytton Strachey that "plots don't matter" and tells Clive Bell that "I shall re-form the novel and capture multitudes of things at present fugitive, enclose the whole, and shape infinite strange shapes."[8] Her own inner logic of vision, what Henry James calls the artist's "one logic," guides her re-formation of the novel: in a letter she gives Violet Dickinson "a specimen of my narrative, which is far from good, seeing that I am forever knotting it and twisting it in conformity with the coils in my own brain."[9] Jean Guiguet makes an important point in this regard about *Mrs. Dalloway;* he notes that the "interlocking" of Clarissa's and Septimus's physical routes

provides only a material framework, a structural device borrowed from the physical world and, actually, a mere allusion. . . . If the structure of *Mrs. Dalloway* consisted in nothing more than this not only would the novel seem to be made of bits and pieces, but moreover it would have no meaning. The clear-cut pattern in space and time is only a substitute for plot. . . . In reality it should be allotted a very minor place and importance, as providing material landmarks for the various stages of the book. The true structure is of another nature: it is homogeneous with the content, and that is why the restriction of the book's substance to precisely defined moments and centres of reference is of capital importance.[10]

The narrational mode of Woolf's novels has attracted substantial critical attention. Yet despite Woolf's avowed reformatory goals, most commentators have concluded that she employs a simple, "old-fashioned" omniscient narrator.[11] Thus Freedman suggests a combination of the poet's lyric self and the omniscient point of view in Woolf, although he notes later the paradox that "the more fully she perfected the conventional device of fiction, the omniscient point of view, the more closely she approached a perfection of poetic form that finds its apex in *The Waves*" (pp. 202, 270). J. Hillis Miller discusses the "omniscient narrator" of *Mrs. Dalloway* and concludes that this narrator has much in common with the narrators of *Vanity Fair*, *Middlemarch*, and *The Last Chronicle of Barset*. James Naremore concurs in general about the omniscience but, in contrast to Miller, notices (about *To the Lighthouse* specifically) "that when she does discuss her characters from the vantage point of traditional omniscience, her voice lacks that tone of certainty that one finds, for example, in George Eliot."[12]

There is one recent critic, however, David Neal Miller, who contradicts the others and suggests the "absence or near-absence of an omniscient narrator" in *Mrs. Dalloway*. He proposes that authorial point of view is established in the novel, not in the usual way that an omniscient narrator would establish his or her viewpoint, but through the use of various devices, such as repetition of words on the linguistic surface of the novel, privileged similes, leitmotiv, discrediting of characters with faulty perception, and the use of extended structure emblematic of the central insight.[13] Woolf thus "does not simply identify Septimus and Clarissa, but rather establishes their insight as the authorial point of view 'behind the backs' of the selected consciousnesses; dimensions of which the characters are ignorant . . . are thus reserved by the narrator for direct communication with the reader."[14] David Neal Miller's approach shows the most evidence of taking into account a rethinking of the function of narration. If we extend his approach to Woolf's other novels—the narrational mode of all her novels from *Jacob's Room* through *Between the Acts* seems much the same despite significant differences in structure—we can better understand what Woolf was trying to do. Superficially, her narrators do resemble the "omniscient narrators" common to pre-Jamesian fiction. They never appear as characters, however, nor do they comment about their narrational function; they are reliable; and while they appear to know what could not be learned strictly by natural means, like the initial narrator of *Lord Jim* they refuse fully to exercise the power they have. They provide the necessary information we need to make the novels cohere, but they never explicitly evaluate characters or action. Instead, as Miller suggests, her narrators use various devices, many of which we especially associate with poetry, to give the reader needed information and connections behind the backs, as it were, of the characters. The "paradox" Freedman notes becomes less troublesome if we recognize how much Woolf departs in her use of this form of narration; she is not only redefining traditional conceptions of fiction but supplanting them as well.

If it is possible to redefine such conceptions *without* supplanting them, then we can say that Henry James and Joseph Conrad work such a redefinition. They tried to work through and around traditional fictional modes in order to express their inner experience. Virginia Woolf, on the other hand, goes beyond merely fictional categories and comes close to doing what Keats does in his poetry: she presents a kind of persona as narrator in her novels like the persona of "Ode on a Grecian Urn" or "Ode on Melancholy" or "To Autumn." In other words, she goes to poetic modes to find a model for her narrators rather than to fictional ones. She seeks Shakespeare's negative capability rather than Wordsworth's egotistical sublime, however; as she notes, while working on some experimental short stories in 1920: "I suppose the danger is the damned egotistical self; which ruins Joyce and [Dorothy] Richardson to my mind."[15] Her novels have much about them that is Wordsworthian; but it is to those poems in which Keats tries to unite the self with the object by knowing it from within, directly, without the agency of the "I," that Woolf turns for her models. In a sense the persona of "Ode on a Grecian Urn" might be called omniscient—his pronouncement, "that is all / Ye know on earth, and all ye need to know" is often read as if it were spoken by an omniscient being—but on the whole the very notion of omniscience is alien to the Romantic experience. So too are the traditional notions of omniscient narration thus irrelevant to the experience of novels like *Mrs. Dalloway, To the Lighthouse,* and *The Waves.*

Virginia Woolf's goals in using a Romantic persona as narrator for her novels are much the same as the Romantic poets'; an assessment by Northrop Frye of Percy Shelley's outlook could equally well apply to Woolf: "There is a world 'behind' the objects we see, and a world 'behind' the subjects that perceive it; these hidden worlds are the same world; poetry is the voice of that world; and the vision of love which contains and transforms all opposites, can realize it."[16] Woolf too seeks to blur the distinction between subject and object to get at that world behind both object and subject (in Woolf's writings, notes David Daiches, "we can often see the ebb and flow between the subjective and the objective attitudes").[17] Some comments of Robert Langbaum are apropos here:

> The romantic lyric or poem of experience . . . is both
> subjective and objective. The poet talks about himself
> by talking about an object; and he talks about an object
> by talking about himself. Nor does he address either
> himself or the object, but both together. He addresses
> the object in order to tell himself something, yet the
> thing he tells himself comes from the object. . . . The
> poet speaks through the observer of the romantic lyric
> the way a playwright speaks through one of his char-
> acters—in that the observer moves through a series of
> intellectual oscillations toward a purpose of which he is
> himself at each point not aware.[18]

The analogy of poet to speaker as playwright to character is a
good one and is useful for a novel like *Mrs. Dalloway* or *To
the Lighthouse*. The narrator of *Mrs. Dalloway* stands in the
same relationship to Clarissa and Septimus Warren Smith as
a playwright to his or her characters; Clarissa and Septimus,
like the observer in a Romantic lyric, move through a series
of intellectual oscillations toward a purpose of which they are
unaware. So do the central characters of *To the Lighthouse* or
The Waves.

This aspect of Woolf's novels (i.e., the manner in which
they treat subject and object) helps to account for what
some critics have called her Bergsonian approach. In the
first place, Bergson's theories are themselves grounded in
Romanticism; he seeks to get at the same kind of experience
that the Romantic poets sought to uncover and participate
in.[19] As Shiv Kumar says in *Bergson and the Stream of Consciousness Novel:* "According to Bergson, there are two ways
of knowing reality: one adopts a point of view in relation to
an object and 'stops at the relative,' while the other seeks an
intuitive identification with the object in an effort to 'possess the original.' " The latter point of view is the Romanticist's. The goal that Kumar assigns to the "new prose-
fiction," which is influenced by Bergson, is inherently

Romantic as well: "The new prose-fiction does not imply a 'withdrawal' from objective reality but constitutes, on the contrary, a deliberate effort to render in a literary medium a new realization of experience as a process of dynamic renewal."[20] Such an attempt to render a process of dynamic renewal had already been assayed in the poetry of the Romantics, whose formulations remain useful "as long as [they return] us to experience, as long as we earn [them], to paraphrase Faust, every day anew" (Langbaum, p. 26).

In *The Poetry of Experience*, Langbaum traces a line of development from the Romantic lyrics of the early years of the nineteenth century through the dramatic monologues of the middle years of the century. Virginia Woolf's fiction develops along a similar line, at least from the lyrical *Jacob's Room* through *The Waves*, which is constructed somewhat like *The Ring and the Book* or "The Waste Land" as a series of monologues. These monologues partake of the quality of the dramatic monologues that Langbaum analyzes. For example, a special trait of the poetry of experience is the way in which characterization is transformed; characters in dramatic monologues are not characters in the "Aristotelian sense of a moral force to be judged morally, but in the modern sense of a pole for sympathy" (p. 52). We saw the consequences of this kind of characterization in both Shelley's *Frankenstein* and Conrad's *Heart of Darkness* and *Lord Jim*. Characterization in Woolf's novels is similarly affected: it too is shaped by the conjunction of dramatic and lyric forces. "Characterization in the dramatic monologue," notes Langbaum, "must be understood as not only a feature of the dramatic element but as the source of the lyric element. This means that the dramatic monologue must use at the same time two opposite methods of characterization. It uses the method of drama, where character is manifested through utterance and action and is determined by what Aristotle calls *ethos* or moral bent. But it also uses the method of the lyric, where the manifestation of character is not by Aristotelian standards *characterization* at all, since it is total rather than determinate and therefore self-expressive and self-justifying rather than teleological and moral" (p. 201). Woolf's fiction is informed by a similar kind of characterization that uses two opposite methods of characterization at once.

Mrs. Dalloway

"The focus of Virginia Woolf's prose fiction," notes Morris Philipson, "is the character of private consciousness, the quality of shared experience, and the place of human life in history and nature."[21] That is, I think, an accurate and fair general assessment. As a generalization, of course, it is not limited solely to Virginia Woolf: one could say very much the same thing about the work of (other) Romantic writers, especially Wordsworth and Keats. Philipson seems to have put his finger on the central effort of, say, *The Prelude* as much as of *Mrs. Dalloway*. That Philipson's comment could almost be a précis of Wordsworth's great poem is not accidental. Woolf's and Wordsworth's literary efforts have much in common. Her affinity with Wordsworth was in fact noted as long ago as 1926 by Edwin Muir, when he remarked that Woolf's treatment of characterization "is less akin to anything else attempted in the novel than to certain kinds of poetry, to poetry such as Wordsworth's, which records not so much a general judgment on life as a moment of serene illumination, a state of soul."[22] Moreover, Woolf herself has expressed admiration for *The Prelude*: "I am reading The Prelude," she writes to Saxon Sydney-Turner. "Dont you think it one of the greatest works ever written? Some of it, anyhow, is sublime; it may get worse."[23] A closer examination of Woolf's relationship to Wordsworth, it would seem, is in order, especially as regards *Mrs. Dalloway*.

Let us begin with this comment by Karl Kroeber in *Romantic Narrative Art*: "What critics of *The Prelude* have stressed insufficiently is that the organization of the poem is founded upon a continuous and systematic dialectic between public and private affairs, between social developments and personal growth, between the objective drama of political events and the subjective drama of psychological change" (pp. 88–89). If Morris Philipson's remark about *Mrs. Dalloway* could apply to *The Prelude*, then, reciprocally, Kroeber's comment about Wordsworth's poem can apply to Woolf's novel. In fact, I think that Kroeber has very nearly described the organization of *Mrs. Dalloway* here. It too is founded on a similar "continuous and systematic dialectic," and just as Wordsworth structures his poem on this dialectic to effect an interpenetration of private and public, so does Woolf seek the same interpenetration between the inner world and the outer through a dialectic. Early in *Mrs. Dalloway* the narrator says through Clarissa's consciousness: "She would not say of any one in the world now that they were this or were that. She felt very young; at the same time unspeakably aged. She sliced like a knife through everything; at the same time was outside, looking on."[24] Over the course of the novel Clarissa's thoughts swing between the poles here set up. We find throughout the novel an alternation between slicing through everything (seeing into the life of things) and observing from outside. The following passage is typical of the pattern or structure of Clarissa's thinking:

> Her only gift was knowing people almost by instinct, she thought, walking on. If you put her in a room with some one, up went her back like a cat's; or she purred. Devonshire House, Bath House, the house with the china cockatoo, she had seen them all lit up once; and remembered Sylvia, Fred, Sally Seton—such hosts of people; and dancing all night; and the waggons plodding past to market; and driving home across the Park. She remembered once throwing a shilling into the Serpentine. But everyone remembered; what she loved was

this, here, now, in front of her; the fat lady in the cab. Did it matter then, she asked herself, walking towards Bond Street, did it matter that she must inevitably cease completely; all this must go on without her; did she resent it, or did it not become consoling to believe that death ended absolutely? but that somehow in the streets of London, on the ebb and flow of things, here, there, she survived, Peter survived, lived in each other, she being part, she was positive, of the trees at home; of the house there, ugly, rambling all to bits and pieces as it was; part of people she had never met; being laid out like a mist between people she knew best, who lifted her on their branches as she had seen the trees lift the mist, but it spread ever so far, her life, herself. (Pp. 11–12)

With the exception of "the objective drama of political events"—which figures in the novel through Richard Dalloway, M.P., and his political connections, and indirectly through the Prime Minister's appearance at Clarissa's party—the categories of the dialectic that Kroeber proposes for *The Prelude* are illustrated, at least in embryo, in this passage from *Mrs. Dalloway.* Here are the grounds for a dialectic between public affairs ("the waggons plodding past to market," "the ebb and flow of things" in "the streets of London") and private affairs ("She remembered once throwing a shilling into the Serpentine"); between social developments ("Devonshire House, Bath House"; "the fat lady in the cab"; "the house there, ugly, rambling all to bits and pieces as it was") and personal growth, the subjective drama of personal change ("did it matter that she must inevitably cease completely; all this must go on without her").

If the dialectic of *The Prelude* occurs within a persona, an "I," the focus of the dialectic of Woolf's novel is Clarissa Dalloway herself. As David Daiches says: "Each character who makes contact with Mrs. Dalloway . . . has some symbolic relation if not to Mrs. Dalloway herself then to the main theme of the book, in the interpretation of which the life and character of Mrs. Dalloway plays such an important part. What first appears to be a random cross-section of life on a summer morning in London in 1919 [*sic*] emerges on closer scrutiny as a subtly organized patterning of experience, with each part having some reference to the other."[25] The organizing principle of that patterning of experience is Clarissa's inner life: "That was her self—pointed; dart-like; definite," Clarissa thinks. "That was her self when some effort, some call on her to be her self, drew the parts together; she alone knew how different, how incompatible and composed so for the world only into one centre, one diamond, one woman who sat in her drawing-room and made a meeting-point, a radiancy no doubt in some dull lives, a refuge for the lonely to come to perhaps" (p. 42). The novel is so structured that its parts are drawn together at the end, at Clarissa's party, where she does become a meeting-point, a radiancy, a center. Even the story of Septimus Warren Smith, which seems at first a parallel subplot, becomes at the end part of a larger pattern of events structured around Clarissa. At the end of the novel she can fairly say with the persona of *The Prelude:* "my theme has been / What passed within me" (III, 173–74).[26]

Clarissa's similarity to the persona of *The Prelude* is threefold. Their response to the world around them follows the same general pattern; they have similar emotional reactions to their experiences; and their intellectual preoccupations are alike, especially in regard to time, eternity, and mutability. Consider the following passage, in which the explanation Wordsworth's persona gives of his characteristic response to the external world might also serve as a paradigm for Clarissa Dalloway's musings on that June day in 1923:

> As if awaken'd, summon'd, rous'd, constrain'd,
> I look'd for universal things; perused
> The common countenance of earth and heaven;

And, turning the mind in upon itself,
Pored, watch'd, expect'd, listen'd; spread my thoughts
And spread them with a wider creeping; felt
Incumbences more awful, visitings
Of the Upholder of the tranquil Soul
Which underneath all passion lives secure
A steadfast life.   (III, 109–17)

Clarissa, turning her mind in upon itself, also pores, watches, expects, and listens on her walk through the London streets and during her preparations at home. She too feels "incumbences more awful," although her thoughts perhaps take on a slightly more sinister air than Wordsworth's persona's because of their juxtaposition with Septimus's madness and suicide. Wordsworth's revision for the 1850 text of *The Prelude* helps sharpen the parallel (it would have been the 1850 text that Woolf read, of course). In this version, Wordsworth writes:

Incumbencies more awful, visitings
Of the Upholder of the tranquil soul,
That tolerates the indignities of Time,
And, from the centre of Eternity,
All finite motions overruling, lives
In glory immutable.[27]

The italicized line from the 1850 text shows the parallel to *Mrs. Dalloway* very clearly. The need to mitigate or obliterate the "indignities of time" is precisely Clarissa's most frequently recurring topic, one which links her to three other consciousnesses in the novel: Peter Walsh's, Septimus Warren Smith's, and the narrator's.

One of the ways Woolf unifies the novel, in fact, is through the characters' "moments," their "spots of time." Clarissa has such a moment early in the novel when she suddenly, intuitively feels what men feel about women:

And whether it was pity, or their beauty, or that she
was older, or some accident—like a faint scent, or a vio-
lin next door (so strange is the power of sounds at certain moments), she did undoubtedly then feel what men
felt. Only for a moment; but it was enough. It was a
sudden revelation, a tinge like a blush which one tried
to check and then, as it spread, one yielded to its expansion, and rushed to the farthest verge and there quiv-
ered and felt the world come closer, swollen with some
astonishing significance, some pressure of rapture,
which split its thin skin and gushed and poured with an
extraordinary alleviation over the cracks and sores. Then,
for that moment, she had seen an illumination; a match
burning in a crocus; an inner meaning almost expressed. But the close withdrew; the hard softened. It
was over—the moment.   (P. 36)

For Clarissa, then, like the persona of *The Prelude,*

> There are in our existence spots of time,
> Which with distinct pre-eminence retain
> A vivifying Virtue, whence, depress'd
> By false opinion and contentious thought,
> Or aught of heavier or more deadly weight
> In trivial occupations, and the round
> Of ordinary intercourse, our minds
> Are nourished and invisibly repair'd,
> A virtue by which pleasure is enhanced
> That penetrates, enables us to mount
> When high, more high, and lifts us up when fallen.
>   (XI, 258–68)

The spots of time experienced by Peter and Septimus are
ironic versions of those experienced by Clarissa and by
Wordsworth's persona. For Peter, the moment is neither
vivifying nor nourishing; instead, it reminds him of a step

taken irrevocably in the past, after which there remains emptiness: "As a cloud crosses the sun, silence falls on London; and falls on the mind. Effort ceases. Time flaps on the mast. There we stop; there we stand. Rigid, the skeleton of habit alone upholds the human frame. Where there is nothing, Peter Walsh said to himself; feeling hollowed out, utterly empty within. Clarissa refused me, he thought. He stood there thinking, Clarissa refused me" (p. 55). When Septimus experiences his revelation, his spot of time, it is not vivifying in the literal sense—it is what sends him into death—but it does ironically give him a kind of life, a kind of victory, since it leads him to a death that frees him from his madness and suffering. Septimus' revelation is a vision of the resurrection of his best friend from the war, the friend whom he saw die: "It was at that moment (Rezia had gone shopping) that the great revelation took place. A voice spoke from behind the screen. Evans was speaking. The dead were with him" (p. 103). From this moment Septimus' suicide is inevitable; his death renders ironic Wordsworth's idea of a "vivifying Virtue" which "enables us to mount / When high, more high, and lifts us up when fallen." By falling upon the spikes of the fence, he is able to mount high, above "loathing, hatred, despair."

Earlier in the novel Septimus has a vision that prepares him for the revelation of Evans speaking to him. He is at Regent's Park with Rezia, his wife. When she says the word *time* he begins to hallucinate: "The word 'time' split its husk; poured its riches over him; and from his lips fell like shells, like shavings from a plane, without his making them, hard, white, imperishable, words, and flew to attach themselves to their places in an ode to Time; an immortal ode to Time" (p. 78). He imagines Evans answering from behind a tree and thinks that a man walking toward him, who turns out to be Peter Walsh, is in fact Evans. For Septimus in his madness, any man passing by could be transformed into Evans; for the reader, it is appropriate that it is

Peter whom Septimus sees while reciting his "Ode to Time," for Peter himself has just been musing on time and the effects of its passage. It is time as well that links Peter to Clarissa through their mutual reflections on the past and its inexorability. Moreover, it is time that the narrator uses to structure the novel, not only through the striking of Big Ben and other clocks, but also through passages like this one, which seems to comment on the effect of the novel's narrative mode at the same time that it provides a narrational transition: "Shredding and slicing, dividing and subdividing, the clocks of Harley Street nibbled at the June day, counselled submission, upheld authority, and pointed out in chorus the supreme advantages that a commercial clock, suspended above a shop in Oxford Street, announced, genially and fraternally, as if it were a pleasure to Messrs. Rigby and Lowndes to give the information gratis, that it was half-past one" (p. 113). Thoughts about time, as well as about the related notions of mortality and eternity, thus join the major characters of the novel together.

The process and pattern Wordsworth describes in that passage from book 3 of *The Prelude* applies to the whole of *Mrs. Dalloway*. Clarissa's thoughts about the flux of life and death, about the indignities of time, reach a culmination in the last scene of the novel, when the Bradshaws arrive late, bringing news of the death of Septimus Warren Smith, a belated casualty of the war. Clarissa is momentarily offended ("What business had the Bradshaws to talk of death at her party?"); but then immediately she finds herself recreating his suicide in her imagination: "Up had flashed the ground; through him, blundering, bruising, went the rusty spikes. There he lay with a thud, thud, thud in his brain, and then a suffocation of blackness. So she saw it." So begins a process of identification with Septimus that ebbs and flows from blame to approbation, from fear to measured pleasure, that weaves through the ordinary as well as the special events of Clarissa's life, past and present, in her mind:

She had once thrown a shilling into the Serpentine,
never any thing more. But he had flung it away. They
went on living (she would have to go back; the rooms
were still crowded; people kept on coming). They (all
day she had been thinking of Bourton, of Peter, of
Sally), they would grow old. A thing there was that mat-
tered; a thing, wreathed about with chatter, defaced,
obscured in her own life, let drop every day in corrup-
tion, lies, chatter. This he had preserved. Death was de-
fiance. Death was an attempt to communicate, people
feeling the impossibility of reaching the centre which,
mystically, evaded them; closeness drew apart; rapture
faded; one was alone. There was an embrace in death.

(P. 202)

From death in general her thoughts return again specifically to "this young man who had killed himself." She imagines that Sir William Bradshaw, for whom she has already
expressed a dislike, has made life intolerable for Septimus.
The horror of his life gets mixed in Clarissa's mind with her
own emotions: "Then (she had felt it only this morning)
there was the terror; the overwhelming incapacity, one's
parents giving it into one's hands, this life, to be lived to
the end, to be walked with serenely; there was in the
depths of her heart an awful fear. Even now, quite often if
Richard had not been there reading the *Times,* so that she
could crouch like a bird and gradually revive, send roaring
up that immeasurable delight, rubbing stick to stick, one
thing with another, she must have perished. She had escaped. But that young man had killed himself" (p. 203).
And so she takes another step toward identification with
Septimus: "Somehow it was her disaster—her disgrace."
She thinks of her own past "disgrace" ("She had schemed;
she had pilfered"), but she remembers her childhood days
at Bourton and this remembrance of past survival of trials
fills her with happiness (this passage is extremely Words-

worthian in subject): "Odd, incredible; she had never been so happy. Nothing could be slow enough; nothing last too long. No pleasure could equal, she thought, straightening the chairs, pushing in one book on the shelf, this having done with the triumphs of youth, lost herself in the process of living, to find it, with a shock of delight, as the sun rose, as the day sank. Many a time had she gone, at Bourton when they were all talking, to look at the sky; or seen it between people's shoulders at dinner; seen it in London when she could not sleep. She walked to the window" (pp. 203–04).

Although Herbert Lindenberger thinks that "the closest prose equivalent to Wordsworth's meditative verse . . . is perhaps the later style of Henry James," passages like this one from *Mrs. Dalloway* would certainly suggest that Virginia Woolf's prose ought also to be considered in such a comparison.[28] In any case, the solace Clarissa takes from emotion recollected in tranquility and from nature enables her to assimilate Septimus' death, to find a meaning in the very ordinariness of the things she does. She walks to the window to look at the sky, as she has done at other times, and she sees the woman who lives across the street preparing to go to bed. The old woman represents for Clarissa the commonplace and the habitual; she is Clarissa's old leech-gatherer, offering much the same kind of resolution to go on with life as Wordsworth's leech-gatherer does for him. That resolution, as well as the beauty of the sky, revives Clarissa, so that she no longer pities Septimus or—for it has become the same thing—herself. Once her identification with him is complete, she can go on living, go on with the routine: "She felt somehow very like him—the young man who had killed himself. She felt glad that he had done it; thrown it away while they went on living. The clock was striking. The leaden circles dissolved in the air. But she must go back. She must assemble. She must find Sally and Peter. And she came in from the little room" (pp. 204–05).

Once Clarissa effects her identification with Septimus, she is freed from similar suicidal feelings; Septimus embodies and carries to fruition her wish for death so that there is literally no longer any need for her to consider death. Her identification with Septimus is a moment of revelation, another of Clarissa's spots of time. Just as the speaker of a dramatic monologue "does not use his utterance to expound a meaning but to pursue one, a meaning which comes to him with the shock of revelation" (Langbaum, p. 189), so Clarissa pursues a meaning in the passages we have just seen rather than expounding one. The unexpected intrusion of death, in the form of the news of Septimus' suicide, interrupts the ebb and flow of her party, but it also provides for Clarissa an illumination, a "shock of revelation"; it is as incongruous as a match burning in a crocus but it becomes, like the match, an image, an image that reveals a deeper pattern of existence under the ordinary events of everyday life.

What Clarissa succeeds in doing, then, is knowing the world in the way that the Romantic poet knows it. She transforms the death of Septimus into a symbol, after having known him through "sympathy or projectiveness . . . the specifically romantic way of knowing" (Langbaum, p. 79). Septimus is a "pole for sympathy" for Clarissa, just as, it turns out, Clarissa is a pole for sympathy for us as readers. The same kind of analogy that we saw in our discussion of *Lord Jim* works here: if Jim is to Marlow as Marlow is to us, then Septimus is to Clarissa as she is to us.

Moreover, just as Jim is a Romantic hero in Conrad's novel, so is Septimus a specifically Romantic character in Woolf's novel.[29] We will remember that Septimus is compared to Keats by Isabel Pole, the woman for whom he has conceived an infatuation before the war (p. 94). And in certain moments of his madness he has a Keatsian perception of beauty and truth: "Beauty, the world seemed to say. And as if to prove it (scientifically) wherever he looked, at the houses, at the railings, at the antelopes stretching over the palings, beauty sprang instantly. . . . Up in the sky swallows swooping, swerving, flinging themselves in and out . . . ; and the flies rising and falling; and the sun spotting now this leaf, now that . . .—all of this, calm and reasonable as it was, made out of ordinary things as it was, was the truth now; beauty, that was the truth now. Beauty was everywhere" (pp. 77–78). But the war destroys his Romantic sensibility, except in his moments of madness; the war causes him to lose all feeling, the worst fate imaginable perhaps for the Romantic. The loss of feeling gradually transforms even his mad vision of beauty into ugliness; as a result literature itself, his former solace, turns ugly: "He could reason; he could read, Dante, for example, quite easily . . . , he could add up his bill; his brain was perfect; it must be the fault of the world then—that he could not feel. . . . Here he opened Shakespeare once more. . . . How Shakespeare loathed humanity—the putting on of clothes, the getting of children, the sordidity of the mouth and the belly! This was now revealed to Septimus; the message hidden in the beauty of words. The secret signal which one generation passes, under disguise, to the next is loathing, hatred, despair" (p. 98).

There is one other aspect of the Romantic form of *Mrs. Dalloway* that we should consider: the specific function of the past for characters in the novel.[30] If the "indignities of time" is Clarissa's—and the novel's—most frequently recurring topic, as I have suggested, then consideration of the past is of paramount importance. Here as elsewhere what we discover is that the novel offers the same consideration of the past as does the work of the Romantic poets. Langbaum has this to say about the Romantic sense of the past: "The famous romantic sense of the past derives its special character from the romanticists' use of the past to give meaning to an admittedly meaningless world. It is just the difference between the romantic and classical sense of the past that the romanticist does not see the present as the heir of the past and does not therefore look to the past for authority as an ethical model. The romanticist sees the past as different from the present and uses the past to explore the full extent of the difference" (p. 12). This is how Clarissa sees her own past and how she uses it in the novel. Throughout the day she thinks of her past and the people she knows not to find an "ethical model" but "to explore the full extent of the difference" between her past and her present. In the morning Clarissa seems to regret the course her life has taken, to regret that she chose to marry Richard Dalloway rather than Peter Walsh; but by evening, the time of her party, Clarissa has a fuller understanding of her present and no longer seems to regret the shape her life has taken. She is able to put into perspective her relationship to her friends from her past, especially Sally Seton and Peter Walsh. Clarissa says: "She [Sally] and Peter had settled down together. They were talking: it seemed so familiar— that they should be talking. They would discuss the past. With the two of them (more even than with Richard) she shared her past; the garden; the trees; old Joseph Breitkopf singing Brahms without any voice; the drawing-room wallpaper; the smell of the mats. A part of this Sally must always be; Peter must always be. But she must leave them" (p. 200).

She must, in other words, leave her past and embrace her present. Through the interruption of Septimus Warren Smith—more precisely, through his suicide—she is able to do just that. What is more (although I have not explicitly called attention to this point, it is implicit in all that I have said about Clarissa), when she resolves the issues that have been bothering her throughout, issues that involve directly the relationship of the past to the present, the novel itself effects a successful transmutation of its narrative elements into a discontinuous structure. That is, while the relationship of the past to the present can be a very ordered one—

chronology is one of the most basic structuring principles, particularly of narratives—*Mrs. Dalloway* offers a discontinuous structure, an ebbing and flowing which results in a nonlogical continuity. The coherence of this novel, then, stems from nearly the same source as the coherence of "Ode to a Nightingale," which "derives almost entirely from the unity of [Keats's persona's] liberated feelings, from the dramatic invasion and counter-invasion of his conflicting sentiments, which do not correlate directly with the objective, external circumstances surrounding his vision" (Kroeber, p. 59). Since Clarissa and Septimus are the selected consciousnesses of this novel, whose insights are established as the authorial point of view (albeit behind their backs), and since they are both Romanticists, *Mrs. Dalloway* should be considered a novel with a Romantic form, a novel that explores the Romantic position in as fully complex a manner as *Lord Jim* or *Frankenstein*.

To the Lighthouse

Although it is the unity of Clarissa Dalloway's liberated feelings and the dramatic invasion and counterinvasion of her conflicting sentiments that lend coherence to *Mrs. Dalloway*, there is no corresponding character in *To the Lighthouse* to perform the same function. There is Mrs. Ramsay, of course, but her death in the opening pages of the second section of the novel prevents her from functioning in the same manner as Clarissa, no matter with how much power we invest her spirit in the final section of the book. There is Lily Briscoe, but as important as she is she plays too little part in the first section to fill Clarissa's role in the earlier novel. Moreover, there is the intriguing middle section, "Time Passes," in which time itself rather than any person is the main "character"; that section seems effectively to block the kind of continuity that Clarissa's presence imposes on *Mrs. Dalloway*. The absence of a character who functions like Clarissa suggests an even more radical experiment in discontinuity, in nonlogical continuity, than we saw in the earlier novel. Consequently, I should like to examine, more specifically than we did for *Mrs. Dalloway,* the manner in which the nature of the narrator as Romantic persona imposes a Romantic form on *To the Lighthouse.* I shall also, however, consider Mrs. Ramsay and Lily Briscoe as Romanticists.

Despite the remarks of critics like Arnold Kettle, who suggests that "it is extremely difficult to say with any sense at all of adequacy what *To the Lighthouse* is about," I think we can say what this novel is about.[31] Its subject is a deeply Romantic one: the value of intuitive art in relation to "scientific" knowledge. Let us turn again to a selection from *Romantic Narrative Art* at which we looked in connection with Conrad's fiction, where Karl Kroeber suggests "that the Romantics found in the poetic tale an effective means for asserting that the truths of intuitive art surpass anything that can be achieved by the methods of rationalistic science. At any rate, we see all the Romantic poets working against the methods of the eighteenth-century philosophers in treating of moral experience. They insist on the unified indivisibility of moral action and demand that it be judged in terms of its own entirety, as a total process. And they deny the ultimate utility of analysis, rejecting any suggestion of a moral calculus" (p. 69). However rationalistic she could be elsewhere, and *Three Guineas* is a model of rational analysis and argument, in *To the Lighthouse* Virginia Woolf argues for a position very close to the one Kroeber delineates above. It is in the service of just such a proposition—that "the truths of intuitive art surpass anything that can be achieved by the methods of rationalistic science"—that Woolf resorts to nonlogical continuity and to a kind of prose that tends to blur distinctions.

The first question to which we must address ourselves is, In what sense can we speak of *To the Lighthouse* as embodying a self-satisfying inner order, a nonlogical continuity? Most critics of the novel are at pains to point out that the planned trip to the lighthouse of the first section is finally undertaken and completed, ten years later, after Mrs. Ramsay's death, in the last section. The significance of this completed journey is sometimes connected to James's winning of his father's approval ("At last he said, triumphantly: 'Well done!' James had steered them like a born sailor");[32] and sometimes it is connected to Lily Briscoe's successful completion of her painting of Mrs. Ramsay. Both points have merit, especially the latter since Woolf herself wanted to make the arrival at the lighthouse and the finishing of Lily's painting simultaneous in the reader's experience. She notes in her diary:

> At this moment I'm casting about for an end. The problem is how to bring Lily and Mr. R. together and make a combination of interest at the end. I am feathering about with various ideas. The last chapter which I begin tomorrow is In the Boat: I had meant to end with R. climbing on to the rock. If so, what becomes of Lily and her picture? Should there be a final page about her and Carmichael looking at the picture and summing up R.'s character? In that case I lose the intensity of the moment. If this intervenes between R. and the lighthouse, there's too much chop and change I think. Could I do it in a parenthesis? So that one had the sense of reading two things at the same time?[33]

As we know, she decided that the final section should be about Lily and her painting; but although Mr. Carmichael does appear in that scene, he and Lily do not sum up Mr. Ramsay's character. Moreover, the intensity of the moment is decidedly not lost; it is in fact enhanced, a peculiar circumstance, one would think, for a novel called *To the Lighthouse*.

It is peculiar, that is, only if one brings ordinary narrative expectations to this novel. I suggest that many critics have felt the need to point out the obvious—the completion of the planned *physical* trip to the lighthouse—precisely because in the typical pre-Jamesian novel the physical arrival would coincide with its metaphorical meaning and would satisfy narrative expectations. Such a journey in such a novel would thus invite analytic reflection. In this novel, however, it is primarily the symbolic arrival at the lighthouse that matters; it is therefore Lily's arrival, symbolized by the completion of her painting (the drawing of a line in the center of the picture), that matters. The line Lily draws is an abstract representation, a symbol, of the lighthouse itself, which plays such an important part in Mrs. Ramsay's thoughts in the first section of the novel. The physical journey of James and Cam and Mr. Ramsay provides the material of Lily's experience: she has an imaginative apprehension of their arrival (" 'He has landed,' she said aloud. 'It is finished' " [p. 319]) that is primary and certain; this apprehension gives her the inspiration to complete her painting. The scene with Lily is thus rightfully the end of the novel, as Woolf obviously finally realized, and it captures rather than loses the intensity of the moment.

To answer the question we raised above: we can say that *To the Lighthouse* embodies a self-satisfying inner order, a nonlogical continuity, in the progression from Mrs. Ramsay's intuitions and experiences to Lily's intuitions and experiences, both of whose experiences are joined by the figure of the lighthouse. Consider this passage which occurs shortly after the light of the lighthouse has been lit and James has been taken off to bed; knitting, Mrs. Ramsay ponders awhile (note particularly the Keatsian nature of her reflections):

No, she thought . . . children never forget. For this reason, it was so important what one said, and what one did, and it was a relief when they went to bed. For now she need not think about anybody. She could be herself, by herself. And that was what now she often felt the need of—to think; well not even to think. To be silent; to be alone. All the being and the doing, expansive, glittering, vocal, evaporated; and one shrunk, with a sense of solemnity, to being oneself, a wedge-shaped core of darkness, something invisible to others. Although she continued to knit, and sat upright, it was thus that she felt herself; and this self having shed its attachments was free for the strangest adventures. When life sank down for a moment, the range of experience seemed limitless. And to everybody there was always this sense of unlimited resources, she supposed; one after another, she, Lily, Augustus Carmichael, must feel, our apparitions, the things you know us by, are simply childish. Beneath it is all dark, it is all spreading, it is unfathomably deep; but now and again we rise to the surface and that is what you see us by. Her horizon seemed to her limitless. There were all the places she had not seen; the Indian plains; she felt herself pushing aside the thick leather curtain of a church in Rome. This core of darkness could go anywhere, for no one saw it. They could not stop it, she thought, exulting. There was freedom, there was peace, there was, most welcome of all, a summoning together, a resting on a platform of stability. Not as oneself did one find rest ever, in her experience (she accomplished here something dexterous with her needles), but as a wedge of darkness. Losing personality, one lost the fret, the hurry, the stir; and there rose to her lips always some exclamation of triumph over life when things came together in this peace, this rest, this eternity; and pausing there she looked out to meet that stroke of the lighthouse, the long steady stroke, the last of the three, which was her stroke, for watching them in this mood always at this hour one could not help attaching oneself to one thing especially of the things one saw; and this thing, the long steady stroke, was her stroke. Often she found herself sitting and looking, sitting and looking, with her work in her hands until she became the thing she looked at—that light for example. (Pp. 99–101)

On the strength of this passage, we can say that Mrs. Ramsay is connected to Lily in several ways, primarily by the nature of their consciousnesses: both are Romanticists, both are artists (although Mrs. Ramsay is an artist only in her imagination).[34] Like Keats, like the Romantic poets in general, Mrs. Ramsay seeks a union between the self and the object—she becomes "the thing she looked at." She wishes to escape "the fret, the hurry, the stir," just as Keats's persona in "Ode to a Nightingale" wants to forget "the weariness, the fever, and the fret." She aspires to the condition of negative capability (what she thinks of as "a wedge-shaped core of darkness"), and once in this state of invisibility her imagination is free to wander anywhere, flying, as it were, "on the viewless wings of Poesy."

Lily Briscoe is an incipient Romanticist who through the intervention of Mrs. Ramsay is able to embrace a Romantic point of view. She wants in the beginning to be like Mrs. Ramsay, to gain strength, to gain a way of knowing from her, but it is not until the end of the novel that she has her vision and is able to complete her painting. Lily struggles to achieve self-confidence, to have the courage of her artistic convictions; she is unable to express on canvas what she sees, however. "She could see it all so clearly, so commandingly, when she looked: it was when she took her brush in hand that the whole thing changed. It was in that moment's flight between the picture and her canvas that the demons set on her who often brought her to the verge of tears and made this passage from conception to work as dreadful as any down a dark passage for a child. Such she often felt herself—struggling against terrific odds to maintain her courage; to say: 'But this is what I see; this is what I see,' and so to clasp some miserable remnant of her vision to her breast, which a thousand forces did their best to pluck from her" (p. 34). Somewhat later Lily "sees" something specific that she is unable to capture (not just on canvas but in reality); she catches a glimpse of Mr. and Mrs. Ramsay together: "Directly one looked up and saw them, what she called 'being in love' flooded them. They became part of that unreal but penetrating and exciting universe which is the world seen through the eyes of love" (p. 76). Shortly after this she encounters Mrs. Ramsay: "Did she lock up within her some secret which certainly Lily Briscoe believed people must have for the world to go on at all?" She wonders: "Could loving, as people called it, make her and Mrs Ramsay one? for it was not knowledge but unity she desired, not inscriptions on tablets, nothing that could be written in any language known to men, but intimacy itself, which is knowledge, she had thought, leaning her head on Mrs. Ramsay's knee" (pp. 82–83).

Lily seeks Mrs. Ramsay's ability to achieve a unity with the object, to become one with the thing she looks at; she seeks this goal by direct physical contact, by leaning her head on Mrs. Ramsay's knee. Such knowledge is not so easily put on, however; it is symbolic in nature, not physical, and cannot be passed on by mere physical contact: "Nothing happened. Nothing! Nothing! as she leant her head against Mrs. Ramsay's knee. And yet, she knew knowledge and wisdom were stored in Mrs. Ramsay's heart. How then, she had asked herself, did one know one thing or another thing about people, sealed as they were?" The answer comes in the form of an image, an analogy; Lily has taken a first step toward the Romanticist's perception, although she is not yet conscious of it: "Only like a bee, drawn by some sweetness or sharpness in the air intangible to touch or taste, one haunted the dome-shaped hives with their murmurs and their stirrings; the hives which were people. Mrs. Ramsay rose. Lily rose. Mrs. Ramsay went. For days there hung about her, as after a dream some subtle change felt in the person one has dreamt of, more vividly than anything she said, the sound of murmuring and, as she sat in the wicker armchair in the drawing-room window she wore, to Lily's eyes, an august shape; the shape of a dome" (p. 83). Lily has at this point the inspiration she needs in Mrs. Ramsay; she has the seeds of her vision, although she still lacks what is necessary to complete it. She begins a painting of Mrs. Ramsay reading to James: she is on the right track—the picture is nonrepresentational, symbolic ("But the picture was not of them, she said. Or, not in his [Mr. Bankes's] sense. There were other senses, too, in which one might reverence them" [p. 85]), but she has not quite achieved what she wants ("It was a question, she remembered, how to connect this mass on the right with that on the left. She might do it by bringing the line of the branch across so. . . . But the danger was that by doing that the unity of the whole might be broken" [p. 86]). This painting remains unfinished.

Another important step in her development happens at dinner. Lily has a Romantic revelation; she penetrates to the heart of the Romantic Image and intuitively understands its nature: "For what happened to her, especially staying with the Ramsays, was to be made to feel violently two opposite things at the same time; that's what you feel was one; that's what I feel was the other, and then they fought together in her mind, as now" (p. 159). It will not be until she can accept these opposite feelings without their fighting together in her mind that she will complete her artistic vision, that she will penetrate into the heart of things and see them as in themselves they really are. That moment comes, ten years later, when she is able to sympathize with Mr. Ramsay; when she extends her sympathy to him she finds the key she needs, she finds an answer to the question with which she opens the third and last section of the novel ("What does it mean then, what can it all mean?" [p. 225]).

We will remember that the most important thing Mr. Ramsay requires is sympathy: "He demanded sympathy. . . . James . . . felt her rise in a rosy-flowered fruit tree laid with leaves and dancing boughs into which the beak of brass, the arid scimitar of his father the egotistical man, plunged and smote, demanding sympathy" (pp. 62–63). Sympathy is precisely what Mrs. Ramsay gives her husband, what she is most able to give; it is the way that she as a Romanticist knows her world. Now Lily has in general no sympathy for Mr. Ramsay: "All Lily wished," when he accosts her just before he is to leave for the lighthouse, "was that this enormous flood of grief, this insatiable hunger for sympathy . . . should leave her" (p. 235). Then suddenly, miraculously, after she has resisted and resisted, she capitulates: she praises his boots, of all things, and he is immensely flattered and relieved. Her sympathy for him overwhelms her: "Why, at this completely inappropriate moment, when he was stooping over her shoes, should she be so tormented with sympathy for him that, as she stooped too, the blood rushed to her face, and, thinking of her callousness (she had called him a play-actor) she felt her eyes swell and tingle with tears?" (pp. 238–39). Whatever the reason, her sympathy with Mr. Ramsay establishes her unity with Mrs. Ramsay, and she is then able to paint. A few moments later she raises her brush: "For a moment it stayed trembling in a painful but exciting ecstasy in the air. Where to begin? . . . With a curious physical sensation, as if she were urged forward and at the same time must hold herself back, she made her first quick decisive stroke. The brush descended. It flickered brown over the white canvas. A second time she did it—a third time. And so pausing and so flickering, she attained a dancing rhythmical movement" (pp. 243–44). And so, through sympathy, through an acceptance and a rejoicing in opposites ("as if she were urged forward and at the same time must hold herself back"), Lily has her vision, her moment: she begins a new painting of

Mrs. Ramsay, a painting she completes in the closing lines of the novel. She becomes a Romanticist at last, Mrs. Ramsay's true heir.

Thus it is through a nonlogical continuity—the continuity of the Romantic visions of Mrs. Ramsay and of Lily Briscoe—that this novel coheres. What Karl Kroeber says of a poem by Keats we can say about Woolf's novel: "Only at the expense of reasonable order do we experience the unified intensity of the poet's trance. Only by surrendering, or, perhaps better, transcending, the ordinary, reasonable processes of perception and conception can we apprehend those distinctions and similarities which form the private unity of the *Ode to a Nightingale*" (p. 61). Once we have so transcended our ordinary processes of perception and conception for Mrs. Ramsay and for Lily, we have a vested interest in what they stand for; and what Mrs. Ramsay represents, in opposition to her husband's extreme rationalism, is intuitive knowledge. So is Lily suspicious of the "scientific" scrutiny of her painting by William Bankes (p. 85). The novel thus endorses Mrs. Ramsay's viewpoint by embodying a demonstration of it in its structure: it defies rational, logical order and argues for the superiority of its own self-satisfying inner order.

But there is more to the novel than Mrs. Ramsay and Lily Briscoe. It is no accident, for instance, that Mrs. Ramsay names Mr. Carmichael, as well as Lily and herself, as someone sharing her views; for he becomes, in the years after her death, a successful lyric poet. Mr. Carmichael joins Mrs. Ramsay and Lily to balance Mr. Ramsay, William Bankes, and Charles Tansley. Such a pattern of intuitive Romantic characters shown in relation to rational, scientific ones is a creation of the implied author. We should look to her to consider the form of the entire novel. But the implied author of *To the Lighthouse*, we discover, is virtually interchangeable with the narrator. It seems more useful then to think of this combined narrator–implied author as a kind of persona; she certainly has more in common with the persona of "Ode on a Grecian Urn" than with the narrator of *Adam Bede*. In fact, as I have already suggested, omniscience is somewhat of a foreign concept to Romanticists.

There is certainly a consciousness directing the action and presenting the characters of *To the Lighthouse*, a single voice, as James Naremore says, that orders the whole.[35] That voice, I suggest, is the voice of a Romanticist. It has the same characteristics as, say, the voice of the persona of "Ode on a Grecian Urn." Naremore notes about Woolf's narrator: "Always, too, there is a clear feeling that the language of the novel has been formed by an omnipresent narrative voice which can take the raw materials of thought and develop from them the poetic motifs which serve to comment on the whole design."[36] In a general sense, Romantic personas engage in the same kind of activity: they take the raw materials of thought and develop from them poetic motifs; but they also develop the whole design of the work of art rather than simply commenting on it. We must add that element to Naremore's assessment to understand the aesthetic experience of *To the Lighthouse*.

The design of the novel is relatively simple and clear: there are three sections, "The Window," "Time Passes," and "The Lighthouse." The first is the longest and it introduces us to the major characters and major themes of the novel. The narrator functions here in the way Naremore suggests: she develops motifs to comment on the whole design. For instance, toward the end of the section, the narrator offers this description, which assumes for us, if not for the characters, a symbolic significance; the major characters of the novel have been brought together around the dinner table; it is evening:

> Now all the candles were lit, and the faces on both sides of the table were brought nearer by the candle light, and composed, as they had not been in the twilight, into a

party around a table, for the night was now shut off by
panes of glass, which, far from giving an accurate view
of the outside world, rippled it so strangely that here,
inside the room, seemed to be order and dry land;
there, outside, a reflection in which things wavered and
vanished, waterily.

Some change at once went through them all, as if this
had really happened, and they were all conscious of
making a party together in a hollow, on an island; had
their common cause against that fluidity out there.

(Pp. 151–52)

Just as Keats's persona creates a reality for the figures on the
urn, so does Woolf's narrator create a reality for the characters of the novel. She sketches a scene of symbolic unity,
a glimmer of light surrounded by darkness (which is what a
lighthouse is after all), a moment of stability in the flux of
life (just as a lighthouse is a fixed point of reference surrounded by the changing of the tides, the motion of the
waves). Once she creates this scene, once she suggests its
existence, the characters go on to embody it. The narrator
consciously seeks to maintain the fiction that the characters
exist independently of her—"as if this had really happened," she says—so that the characters stand in the same
relationship to her as the characters carved or depicted on
the urn stand to Keats's persona. He endows the "marble
men and maidens overwrought" with significance; he
creates a story, an existence, for them; the urn "dost tease
[him] out of thought" (44) and he effects an imaginative
identification with it. Thus does the narrator of *To the Lighthouse* behave; she seeks to create the illusion that the characters of the novel exist in the same way that the characters
on the urn exist and then to comment on their existence in
the same manner that Keats's persona does. She consciously
and explicitly endows them with symbolic importance,
however, while Keats's persona works by implication:

"And suddenly the meaning which, for no reason at all, as perhaps they are stepping out of the Tube or ringing a doorbell, descends on people, making them symbolical, making them representative, came upon them, and made them in the dusk standing, looking, the symbols of marriage, husband and wife. Then, after an instant, the symbolical outline which transcended the real figures sank down again, and they became, as they met them, Mr. and Mrs. Ramsay watching the children throwing catches" (pp. 114–15).

The narrator functions in much the same way in the last section, "The Lighthouse." Since she does not have the convenient fiction of a preexistent urn, however, she must also do what ordinary narrators do—tell us what goes on, what the characters do as well as what they think and say. The symbolic nature of the lighthouse is completely her creation, however, since the characters never explicitly comment on its significance. She is thus responsible for the nonlogical continuity that we spoke of above; it is the lighthouse that provides the final symbolic link between Mrs. Ramsay and Lily. In the first and third sections of the novel, the narrator relies on explicit symbols to provide connections and impose meaning; the inner order of the novel depends on the narrator's symbol-making activity.

We come then to the famous middle section of the novel, "Time Passes," the section that Woolf herself describes as lyric.[37] Ralph Freedman suggests that this section "clarifies the epistemological relationships within the novel as a whole. As the glare of the lighthouse penetrates the window and, like Bergson's duration, 'gnaws' on the things within, it establishes an active function of the imagination. The dialectic of window and lighthouse has continued even in the absence of people. Seeing their relationship to one another in a purely formal context, the reader has been prepared for the turnabout of the conclusion" (p. 235). If the lighthouse is the symbol by which a unity is achieved be-

tween Lily and Mrs. Ramsay, it is also the means by which
the unity of the whole novel is achieved. Freedman points
out one of its functions: "It depicts the moment through
images, transforming it finally into a larger image of time
itself. Freed from its dependence on human beings, it
renders, in a more abstract form, the interrelation between
the inner and outer worlds of protagonists on the one hand
and a symbolic world on the other" (p. 234).

There is another way in which the lighthouse functions. In
the first section, Mrs. Ramsay identifies herself with its light.
She imagines herself to be invisible, a core of darkness that
paradoxically becomes one with the beam of light; the union
of Mrs. Ramsay and the lightbeam makes the lighthouse itself a kind of Romantic Image. (Like a Romantic Image it
contains opposites: physically, it is both black and white [see
pp. 286, 311].) In the middle section of the novel Mrs. Ramsay becomes literally invisible for us as readers. She dies, not
to appear again except in another character's memory, and in
her place we have the beam of the lighthouse that flashes
through the empty house, the beam being all that is left to
represent her. Her physical reality ceases and she becomes
solely symbolic. That is why her death occurs for us in a
subordinate clause in a sentence within brackets: "[Mr.
Ramsay stumbling along a passage stretched his arms out
one dark morning, but, Mrs. Ramsay having died rather suddenly the night before, he stretched his arms out. They remained empty]" (pp. 199–200). Her death is announced this
way to signal that the fate of her physical being is of much
less importance than her symbolic power. Our physical lives
are part of the flux; what gains a measure of endurance outside the flux is the power of the symbolic. Thus, while time
passes, the symbol (as it is embodied in art) endures. The
persona of "Ode on a Grecian Urn" is mortal but the figures
on the urn are immortal; the persona of "Ode to a Nightingale" is mortal but the song of the bird is immortal. The
lighthouse, which subsumes Mrs. Ramsay and makes her

part of it, takes on the same function as the Grecian urn and the nightingale's song. The urn and the story of its figures are merely the occasion for an inquiry, an aesthetic investigation, into the nature of beauty and truth, of time and experience; the story of the Ramsays and of Lily Briscoe is also just such an occasion for an investigation into the nature of beauty and truth, the beauty and truth of art, an inquiry into the nature of time and experience.

In conclusion, we can say that *To the Lighthouse,* perhaps more subtly and more fully even than *Mrs. Dalloway,* embodies the Romantic vision of experience. If Virginia Woolf strove to write novels that were poetic in form, the kind of "poetry" she wrote, we can now say, was Romantic poetry. It is not surprising that it should be so. After all, as we have seen elsewhere in this study, the Romantic impulse is a continuing one; and modern novelists, fully as much as modern poets, were affected by it. Far from being a private, personal, and idiosyncratic vision that was exclusive and limited, Woolf's vision is central to the fictional endeavors of her day; it is no more personal and private than Conrad's, or James's, or Lawrence's, or Joyce's. Her methods are more extreme perhaps than those of her two colleagues whom we have examined in this study—Henry James and Joseph Conrad— but her efforts are directed at the same goal: to impose the appropriate form on experience, the form that best helps us deal with it in a meaningful way. That form embodies the underlying principle of the Romantic poetry of experience: that immediate apprehension gained through experience is primary and certain. The effort of all Romantic writers is to make that experience be the experience of their readers; it is an effort to turn their readers into Mrs. Ramsays and Lily Briscoes, at least symbolically; it is an effort—and here Virginia Woolf succeeds superlatively—to send their readers on a journey to the Lighthouse.

SEVEN

Afterword

Henry James, Joseph Conrad, and Virginia Woolf figure on everyone's list of major modern novelists, but there is a large area of modern fiction I have not touched on. In the few remaining pages I should like to sketch in, broadly and roughly, an outline for the further examination of the Romantic nature of modern fiction. My remarks are intended to be suggestive rather than conclusive and concern the fiction of this century up to 1945. We are still too close to the period after World War II to see the forest for the trees.

Modern novelists are linked to one another not so much by common subjects as by a shared attitude toward experience, an attitude derived, as I have tried to show here, from Romanticism. The primary characteristic of this attitude is a pervasive uncertainty that challenges the idea of a universal human experience or at least questions our ability to know that what we feel and experience is felt and experienced by others. In David Daiches' words, what is lost is "a public agreement about what is significant in experience and therefore about what the novelist ought to select."[1] One consequence of this loss is a transformation of aesthetic ideas about narration: the traditional narrative of events and encounters is replaced by a narrative of experience. Characters and events are seen as part of someone's experience, be it that of one character, the narrator, the implied author, or even the reader, but not of everyone's, not of society's at large. The underlying proposition is not just that each person's experience is unique—for in some area it must be—but that we can never speak with assurance of the

experience of others. What we know must always be quali-
fied by who we are—which is why identity is a major concern of modern fiction, as it is of Romantic poetry.

The shift in narrative emphasis is the crucial fact of modern fiction that distinguishes it from earlier fiction. To single
out the change in perspective, however, is in some ways to
exaggerate it. In the first place, while the change in the novel
is significant, the differences between modern and traditional novels are not in total greater than the similarities. We
are examining not a new genre but a change in an existing
one. In the second place, the change did not happen suddenly. It was effected gradually over the course of the nineteenth century. What was sudden was the appearance of ad-
vocates of that change in the front ranks of novelists. All in a
rush, or so it seems, there were Conrad, Joyce, Lawrence,
and Woolf, ready to take James's ideas further than even he
probably would have expected. But just as the beginnings of
Romanticism can be seen in the eighteenth century, so the
beginnings of the modern fictional aesthetic can be traced in
the nineteenth century. Even George Eliot, whose *Adam Bede*
I have used as a representative Victorian novel, was affected
by the breakdown of a shared sense of public significance,
and her later novels do not have the certainty of tone that we
find in her earlier work.

Forewarned, then, about the risk of exaggeration, let us
see in what ways the Romantic aesthetic might play a part
in the work of other modern novelists. An obvious place to
begin is with D. H. Lawrence. On first glance, his two
major achievements, *The Rainbow* and *Women in Love,* seem
Romantic in subject matter, an impression that is confirmed
on closer examination, since the theme of both novels is a
Shelleyan quest for wholeness and for the lover's union
with another. One might profitably explore in fact the af-
finities between *Women in Love* and "Epipsychidion." These
lines, in which Shelley mingles the rapture of the lovers'
union with the fear of the loss of self in that union, might

almost be a gloss for the two sets of relationships Lawrence gives us in the novel:

> One hope within two wills, one will beneath
> Two overshadowing minds, one life, one death,
> One Heaven, one Hell, one immortality,
> And one annihilation.[2]

Lawrence's recurring theme is the lover's fear that his will will be annihilated or overshadowed, yet without the "one hope within two wills," the lover is incomplete. Only Ursula and Birkin come close; Gerald and Gudrun fail, and Gerald is annihilated in a different manner than here suggested.

Even more strikingly Romantic, however, is what Lawrence does with narrative. One of the chief characteristics of Romantic fiction is a discontinuous, nonnarrative structure. Long stretches of *The Rainbow* can best be described in this way. The narrator mixes together different time-schemes so that the novel, which is at bottom a chronicle of several generations, seems to proceed at one point by fits and starts and at another by the blending of the characters' emotions and experiences into a seamless whole. Notice in the following passage, for example, how the point of view shifts from Will to Anna and back again:

> And ever and again, the pure love came in sunbeams between them, when she was like a flower in the sun to him, so beautiful, so shining, so intensely dear that he could scarcely bear it. Then as if his soul had six wings of bliss he stood absorbed in praise, feeling the radiance from the Almighty beat through him like a pulse, as he stood in the upright flame of praise, transmitting the pulse of Creation.
>   And ever and again he appeared to her as the dread flame of power. Sometimes, when he stood in the doorway, his face lit up, he seemed like an Annunciation to

her, her heart beat fast. And she watched him, suspended. He had a dark, burning being that she dreaded
and resisted. She was subject to him as to the Angel of
the Presence. She waited upon him and heard his will,
and she trembled in his service.

Then all this passed away. Then he loved her for her
childishness and for her strangeness to him, for the
wonder of her soul which was different from his soul, and
which made him genuine when he would be false. And
she loved him for the way he sat loosely in a chair, or for
the way he came through a door with his face open and
eager. She loved his ringing, eager voice, and the touch of
the unknown about him, his absolute simplicity.

Yet neither of them was quite satisfied. He felt, some-
where, that she did not respect him. She only respected
him as far as he was related to herself. For what he was,
beyond her, she had no care. She did not care for what
he represented in himself. It is true, he did not know
himself what he represented. But whatever it was she
did not really honour it.[3]

By traditional standards this passage seems discontinuous:
the narrative voice swings back and forth between the characters, and readers could be uncertain where their attention
should be directed. They would be uncertain, that is, if
their point of comparison were Jane Austen, George Eliot,
or Anthony Trollope. Readers familiar with modern fiction,
however, can follow this passage with little difficulty. They
understand that the focus here, like that of all Romantic
literature, is so totally on what the characters experience
that everything else is subservient to it. The plot does advance, but it does so rather in the manner of "Ode to a
Nightingale"—associatively, experientially.

One cannot get a proper sense of the discontinuous nature of Lawrence's narratives from a short extract. His long
chapters must be read in full to appreciate his disregard of

traditional patterns of fictional organization. This disregard shows up in his novels' structural aspects as well. His novels often seem disproportionate or even lopsided. *Sons and Lovers*, for example, seems out of balance, with Paul Morel's later life slighted in comparison to his adolescence or childhood, his artistic life only hinted at (although it is essential in understanding his motivations) in comparison to his emotional life, his relationship with Miriam so much more fully considered than his relationship with Clara. Lawrence seems to be belaboring his characters' emotional experiences for very much the same reasons Marlow is compelled to tell his stories of Kurtz and Jim. Both, like the Romanticist, seek a wider, more inclusive mystery.

Joyce's fiction is Romantic in a different manner from Lawrence's. His general effort is the same—to concentrate the reader's attention on his characters' inner experiences— but his methods are different. Like *Sons and Lovers*, *A Portrait of the Artist* shows us the developing psychology of a young (male) artist, and like Lawrence's novel, it presents that psychology from the inside. But whereas Lawrence tells us, in painstaking specificity, what Paul is thinking, Joyce relies on the stream-of-consciousness technique to dramatize Stephen Dedalus's psyche and the struggles within it. An obvious avenue of exploration here is the connection between stream-of-consciousness in fiction and the dramatic monologue in poetry. More generally, the way to analyze *Portrait* as Romantic is to trace the manner in which the "process of experience" becomes for Stephen "a process of self-realization" (to use Langbaum's words again).[4] As the novel progresses we see its protagonist, like the Romanticist, in a continual endeavor to formulate and reformulate values, though never arriving at a final formulation (as *Ulysses* further demonstrates). In one sense, Stephen becomes an artist when he realizes the very thing that the Romanticist knows, that "the process of experience is . . . a process of self-realization, of a constantly expanding discovery of the self through discoveries of its imprint on the external world" (Langbaum, p. 25).

In addition, *Portrait* is structured to emphasize the process of self-discovery. Stephen's first words in the novel reveal just such a process. He transforms the words of a song from "O, the wild rose blossoms" into "O, the green wothe botheth," and by so doing he puts his imprint on the outside world. The entire novel elaborates this process as Stephen moves from his small, schoolchild's world to the political and religious reality of early twentieth-century Ireland. By the end of the fourth chapter, when he has his epiphany on the beach that confirms him as an artist, he has matured enough to seek, consciously, self-realization the way the Romanticist does. He is ready then to turn knowledge into experience, as his villanelle ("Are you not weary of ardent ways") is an attempt to do.

On a much larger scale and in a more complex way, *Ulysses* also shows us how knowledge is turned into experience. It is a chronicle of Leopold Bloom's discovery of his imprint on the external world fully as much as *Portrait* is of Stephen's. Bloom's imagination ranges more widely than Stephen's though, so that his quest on that June day in 1904 is much more fully imbued with national, political, and religious overtones than Stephen's. Whereas it is Stephen who announces at the end of *Portrait*, "I go to encounter for the millionth time the reality of experience and to forge in the smithy of my soul the uncreated conscience of my race," it is Leopold Bloom who more completely effects such an encounter in *Ulysses*.[5] The affinity between the two characters is in part that each recognizes that "it makes no difference whether [he] arrives in the end at a new formulation [of the meaning of his experience] or returns to an old one. It is the process of denial and reaffirmation which distinguishes him both from those who have never denied and those who, having denied, have never reaffirmed" (Langbaum, p. 20). An analysis of *Ulysses* to show us in detail Bloom's and

Stephen's "process of denial and reaffirmation" would help to demonstrate the novel's Romantic nature.

Another way to approach what is Romantic about Joyce's fiction is to start with the idea of the epiphany. We have noted already its connection to Wordsworth's "spots of time" and Woolf's "moments." Langbaum assesses it this way in *The Poetry of Experience:*

> The epiphany, in the literary sense, is a way of apprehending value when value is no longer objective—when it is no longer in nature, which is to say in a publicly accepted order of ideas about nature. The epiphany grounds the statement of value in perception; it gives the idea with its genesis, establishing its validity not as conforming to a public order of values but as the genuine experience of an identifiable person. It gives us the idea, in other words, before we have to pass judgment on its truth or falsity—while it is still in union with emotion and the perceived object. (P. 46)

A reexamination of Joyce's use of the epiphany, in *Dubliners* as well as *Portrait* and *Ulysses,* from the perspective Langbaum here provides would add substantially to our understanding of the Romantic aspects of modern fiction, especially if connections were drawn between Joyce's use of the epiphany and fictional equivalents of the dramatic monologue and Woolf's use of the moment and of such monologues. A comparison of *Ulysses* and *The Waves* with *The Ring and the Book* might yield valuable insights in this area as well.

Although the five novelists considered thus far—James, Conrad, Woolf, Lawrence, and Joyce—are the major novelists of the modern period, their contemporaries and their successors have also been influenced by the Romantic aesthetic. The novels of Ford Madox Ford, for instance, demonstrate a nonnarrative, discontinuous structure as thoroughly as any book one could name. The four volumes that make up *Parade's End* abandon all sense of conventional narrative. Their structure is best described as elliptical, just as their style is characterized by a heavy use of ellipses (as in *Some Do Not . . .* , the title of the first volume). Ordinary connections between one character and another or between one event and another are lacking; rather, the reader is plunged into the midst of events very much in the manner that Tietjens, the main character of the tetralogy, is thrown into the chaos of trench warfare in *A Man Could Stand Up—*. The dash in this title, like the ellipsis of *Some Do Not . . .* , points up the inconclusiveness of the characters' experiences, but that inconclusiveness is like Marlow's in *Heart of Darkness*. It signals a dissatisfaction with traditional explanations and reveals a Romantic outlook: Tietjens must struggle to formulate his values every day anew. He is like Marlow in that he starts as the conservative, the believer in a fixed standard of moral conduct, but he moves beyond Marlow when he comes to understand how thoroughly the first World War has obliterated the old life. In the final volume, *Last Post,* he goes back to Groby, the family estate, but he returns with a new sense of the need for a continuing process of denial and reaffirmation.

Ford's best and most well known novel, *The Good Soldier,* is also perhaps the most extreme example of the uncertainty of modern fiction. Because Dowell, the narrator, deliberately lies to us, we are thrown adrift and must piece together what has happened ourselves, primarily by catching him up in inconsistencies. The reader is forced to assume the role of narrator. We saw that happen with *Frankenstein,* where the conflicting stories of the narrators left the reader's sympathies divided. The purpose is the same here: to make you see from within, to make you sympathize rather than judge, and to cut you off from traditional doctrines. The whole novel comes to resemble one of Browning's dramatic monologues, in which we discover, in Langbaum's words, "passion, power, strength of will and intellect, just those existential virtues which are independent of logical and moral correctness and are therefore best made out through sympathy and when clearly separated from, even opposed to, other virtues" (p. 86).

This kind of literary effect, in which one is asked to sympathize with characters whom one might otherwise or also morally condemn, is a clear legacy of Romanticism. When we find it in fiction, we should suspect that an analysis of the kind I have been doing here will be helpful. Examples abound in modern fiction, from James's short stories to Ford's novel. Likewise, when we discover the reader being asked to take on the role of narrator, we should investigate a possible connection to Romanticism. William Faulkner's work comes to mind, especially *The Sound and the Fury* and *Absalom, Absalom!*, which are both constructed as a series of dramatic monologues, different characters each narrating his or her version of the same or overlapping events. The true version, if it exists at all, exists only in readers' minds after it has been pieced together by those readers themselves, rather than by a single narrator.

Faulkner is not the only American novelist of this century whom we might examine as Romantic. If his work seems influenced by the experiments of James and Ford, as well as by those of Joyce, Scott Fitzgerald inherits a Conradian legacy and, with it, a Romantic one. A comparison of *The Great Gatsby* with *Lord Jim* is fruitful. Like Jim, Gatsby is a Romantic hero. He fits in part Northrop Frye's definition: "A solitary, an outcast. . . . He has great energy, often great powers of leadership, and even his vices are dignified enough to have some aesthetic attraction."[6] Like Jim, he lives for an unachievable dream, and his death is equally ironic and ambiguous in its Romanticism: both sacrifice themselves for a dubious ideal—Jim for an empty heroism, Gatsby for an empty love. Gatsby is also similar to Kurtz: he too is hollow at the core, yet his futile dream is compelling and somehow admirable. He has kicked himself free of the earth, and been corrupted too, but his victory is a moral one in the same ironic sense that Kurtz's is. Nick Carraway, Fitzgerald's narrator, is much like Marlow, in that he is driven to penetrate the mystery of a character unlike himself. His fascination with Gatsby could be analyzed in the same way as Marlow's with Kurtz or Jim.

I have offered just a few suggestions for how a further examination of the Romantic nature of modern fiction might be carried forth. Although I have mentioned only novelists writing in English, a line of investigation might certainly be pursued that would start with Proust and Gide and continue up to Camus and the New Novelists, especially Robbe-Grillet. Robert Musil and Hermann Hesse would also lend themselves to such an investigation. It is important, though, that these suggestions not be seen as the mechanical plugging of Romantic characteristics into modern novels. I have tried, rather, to identify those areas where knowledge of the Romantic aesthetic will help to illuminate individual fictional worlds. The value of such an endeavor consists in the increased understanding of modern fiction that it affords us. A fuller grasp of the ways in which much of the literature of the past two centuries can be considered as part of an ongoing literary tradition—a tradition for which we have only the inadequate and perhaps misleading name of Romanticism—ought to help us to perceive the true nature of that literature. Such an effort is undertaken not to diminish modern fiction but to bring its full significance to our attention.

NOTES

INDEX

Notes

1. Introduction

1. *The Sacred Wood* (1920; rpt. London: Methuen, 1964), p. 32. The most notable exception to Eliot's ideas is Jacques Barzun's study in 1943, *Romanticism and the Modern Ego;* a second, revised edition was published as *Classic, Romantic and Modern* (1961; rpt. Chicago: Univ. of Chicago Press, 1975).

2. See Frank Kermode, *Romantic Image* (1957; rpt. New York: Vintage, n.d.), pp. 119–37; Graham Hough, *Image and Experience* (Lincoln: Univ. of Nebraska Press, 1960), esp. pp. 28–56; Murray Krieger, "The Ambiguous Anti-Romanticism of T. E. Hulme," *ELH*, 20 (1953), 300–14, and "T. E. Hulme: Classicism and Imagination," in *The New Apologists for Poetry* (Bloomington: Indiana Univ. Press, 1963), pp. 31–45; Carl Woodring, *Politics in English Romantic Poetry* (Cambridge: Harvard Univ. Press, 1970), p. 25. For a more recent attempt to sort out Hulme's confused ideas, see Ronald Primeau, "On the Discrimination of Hulmes: Toward a Theory of the 'Anti-romantic' Romanticism of Modern Poetry," *Journal of Modern Literature*, 3 (July 1974), 1104–22. Primeau suggests that modern literature shows both a continuity with Romanticism and a departure from it that "create a distinctive movement" (p. 1118). His discussion does not demonstrate to my satisfaction that the "modifications" the moderns performed on Romantic ideas are evidence enough to speak of a "distinctive movement"; they would seem to suggest, on the contrary, that what we have is merely a modified Romanticism (see pp. 1118–20).

3. Ralph Freedman, *The Lyrical Novel: Studies in Hermann Hesse, André Gide, and Virginia Woolf* (1963; rpt. Princeton: Univ. of Princeton Press, 1970). Further references are included in the text.

4. (New Haven: Yale Univ. Press, 1974), p. xi. For an attempt to discuss D. H. Lawrence as a Romanticist, see Colin Clarke, *River of Dissolution: D. H. Lawrence and English Romanticism* (New York: Barnes and Noble, 1969).

5. Maurice Beebe, "*Ulysses* and the Age of Modernism," *James Joyce Quarterly*, 10 (Fall 1972), 175.

6. *Journal of Modern Literature*, 3 (July 1974), 1075.

7. Pp. 176–77.

8. "Romanticism and Antiself-consciousness," in *Romanticism: Points of View*, ed. Robert F. Gleckner and Gerald E. Enscoe, 2nd ed. (Englewood Cliffs, N.J.: Prentice-Hall, 1970), p. 296.

9. (1946; rpt. New York: Harper Torchbooks, 1961), p. 168.

10. *English Romantic Poetry* (Berkeley and Los Angeles: Univ. of Calif. Press, 1968), p. 261. Further references are included in the text.

11. (Cambridge: Harvard Univ. Press, 1972). See also Walter L. Reed, *Meditations on the Hero: A Study of the Romantic Hero in Nineteenth-Century Fiction* (New Haven: Yale Univ. Press, 1974).

12. Beebe, "What Modernism Was," p. 1075. For an illuminating discussion of James's critical ideas, that implicitly refutes Beebe, see James E. Miller, Jr., "Henry James in Reality," *Critical Inquiry*, 2 (Spring 1976), 585–604.

13. R. A. Foakes, *The Romantic Assertion* (London: Methuen, 1958), p. 45; Graham Hough, *The Romantic Poets*, 3rd ed. (London: Hutchinson Univ. Library, 1967), p. 57.

14. Henry James, "The Art of Fiction," in *Partial Portraits* (1888; rpt. Ann Arbor: Univ. of Michigan Press, 1970), p. 398.

15. J. Hillis Miller, *Poets of Reality* (Cambridge: Belknap Press of Harvard Univ. Press, 1965), p. 1.

16. (Rev. ed., 1960; rpt. Chicago: Phoenix Books, 1967); (1955; rpt. New York: Grove Press, n.d.); (New York: Oxford, 1966). For two different approaches to the question of a change in the novel, see William C. Frierson, *The English Novel in Transition 1885–1940* (Norman: Univ. of Oklahoma Press, 1942), and Donald D. Stone, *Novelists in a Changing World: Meredith, James, and the Transformation of English Fiction in the 1880's* (Cambridge: Harvard Univ. Press, 1972). See also Peter Garrett, *Scene and Symbol from George Eliot to James Joyce: Studies in Changing Fictional Mode* (New Haven: Yale Univ. Press, 1969), and Max F. Schulz, "Characters (Contra Characterization) in the Contemporary Novel," in *The Theory of the Novel: New Essays*, ed. John Halperin (New York: Oxford, 1974), pp. 141–54.

17. See also G. S. Fraser, *The Modern Writer and His World* (1953; rev. ed. Baltimore, Md.: Penguin Books, 1964), p. 79: "Behind the great novels of the past lay the writer's awareness of an established order, which he might judge to be in the main good or evil, but which was in either case reliably *there*; today there is no constant order for the novelist either to accept or to rebel against. All social and political arrangements—indeed, the continued existence of civilized human society and of the human race—have today a provisional air; the marks of our time are uncertainty and anxiety, but also a certain fatalism and apathy, coming from the powerlessness of the individual." See also Max F. Schulz, "The Perseverance of Romanticism: From Organism to Artifact," *Clio: An Interdisciplinary Journal of Literature, History, and the Philosophy of History* (Univ. of Wisconsin), 3 (1974), 165–86.

18. Here is a sampling of studies which discuss in some way a continuity between nineteenth- and twentieth-century literature: M. H. Abrams, *The Mirror and the Lamp* (1953; rpt. New York: Norton, 1958), and *Natural Supernaturalism* (New York: Norton, 1971), although in the latter Abrams has expressed his reservations about how widespread the Romantic influence is in modern literature; Jacques Barzun, *Classic, Romantic and Modern* (1961; rpt. Chicago: Univ. of Chicago Press, 1975); John Bayley, *The Romantic Survival: A Study in Poetic Evolution* (London: Constable, 1967); Harold Bloom, "The Internalization of the Quest-Romance," in *Romanticism and Consciousness* (New York: Norton, 1970); Edward E. Bostetter, *The Romantic Ventriloquists* (Seattle: Univ. of Washington Press, 1963); Northrop Frye, *A Study of English Romanticism* (New York: Random House, 1968); Geoffrey Hartman, *Beyond Formalism* (New Haven: Yale Univ. Press, 1970); Graham Hough, *The Last Romantics* (1947; rpt. London: Methuen, 1961); Randall Jarrell, "The End of the Line," in *Literary Modernism,* ed. Irving Howe (New York: Fawcett, 1967); Frank Kermode, *Romantic Image* (1957; rpt. New York: Vintage, n.d.); Robert Langbaum, *The Modern Spirit: Essays on the Continuity of Nineteenth- and Twentieth-Century Literature* (New York: Oxford, 1970), and *The Poetry of Experience* (1957; rpt. New York: Norton, 1963); Morse Peckham, *Romanticism: The Culture of the Nineteenth Century* (Columbia: Univ. of South Carolina Press, 1970); David Thorburn, *Conrad's Romanticism;* and David Thorburn and Geoffrey Hartman, eds., *Romanticism: Vistas, Instances, Continuities* (Ithaca, N.Y.: Cornell Univ. Press, 1973).

19. P. 15. Cf. Virginia Woolf's essay, "The Narrow Bridge of Art" (1927), where she remarks: "Nobody indeed can read much modern literature without being aware that some dissatisfaction, some difficulty, is lying in our way. On all sides writers are attempting what they cannot achieve, are forcing the form they use to contain a meaning which is strange to it. Many reasons might be given, but here let us select only one, and that is the failure of poetry to serve us as it has served so many generations of our fathers" (*Granite and Rainbow* [New York: Harcourt Brace Jovanovich, 1958], p. 11).

20. (1960; rpt. Madison: Univ. of Wisconsin Press, 1966), pp. 47, 41.

21. For a comprehensive discussion of the aesthetics of the major modern novelists, see John Paterson, *The Novel as Faith: The Gospel According to James, Hardy, Conrad, Joyce, Lawrence, and Virginia Woolf* (Boston: Gambit, 1973).

22. Cf. Robert Scholes and Robert Kellogg, *The Nature of Narrative* (New York: Oxford, 1966), p. 156: "The raw material of human existence remains ever the same, the molds by which it is given significance and recognizable shape are forever being re-created by the writers of empirical narrative and drama. The new in empirical narrative depends upon an originality of

vision, a creation of new types of actuality, and not upon a flight of the imagination away from the actual."

23. Wayne Booth, *The Rhetoric of Fiction* (Chicago: Univ. of Chicago Press, 1961), p. 321. Further references are included in the text.

24. In support of my position, see M. H. Abrams, "What's the Use of Theorizing about the Arts?" in *In Search of Literary Theory*, ed. Morton Bloomfield (Ithaca, N.Y.: Cornell Univ. Press, 1972), p. 50: "But we will get clear about what we are really doing in artistic criticism, and in various related areas of inquiry, only if we face up to the full consequences of the realization that these pursuits are neither logic nor science, but their own kinds of discourse, adapted to their own kinds of problems, having their own criteria of rationality, and yielding their own kinds of knowledge, to which the term 'certainty' does not apply. But if this knowledge is not 'certain,' neither is it, strictly speaking, 'uncertain'; both terms, insofar as they are tied to alien modes of discourse, are misleading."

25. T. E. Hulme, *Speculations* (1927; rpt. New York: Harvest Books, n.d.), p. 127.

26. See Geoffrey Hartman, *Beyond Formalism* (New Haven: Yale Univ. Press, 1970), pp. 67–68. Frank Kermode has even suggested that reading modern fiction has helped us see new aspects of earlier narratives; see "Novel and Narrative," in *The Theory of the Novel: New Essays*, ed. John Halperin (New York: Oxford, 1974), pp. 172–73.

27. Bayley, *Romantic Survival*, p. 20. Cf. Geoffrey Hartman, *Wordsworth's Poetry 1787–1814* (New Haven: Yale Univ. Press, 1964), p. 295.

2. Romantic Form: Poetry

1. Robert Langbaum, *The Modern Spirit* (New York: Oxford, 1970), p. 44.

2. *The Philosophy of Symbolic Forms*, trans. Ralph Manheim, I (1953; rpt. New Haven: Yale Univ. Press, 1968), 154.

3. (London: Hutchinson Univ. Library, 1967), p. 57.

4. Albert Gérard, *English Romantic Poetry* (Berkeley and Los Angeles: Univ. of Calif. Press, 1968), p. 206. Further references are included in the text.

5. Karl Kroeber, *Romantic Narrative Art* (1960; rpt. Madison: Univ. of Wisconsin Press, 1966), p. 51. Further references are included in the text.

6. *A Study of English Romanticism* (New York: Random House, 1968), p. 68.

7. "On Reading Romantic Poetry," *PMLA*, 86 (Oct. 1971), 977.

8. Robert Langbaum, *The Poetry of Experience* (1957; rpt. New York: Norton, 1963), pp. 35–36, 26, 25. Further references are included in the text.

9. (1953; rpt. New York: Norton, 1958), p. 22. See also Frank Kermode, *Romantic Image* (1957; rpt. New York: Vintage, n.d.), p. 93.

10. Albert Gérard, "On the Logic of Romanticism," in *Romanticism: Points of View*, ed. Robert Gleckner and Gerald Enscoe, 2nd ed. (Englewood Cliffs, N.J.: Prentice-Hall, 1970), p. 264.

11. R. A. Foakes, *The Romantic Assertion* (London: Methuen, 1958), pp. 39, 41–42.

12. *Romantic Assertion*, p. 45.

13. Ibid., p. 44.

14. *Alexander Pope: Selected Poetry and Prose*, ed. William K. Wimsatt (New York: Holt, Rinehart, and Winston, 1968), p. 55. Further references by line number are in the text.

15. See John Butt, ed., *The Poems of Alexander Pope* (New Haven: Yale Univ. Press, 1963), p. 139n.

16. "On the Logic of Romanticism," p. 266.

17. Ibid., p. 264.

18. *Lives of the Poets*, ed. George Birbeck Hill (Oxford: The Clarendon Press, 1905), III, 228.

19. Cf. Gérard, *English Romantic Poetry*, p. 17.

20. *The Complete Poetry and Selected Prose of John Keats*, ed. H. E. Briggs (New York: Modern Library, 1951), p. 290. References by line number are in the text.

21. Cf. Liane Norman, "Risk and Redundancy," *PMLA*, 90 (March 1975), 290: "The critical habit of seeing a piece of literature as a whole design, a symmetrical object in space, as it were, rather than an event apprehended in time, often obscures many of the structural functions of particular stratagems. Information is given the reader one piece before the next. The recipient of information has a memory (which is the reason language is possible) so that the effects of information are cumulative. On the basis of accumulated evidence the reader is expected to draw and correct his conclusions."

22. As an apprentice to an apothecary, Keats would have been familiar with various drugs and their effects. See Stuart Sperry, "Keats and the Chemistry of Poetic Creation," *PMLA*, 85 (1970), 268–77.

23. See Kroeber, *Romantic Narrative Art*, p. 70.

3. Romantic Form: Fiction

1. Karl Kroeber, *Romantic Narrative Art* (1960; rpt. Univ. of Wisconsin Press, 1966), pp. 6–7. Further references are included in the text.

2. See Robert Scholes and Robert Kellogg, *The Nature of Narrative* (New York: Oxford, 1966), p. 275.

3. Wayne Booth, *The Rhetoric of Fiction* (Chicago: Univ. of Chicago Press, 1961), p. 160. See chapter 6, "Types of Narration," pp. 147–65. Further references are included in the text.

4. It is related to the issue of publicly shared values that arose in our discussion of Pope and Keats in chapter two when we considered the persona of "Ode for Music" as speaking generally, universally, and omnisciently of publicly shared values, while the persona of "Ode to a Nightingale" spoke idiosyncratically of his own limited, private, personal experience.

5. David Daiches, *The Novel and the Modern World*, rev. ed. (1960; rpt. Chicago: Phoenix Books, 1967), p. 5; John Bayley, *The Romantic Survival* (London: Constable, 1967), p. 77.

6. See D. H. Stewart, *"Vanity Fair:* Life in the Void," *College English,* 25 (1963), 209–14; William Marshall, *The World of the Victorian Novel* (New York: New York Univ. Press, 1967), p. 259.

7. See Daiches, *The Novel and the Modern World,* p. 3: "Much Victorian fiction investigates the limits of hypocrisy, the ways in which and the degree to which vice can achieve the reputation of virtue by manifesting virtue's outward signs."

8. Cf. David Thorburn, *Conrad's Romanticism* (New Haven: Yale Univ. Press, 1974), p. 125.

9. *The Romantic Novel in England* (Cambridge, Mass.: Harvard Univ. Press, 1972), p. 1. Further references are in the text.

10. For a discussion of this point, see U. C. Knoepflmacher, *George Eliot's Early Novels* (Berkeley and Los Angeles: Univ. of Calif. Press, 1968), chapter 4, "Pastoralism and the Justification for Suffering: *Adam Bede,"* pp. 89–127. See also an earlier version of some of this material, "The Post-Romantic Imagination: *Adam Bede,* Wordsworth, and Milton," *ELH,* 34 (1967), 518–40.

11. Mary Shelley, *Frankenstein* (1831; rpt. New York: Signet, 1965), p. 95, hereafter cited in the text. This edition is based on the third London edition of 1831. Although Shelley revised the first edition (1818) substantially, her revisions do not materially affect my discussion of the novel.

12. As Henry James says, the novel for George Eliot "was not primarily a picture of life, capable of deriving a high value from its form, but a moralised fable, the last word of a philosophy endeavouring to teach by example." See "The Life of George Eliot" (1885) in James E. Miller, Jr., ed., *Theory of Fiction: Henry James* (Lincoln: Univ. of Nebraska Press, 1972), p. 94.

13. *Aspects of the Novel* (1927; rpt. New York: Harvest Books, n.d.), p. 52.

14. W. J. Harvey, *The Art of George Eliot* (1961; rpt. New York: Oxford, 1969), pp. 71–72. Further references are included in the text.

15. George Eliot, *Adam Bede,* ed. John Paterson (Boston: Houghton-Mifflin, 1968), p. xx. Further references to this edition of *Adam Bede* (1859) are included in the text.

16. See U. C. Knoepflmacher, *Religious Humanism and the Victorian Novel* (Princeton: Princeton Univ. Press, 1965).

17. Notably Dorothy Van Ghent, *The English Novel: Form and Function* (1953; rpt. New York: Perennial Library, 1967), pp. 209–21.

18. Karl Kroeber, *Styles in Fictional Structure* (Princeton: Princeton Univ. Press, 1971), pp. 33, 39. Harvey makes a similar point in *The Art of George Eliot* when he speaks of a "series of interconnected but ever-enlargening perspectives which demand of us greater and greater knowledge, sympathy and insight. By this means each of her characters is seen in a number of interacting relationships—man in relation to himself, his family, trade, local community and to the whole of his historical society" (p. 41). See also Harvey, p. 147.

19. Robert Langbaum, *The Poetry of Experience* (1957; rpt. New York: Norton, 1963), p. 35. Further references are included in the text.

20. "Gothic as Vortex: The Form of Horror in Capote, Faulkner, and Styron," *Modern Fiction Studies,* 19 (Summer 1973), 154.

21. *The Form of Victorian Fiction* (Notre Dame: Univ. of Notre Dame Press, 1968), p. 35, as quoted in Perry, "Gothic as Vortex," p. 155.

22. This is how the film versions of the twentieth century have tended to treat the story; occasionally a movie monster will make a human gesture but the viewer is never allowed to see from his point of view as the reader of the novel is. Christopher Isherwood's television version, *"Frankenstein: The True Story"* (1973), was unusual in that it presented the monster as sympathetic; unfortunately, it was in every other way a completely perverted version of the true story of Shelley's novel.

23. Larry Swingle, "On Reading Romantic Poetry," *PMLA,* 86 (Oct. 1971), 975. Further references are included in the text. Swingle himself has examined *Frankenstein,* but his emphases are different from mine. See "Frankenstein's Monster and Its Romantic Relatives: Problems of Knowledge in English Romanticism," *Texas Studies in Literature and Language,* 15 (Spring 1973), 51–66. See also Richard J. Dunn, "Narrative Distance in *Frankenstein,"* *Studies in the Novel,* 6 (Winter 1974), 408–17.

24. See Harold Bloom's afterword to the Signet edition of *Frankenstein* (p. 213). As Bloom notes, Muriel Spark's antithesis between Frankenstein as the feelings and the monster as the intellect is not supported by the text; Bloom's own suggestion that the monster is a shadow or double of Frankenstein seems gratuitous. Their personalities and desires are distinct; what similarities there are do not require us to see the two characters as doubles. To read these characters as two halves of the same being or as doubles reduces Shelley's perceptions of human nature to simplistic terms; the subtle differences in their personalities give the novel its quality of moral complexity.

25. William Walling, *Mary Shelley* (New York: Twayne Publishers, 1972), p. 39. Walling cites for support M. A. Goldberg, "Moral and Myth in Mrs. Shelley's *Frankenstein,"* *Keats-Shelley Journal,* 8 (Part 1, 1959), 27–38.

26. "Female Gothic: The Monster's Mother," *New York Review of Books,* 21 March 1974, p. 25. Cf. Kiely's discussion (*Romantic Novel in England,* pp. 164–66) of Frankenstein's "attempt to usurp the power of women."

27. *The Philosophy of Symbolic Forms,* trans. Ralph Manheim, II (1955; rpt. New Haven: Yale Univ. Press, 1970), 108.

4. Henry James

1. 'What Modernism Was," *Journal of Modern Literature,* 3 (July 1974), 1075.

2. "The Art of Fiction," in *Partial Portraits* (1888; rpt. Ann Arbor: Univ. of Michigan Press, 1970), p. 396. Further references appear parenthetically in the text, prefixed AF.

3. *Poetical Works,* ed. Thomas Hutchinson, rev. ed. Ernest de Selincourt (1936; rpt. London: Oxford, 1966), p. 737. Further references are included in the text.

4. Henry James, *The Art of the Novel: Critical Prefaces by Henry James,* intro. R. P. Blackmur (New York: Scribner's, 1934), pp. 122–23. Further references appear parenthetically in the text.

5. See *The Art of the Novel,* pp. 15, 25, 36, 83, 84, 101, 106, 122–23, 136, 139, 140, 151, 219, 230, 233–34, 305, 339, and 342.

6. Most notably by Wayne Booth, *The Rhetoric of Fiction* (Chicago: Univ. of Chicago Press, 1961); and W. J. Harvey, *The Art of George Eliot* (1961; rpt. New York: Oxford, 1969), and *Character and the Novel* (Ithaca, N.Y.: Cornell Univ. Press, 1965). Further references to *The Rhetoric of Fiction* are included in the text.

7. See also *The Art of the Novel,* pp. 33, 80, 151, 182, and 214.

8. Harold T. McCarthy, *Henry James: The Creative Process* (New York: Thomas Yoseloff, 1958), p. 69. McCarthy also notes a relationship between James's methods and one of the cardinal principles of Romanticism. Speaking of James's development of one of his *données,* McCarthy comments: "He had to be free to feel where the interest lay in his impression and free to develop it according to his own sense of things. In this respect, he seems to have had the quality which Keats observed Shakespeare to have possessed so enormously, 'Negative Capability' " (p. 66). In *The Search for Form* (Chapel Hill: Univ. of North Carolina Press, 1967), J. A. Ward also discusses the organic nature of James's means of composition; see chapter 1, "The Organic and the Scientific," pp. 3–28, esp. 16–17. I think Ward is mistaken in calling James "neoclassic" as well as Romantic (see pp. 4, viii). Ward seems to think that a concern for form is inconsistent with Romantic concerns, but Gérard's *English Romantic Poetry* should be sufficient to refute that position.

9. See *The Art of the Novel,* pp. 15, 33, 37, 62, 66, 68, 138, 143, 164, 176, 196, 214, 233, 251, 259, 263, 281, 300, 318, 326, and 330. See also *Partial Portraits,* p. 384, and James's "Project of Novel" for *The Ambassadors* in F. O. Matthiessen and Kenneth Murdock, eds., *The Notebooks of Henry James* (1947; rpt. New York: Oxford, 1961), pp. 372–415 passim.

10. H. F. B. Brett-Smith, ed., *Shelley's Defence of Poetry,* 2nd ed. (1923; rpt. Oxford: Basil Blackwell, 1967), p. 33.

11. Letter to George and Tom Keats, 21, 27 (?) December 1817, in Robert Gittings, ed., *Letters of John Keats* (New York: Oxford, 1970), p. 42.

12. *The Poetry of Experience* (1957; rpt. New York: Norton, 1963), p. 46. Further references are included in the text.

13. Langbaum, *The Poetry of Experience,* p. 46; M. H. Abrams, *Natural Supernaturalism* (New York: Norton, 1971), p. 419.

14. M. H. Abrams, *The Mirror and the Lamp* (1953; rpt. New York: Norton, 1958), p. 22.

15. McCarthy, *Henry James,* p. 133.

16. *The Art of George Eliot* (1961; rpt. New York: Oxford, 1969), p. 79. Cf. McCarthy, *Henry James,* p. 70, where he notes that the reader in James "is thrown upon his own resources and to a great extent the value of the experience will depend upon what he, himself, can bring to it."

17. Karl Kroeber, *Romantic Narrative Art* (1960; rpt. Madison: Univ. of Wisconsin Press, 1966), pp. 6–7. Further references are included in the text.

18. *Partisan Review,* 36 (1969), 57–58.

19. Abrams, *Natural Supernaturalism,* pp. 356–57. For an illuminating discussion of freedom and liberty in relation to Romanticism, see Northrop Frye, *A Study of English Romanticism* (New York: Random House, 1968). For example: "For Shelley a universal idea is actualizing itself in the world by the containing and transforming of opposites: this idea is the idea of liberty, and liberty is a creative force in a cosmological sense, the principle of order in the chaos, or debased creation, of Jupiter's and Prometheus's torment" (p. 112). We shall see later how James uses Romantic Images to contain and transform opposites in *The Golden Bowl* and *The Wings of the Dove.*

20. *Theory of Fiction: Henry James,* ed. James E. Miller, Jr., (Lincoln: Univ. of Nebraska Press, 1972), p. 321.

21. E.g., see Henry James, *The Ambassadors,* ed. S. P. Rosenbaum (1903; rpt. New York: Norton, 1964), pp. 39, 41, 48, 60, 70, 78, 97, 103, 104, 111, 112, 113, 114, 117, 127, 128, 131, 132, 149, 154, 155, 168, 209, 213, 223, 230, 281, 289, 303. Further references (by book and chapter as well as page number) to this edition are included parenthetically in the text. I cite this paperback edition since it is more widely available in the United States than the New York edition and offers a definitive text.

22. For a fuller discussion of the relationship between Strether and Chad, see Laurence Holland, *The Expense of Vision* (Princeton: Princeton Univ. Press, 1964), chapter 4, section 1, "Chad's Transformation and the Vicarious Imagination," pp. 229–48.

23. *Language of Fiction* (London: Routledge & Kegan Paul, 1966), p. 197.

24. See John Carlos Rowe, "The Symbolization of Milly Theale: Henry James's *Wings of the Dove*," *ELH*, 40 (1973), 134: "Unlike the metaphysic implicit in the Scriptural texts, a novel is a limited linguistic world. The tissue of words and signs which constitute the text are the only reality of the work."

25. See II.ii.65: "Though indeed our friend felt, while he prolonged the meditation I describe, that for himself even already a certain measure had been reached."

26. See Matthiessen and Murdock, *Notebooks*, p. 372. The reader, H. M. Alden, reported that the story "centres about an American youth in Paris," but gives no indication that a character named Strether even figures in the novel.

27. Lodge, *Language of Fiction*, p. 194.

28. Henry James, *The Golden Bowl* (1904; rpt. New York: Scribner's, 1909), I, 189. I shall cite future references to the New York edition of James's works in the text by volume and page number; but since the two paperback editions of this novel which are most widely available in the United States (New York: Popular Library, n.d., ed. John Halperin; New York: Dell, 1963, intro. R. P. Blackmur) both number the chapters consecutively, I shall cite their chapter numbers as well. Thus, the full reference for this quotation would appear as: I, 189; ch. 10.

29. I have counted at least seven appearances of the narrative "I" in chapters 1 (I, 18, 19), 11 (I, 202), 12 (I, 210), 25 (II, 22), 38 (II, 283, 287); and some sixteen appearances of the first-person plural, mostly in the construction *our* friend or *our* concern.

30. I have counted over thirty instances of the use of the words *free, freely,* and *freedom.*

31. F. O. Matthiessen, *Henry James: The Major Phase* (New York: Oxford, 1944), pp. 82–87.

32. Holland, *The Expense of Vision,* p. 348.

33. Frank Kermode, *Romantic Image* (1957; rpt. New York: Vintage, n.d.), p. 43. Further references are included in the text.

34. When the narrator does comment directly, his voice carries much weight since his judgments are usually implicit rather than explicit.

35. Matthiessen, *Henry James,* p. 100.

36. The application of the cage image to Amerigo is prefigured in ch. 34 (II, 192): "She felt with her sharpest thrill how he was straitened and tied,

and with the miserable pity of it her present conscious purpose of keeping him so could none the less perfectly accord."

37. Henry James, *The Wings of the Dove* (1902; rpt. New York: Scribner's, 1909), II, 218–19. Again, since the most readily available paperback edition of the novel (New York: Signet, 1964) numbers its chapters consecutively, I shall include chapter numbers parenthetically in the text along with the volume and page reference to the New York edition. The present passage appears in chapter 28.

38. Without connecting it to Romanticism, Laurence Holland discusses this point at some length in *The Expense of Vision*, pp. 319 ff. "In the rhythm of *The Wings of the Dove*," he says, "the form is made to be analogous to the action which the novel is about. Instead of merely describing its subject, the form acts it out. The form enacts the passion which lies at the novel's center and is revealed, chiefly through Milly's sacrifice, in the action which she, helped by the others, brings to pass" (p. 320).

39. Those seven chapters are 2, 11, 14, 27, 31, 36, and 37. I have counted over seventy-five instances of those words in the other thirty-one chapters.

40. "The Abyss and *The Wings of the Dove*: The Image as a Revelation," *Nineteenth-Century Fiction*, 10 (March 1956), 283.

41. Her "suicide" is surely meant to be taken metaphorically, as I say, not literally, as Robert C. McLean has suggested in " 'Love by the Doctor's Direction': Disease and Death in *The Wings of the Dove*," *Papers on Language and Literature*, 8 (1972), supp. 128–48.

42. "The Narrator as Center in 'The Wings of the Dove,' " *Modern Fiction Studies*, 6 (Summer 1960), 138, 142.

43. Cf. Kroeber, *Romantic Narrative Art*, p. 159: "From Canto VIII on [Juan] participates in events of which he is not the prime mover, in which he is only peripherally or accidentally concerned. Juan loses all resemblance to a picaro. He becomes something like a Jamesian 'central intelligence,' a lens for focussing and illuminating the actions of others."

44. See pp. 15, 37, 49, 51, 68, 84, 85, 89–90, 143, 157, 233, 294, 296, 300, 305, 307, 311, and 317. James often expresses interest in the aesthetic goal of "roundness" as well; see pp. 52, 172, 233, 237, and 296.

45. Ernest Sandeen, "*The Wings of the Dove* and *The Portrait of a Lady*: A Study of Henry James's Later Phase," *PMLA*, 69 (Dec. 1954), 1071.

46. "The River and the Whirlpool: Water Imagery in *The Ambassadors*," *Ball State University Forum*, 12, ii (1971), 72.

47. *The Negative Imagination* (Ithaca, N.Y.: Cornell Univ. Press, 1968), p. 85. This "paradoxical sense of things" is characteristic of the Romantic imagination in general, and the idea of "antithetical modes of structuring and comprehending reality" informed our discussion of *Frankenstein* and the nature of its Romantic form.

5. Joseph Conrad

1. David Thorburn, *Conrad's Romanticism* (New Haven: Yale Univ. Press, 1974), p. x. Further references are included in the text.

2. Robert Scholes and Robert Kellogg, *The Nature of Narrative* (New York: Oxford, 1966), p. 158. For discussions of related issues, see James Guetti, *The Limits of Metaphor: A Study of Melville, Conrad, and Faulkner* (Ithaca, N.Y.: Cornell Univ. Press, 1967), pp. 57, 59–60; Bruce Johnson, *Conrad's Models of Mind* (Minneapolis: Univ. of Minnesota Press, 1971), pp. 76–87; and Edward Said, *Joseph Conrad and the Fiction of Autobiography* (Cambridge: Harvard Univ. Press, 1966), pp. 96, 99. Further references to Said's study are included in the text.

3. Scholes and Kellogg, *Nature of Narrative,* p. 157. In reference specifically to the *Confessions,* they say: "It is the old narrator's task because if the young man could have spoken, it would not have been an experience worth recording." Cf. Thorburn on *Lord Jim:* "This compelling vision of a man caught in the imprisoning privacy of his own experience defines one of Conrad's deepest fears, enacts one of this novel's crucial insights and, finally, begins to explain the fevered erratic shifting of the book's narrative form" (*Conrad's Romanticism,* p. 116). For some remarks on the relationship between Rousseau and Conrad, see Said, *Joseph Conrad,* p. 53.

4. For a comparison of *Lord Jim* and Coleridge's poem, see M. H. Begnal, "*Lord Jim* and 'The Rime of the Ancient Mariner,' " *Conradiana,* I, ii (1968), 54; see also Warren Ober, "*Heart of Darkness:* 'The Ancient Mariner' a Hundred Years Later," *Dalhousie Review,* 45 (Autumn 1965), 333–37. Cf. Albert Guerard, *Conrad the Novelist* (1958; rpt. New York: Atheneum, 1970), p. 1: "For we are concerned with a style that is unmistakably a speaking voice." Further references to Guerard are included in the text.

5. See Guerard, p. 142: "*Lord Jim* is a novel of intellectual and moral suspense, and the mystery to be solved, or conclusion to be reached, lies not in Jim but in ourselves." See also Dorothy Van Ghent, *The English Novel: Form and Function* (1953; rpt. New York: Perennial Library, 1967), p. 277, where she notes that the enigma "is not what Jim is but what we are, and not only what we are, but 'how to be' what we are."

6. Guerard's earlier discussion of the role of the "casual reader" (pp. 131 ff.) raises different points. I think he goes somewhat astray there, but I do not think we need to consider that point in any detail. Guerard and I may disagree about the nature of the reader's participation but the fact of that participation is not in dispute.

7. Robert Langbaum, *The Poetry of Experience* (1957; rpt. New York: Norton, 1963), p. 46. Further references are included in the text. Cf. Murray Krieger, "The Varieties of Experience: *Lord Jim,*" in Thomas Moser, ed., *Lord Jim,* by Joseph Conrad (New York: Norton Critical Edition, 1968), p.

441: "The facts are laid out again and again, in inexhaustible and repetitious detail. But ironically, the real mystery has not been solved; it has only deepened." (This essay is a selection from *The Tragic Vision: Variations on a Theme in Literary Interpretation* [New York: Holt, Rinehart, and Winston, 1960], pp. 165–79.) Cf. W. Y. Tindall, "Apology for Marlow," in *From Jane Austen to Joseph Conrad,* ed. Robert Rathburn and Martin Steinmann (Minneapolis: Univ. of Minnesota Press, 1958), p. 280: "The emphasis on enigma that Leavis finds lamentable is not there to make a virtue of ignorance. Not only the heart of Marlow's darkness, it is also a consequence of his symbolist position. For romantic symbolists there can be no definite conclusions; and however certain Marlow may be about some images, his tale, as listening Conrad says, is 'inconclusive.' "

8. See Tindall, "Apology for Marlow," for a comparison of the Marlow of each of the four works in which he figures. Tindall suggests a progressive maturing of the character from "Youth" to *Chance.*

9. Ian Watt, "Conrad, James, and *Chance,*" in *Imagined Worlds: Essays in Honor of John Butt,* ed. Maynard Mack and Ian Gregor (London: Methuen, 1968), p. 306. Dale Kramer also calls Marlow a Jamesian character; see "Marlow, Myth, and Structure in *Lord Jim,*" *Criticism,* 8 (Summer 1966), 264.

10. Henry James, *The Art of the Novel: Critical Prefaces by Henry James,* intro. R. P. Blackmur (New York: Scribner's, 1934), pp. 320, 321.

11. See also Tony Tanner, *Conrad: Lord Jim* (London: Edward Arnold, 1963), p. 13: "It is impossible to remain outside the circle of Marlow's auditors. He professes a range of values which are too central, civilised and humane to permit of any disaffiliation on our part. His doubts and questions, his speculations and assertions, his tolerance and self-effacement, the leisurely quest of his memory, the feeling he conveys of being aware yet incapable of the extremes of human behaviour—all these things bring us into the story."

12. See W. Y. Tindall's remark about "Youth" in "Apology for Marlow," p. 278: "An amateur as yet at telling tales and otherwise imperfect, Marlow is allowed by Conrad to expose himself—in a kind of double exposure. While old Marlow exposes young Marlow to sentimental irony, ironic Conrad, aloof, silent, and listening among men of affairs, lets innocent old Marlow show old Marlow up. The anxious awkwardness and sentimentality that he displays are important for the nature of Marlow is the theme."

13. See also Guerard, p. 147: "*Lord Jim* is perhaps the first major novel solidly built on a true intuitive understanding of sympathetic identification as a psychic process, and as a process which may operate both consciously and less than consciously."

14. Northrop Frye, *A Study of English Romanticism* (New York: Random House, 1968), p. 26. Further references are included in the text.

15. Cf. Conrad's own remark about *Heart of Darkness* in the "Author's Note" (1917) to "Youth": "That sombre theme had to be given a sinister resonance, a tonality of its own, a continued vibration that, I hoped, would hang in the air and dwell on the ear after the last note had been struck" (Robert Kimbrough, ed., *Heart of Darkness*, by Joseph Conrad [1963; rpt. New York: Norton Critical Edition, 1971], p. 160. Citations in the text are to this edition.)

16. Guetti, *Limits of Metaphor*, p. 57.

17. *Romantic Narrative Art* (1960; rpt. Madison: Univ. of Wisconsin Press, 1966), p. 58. Further references are included in the text. See also Tanner, *Conrad: Lord Jim*, pp. 10–11.

18. F. R. Leavis, *The Great Tradition* (1948; rpt. Harmondsworth, Eng.: Penguin Books, 1967), p. 200. Compare pp. 196–97: "The same vocabulary, the same adjectival insistence upon inexpressible and incomprehensible mystery, is applied to the evaluation of human profoundities and spiritual horrors; to magnifying a thrilled sense of the unspeakable potentialities of the human soul. The actual effect is not to magnify but rather to muffle."

19. Ralph Maud, "The Plain Tale of *Heart of Darkness*," in Kimbrough, ed., *Heart of Darkness*. p. 205.

20. But see Robert F. Haugh, "*Heart of Darkness:* Problems for Critics," in Kimbrough, ed., *Heart of Darkness*, p. 165.

21. "Marlow's Quest" in Kimbrough, ed., *Heart of Darkness*, p. 178. See also Johnson, *Conrad's Models of Mind*, pp. 85, 86–87.

22. For a very different reading of Kurtz that draws upon Christian conceptions, see Robert Andreach, *The Slain and Resurrected God: Conrad, Ford, and the Christian Myth* (New York: New York Univ. Press, 1970), pp. 44 ff.

23. See ibid., p. 52.

24. Letter of 31 May 1902 to William Blackwood, in *Joseph Conrad: Letters to William Blackwood and David S. Meldrum,* ed. William Blackburn (Durham, N.C.: Duke Univ. Press, 1958), p. 154.

25. Compare Donald R. Benson, "*Heart of Darkness:* The Grounds of Civilization in an Alien Universe," in Kimbrough, ed., *Heart of Darkness*, pp. 210–17.

26. J. Hillis Miller, "The Interpretation of *Lord Jim*," in *The Interpretation of Narrative: Theory and Practice*, ed. Morton Bloomfield (Cambridge: Harvard Univ. Press, 1970), pp. 217–18. Further references are included in the text.

27. Cf. Dale Kramer, "Marlow, Myth, and Structure in *Lord Jim*," *Criticism*, 8 (Summer 1966), 226: "The similarity [between Jim's outlook and Marlow's] is not simply that both are romantic, but that both are rigid adherents to mystical codes of ethics. Paradoxically, however, and it is this that seems to account for Marlow's fascination with Jim, their codes are

mutually contradictory. Marlow's personality is a reflector of the forces that create a solidarity among men to oppose the unfathomable dark powers that threaten from within and without. Although intrinsically lacking certitude by his own finely tuned consciousness, Marlow defends 'the sovereign power enthroned in a fixed standard of conduct.' Jim—despite the powerfully mythic force he acquires in the society he 'creates' on Patusan—has as his final arbiter of values an insistent force within himself, that must seek a perfect manifestation of the self's sufficiency according to conditions it has itself established."

28. Guetti, *The Limits of Metaphor*, pp. 59–60.

29. Joseph Conrad, *Lord Jim*, ed. Thomas Moser (1900; rpt. New York: Norton Critical Editions, 1968), p. 61. Further references are included in the text.

30. For a similar discussion, see Thorburn, *Conrad's Romanticism*, pp. 116–19.

31. Janet Burstein, "On Ways of Knowing in *Lord Jim*," *Nineteenth-Century Fiction*, 26 (1971), 465. Further references are included in the text.

32. Ernst Cassirer, *The Philosophy of Symbolic Forms*, trans. Ralph Manhein, II (1955; rpt. New Haven: Yale Univ. Press, 1970), 35.

33. I thought of lines from "On First Looking into Chapman's Homer" ("Oft of one wide expanse had I been told") and "After Dark Vapours" ("After dark vapours have oppressed our plains"); Marlow's phrase "throwing the impalpable poesy of its dimness" also has the same kind of cadence as Keats's prose in his letters. We might have used as well Keatsian terminology above in discussing Marlow's (and Conrad's) need to deal with mystery. For example, Keats says, in one of his most famous remarks from the letters: "I mean *Negative Capability*, that is when man is capable of being in uncertainties, Mysteries, doubts, without any irritable reaching after fact & reason" (Letter to George and Tom Keats, 21, 27 [?] December 1817, in Robert Gittings, ed., *Letters of John Keats* [New York: Oxford, 1970], p. 43). We could say that Marlow seeks negative capability, that part of his problem is that he is incapable of "being in uncertainties . . . without any irritable reaching after fact & reason." Compare also this by Keats in a letter to J. H. Reynolds, 3 May 1818: "An extensive knowledge is needful to thinking people—it takes away the heat fever; and helps, by widening speculation, to ease the Burden of the Mystery" (Gittings, *Letters*, p. 92).

34. Miller, "Interpretation of *Lord Jim*," p. 221: "The narrator may have been brought back briefly near the end of the novel to suggest that the reader might be wise to put in question Marlow's interpretation of Jim, even though he cannot or will not provide the reader with any solid alternative ground on which to stand."

6. Virginia Woolf

1. See Ralph Freedman, *The Lyrical Novel: Studies in Hermann Hesse, André Gide, and Virginia Woolf* (1963; rpt. Princeton: Princeton Univ. Press, 1970); Margaret Beede, "Virginia Woolf: Romantic," *North Dakota Quarterly*, 27 (1959), 27–29; Irma Rantavaara, "Romantic Imagery in Virginia Woolf's *The Waves* with a Special Reference to Antithesis," *Neuphilologische Mitteilungen*, 60 (April 1959), 72–89; as well as Joan Bennett, *Virginia Woolf: Her Art as Novelist*, 2nd ed. (Cambridge: Cambridge Univ. Press, 1964), pp. 69, 71, 106; Bernard Blackstone, *Virginia Woolf: A Commentary* (New York: Harvest Books, n.d.), p. 210; Frank D. McConnell, " 'Death Among the Apple Trees': *The Waves* and the World of Things," in *Virginia Woolf: A Collection of Critical Essays*, ed. Claire Sprague (Englewood Cliffs, N.J.: Prentice-Hall, 1971), pp. 117–20, 124, 126; and James Naremore, *The World Without a Self: Virginia Woolf and the Novel* (New Haven: Yale Univ. Press, 1973), pp. 140, 245.

2. *A Writer's Diary* (New York: Harvest Books, 1954), p. 104.

3. Letter to Virginia Woolf, 23 October 1931, in *Virginia Woolf: The Critical Heritage*, ed. Robin Majumdar and Allen McLaurin (London: Routledge & Kegan Paul, 1975), p. 271.

4. See David Daiches, *Virginia Woolf* (1943; rev. ed. New York: New Directions, 1963), p. 36; and Morris Philipson, "*Mrs. Dalloway*, 'What's the Sense of Your Parties?' " *Critical Inquiry*, 1 (Sept. 1974), 138. See also, e.g., Leon Edel, *The Modern Psychological Novel* (1955; rpt. New York: Grove Press, n.d.), pp. 127–30; Bennett, *Virginia Woolf*, p. 18; R. L. Chambers, *The Novels of Virginia Woolf* (Edinburgh: Oliver and Boyd, 1947), p. 16–17; Jean Guiguet, *Virginia Woolf and Her Works* (1962), trans. Jean Stewart (London: The Hogarth Press, 1965), pp. 284, 379; Stuart Rosenberg, "The Match in the Crocus: Obtrusive Art in Virginia Woolf's *Mrs. Dalloway*," *Modern Fiction Studies*, 13 (Summer 1967), 219–20; and Naremore, *World Without a Self*, pp. 17, 241–43. Jean O. Love writes on a number of issues related to my discussion here, but the terms of her discussion are quite different from mine; see *Worlds in Consciousness: Mythopoetic Thought in the Novels of Virginia Woolf* (Berkeley and Los Angeles: Univ. of Calif. Press, 1970).

5. Freedman, *Lyrical Novel*, pp. 185, 202–03. Further references appear parenthetically in the text.

6. Majumdar and McLaurin, *Critical Heritage*, p. 177.

7. Karl Kroeber, *Romantic Narrative Art* (1960; rpt. Madison: Univ. of Wisconsin Press, 1966), p. 47. Further references are included in the text.

8. Woolf, *A Writer's Diary*, p. 138; *The Letters of Virginia Woolf*, ed. Nigel Nicolson and Joanne Trautmann, vol. I: 1888–1912 (New York: Harcourt Brace Jovanovich, 1975), 370, 356.

9. Woolf, *Letters*, I, 300.

10. Guiguet, *Virginia Woolf and Her Works*, p. 429.

11. J. Hillis Miller, "Virginia Woolf's All Soul's Day: The Omniscient Narrator in *Mrs. Dalloway*," in *The Shaken Realist*, ed. Melvin Friedman and John Vickery (Baton Rouge: Louisiana State Univ. Press, 1970), pp. 102–05; see also Chambers, *Novels of Virginia Woolf*, p. 44; Rosenberg, "The Match in the Crocus," pp. 212–18; Barry S. Morgenstern, "The Self-Conscious Narrator in *Jacob's Room*," *Modern Fiction Studies*, 18 (Fall 1972), 352; Philipson, "*Mrs. Dalloway*," p. 126. Cf. James Hafley, *The Glass Roof: Virginia Woolf as Novelist* (Berkeley and Los Angeles: Univ. of Calif. Press, 1954), pp. 74, 90.

12. Naremore, *World Without a Self*, p. 126; see also pp. 92–100, 132.

13. David Neal Miller, "Authorial Point of View in Virginia Woolf's *Mrs. Dalloway*," *Journal of Narrative Technique*, 2 (1972), 125, 131–32.

14. Ibid., p. 130.

15. Woolf, *A Writer's Diary*, p. 22. See also Freedman, *Lyrical Novel*, p. 206: "This is Virginia Woolf's approach to poetry: the evolution of the self toward a depersonalized image."

16. Northrop Frye, *A Study of English Romanticism* (New York: Random House, 1968), p. 112. Frye also notes: "We have seen that the Kantian riddle of a distinction between things as known and things in themselves informs a great deal of Romantic imagery. In literature the noumenal world becomes a mysterious world hidden within or behind the world of ordinary experience" (p. 111). Much of Woolf's imagery is founded on this distinction as well. Cf. Kroeber, *Romantic Narrative Art*, p. 83: "The synthesis of a unified continuous action out of the interinfluence of elemental contraries seems to have been congenial to the early Romantic poets because it enabled them to be at the same time personal and impersonal, subjective and objective." Cf. also Ralph Freedman's remarks about Woolf's essay, "The Moment: Summer's Night." He says that it is a "shrewd analysis of the components of consciousness. Equating the subject and the object of awareness with the 'inner' and the 'outer,' Virginia Woolf suggests that both are included in a single whole. The mind recognizes relations between experience and its objects, isolated from the stream of experience upon intense concentration but incapable of enduring in time" (*Lyrical Novel*, p. 199).

17. Daiches, *Virginia Woolf*, p. 12.

18. Robert Langbaum, *The Poetry of Experience* (1957; New York: Norton, 1963), p. 53. Further references are included in the text.

19. As long ago as 1914, A. O. Lovejoy discussed Bergson's Romanticism; see *Bergson and Romantic Evolutionism* (Berkeley and Los Angeles: Univ. of Calif. Press, 1914).

20. (1962; rpt. New York: New York Univ. Press, 1963), pp. 19, 2.

21. Philipson, "*Mrs. Dalloway*," p. 145.

22. "Virginia Woolf" (17 April 1926), in Majumdar and McLaurin, *Critical Heritage*, p. 184.

23. Woolf, *Letters*, I, 480.

24. Virginia Woolf, *Mrs. Dalloway* (1925; rpt. London: The Hogarth Press, 1968), p. 10. Further references appear parenthetically in the text.

25. Daiches, *Virginia Woolf*, pp. 62–63.

26. *The Prelude, Or the Growth of a Poet's Mind* (text of 1805), ed. Ernest de Selincourt (1933; rev. ed. London: Oxford, 1960), pp. 38–39. See Langbaum, *Poetry of Experience*, p. 226, and M. H. Abrams, *Natural Supernaturalism* (New York: Norton, 1971), p. 419.

27. III, 116–21 of the 1850 text; see William Wordsworth, *Poetical Works*, ed. Thomas Hutchinson, rev. ed. Ernest de Selincourt (1936; rpt. London: Oxford, 1966), p. 509.

28. *On Wordsworth's Prelude* (1963; rpt. Princeton: Princeton Univ. Press, 1966), p. 65.

29. Cf. Freedman's comment that Septimus is "the romantic hero in reverse" (*Lyrical Novel*, p. 215).

30. Peter Walsh considers the past explicitly on a number of occasions (pp. 48, 55, 62, and 207); unlike Clarissa, he has a harder time seeing that the past is not an "ethical model" for the present. It is also interesting that old Miss Helena Parry, Clarissa's aunt, is still alive—a living representative of the past come to the party. She helps Clarissa, Peter, Sally, and Hugh to realize the full extent of the difference between their past and their present.

31. *An Introduction to the English Novel*, 2 vols., 2nd ed. (London: Hutchinson Univ. Library, 1969), II, 91. See also Arnold Bennett, "Another Criticism of the New School" (2 December 1926), in Majumdar and McLaurin, *Critical Heritage*, p. 189: "I have read two and a half of Mrs. Woolf's books. First, *The Common Reader*, which is an agreeable collection of elegant essays on literary subjects. Second, *Jacob's Room*, which I achieved with great difficulty. Third, *Mrs. Dalloway*, which beat me. I could not finish it, because I could not discover what it was really about, what was its direction, and what Mrs. Woolf intended to demonstrate by it."

32. Virginia Woolf, *To the Lighthouse* (1927; rpt. London: The Hogarth Press, 1967), p. 316. Further references are in the text.

33. Woolf, *A Writer's Diary*, p. 98.

34. Lily specifically thinks of Mrs. Ramsay as an artist: "She brought together this and that and then this, and so made out of that miserable stillness and spite . . . something . . . which survived, after all the years, complete, so that she dipped into it to re-fashion her memory of him, and it stayed in the mind almost like a work of art. 'Like a work of art,' she repeated" (pp. 248–49).

35. Cf. Naremore, *World Without a Self*, pp. 112–13: "The method here is essentially the same as that used in *Mrs. Dalloway*, but it has become more

complex and subtle. The text is divided into parts and sections, so that the action seems not so much all of a piece. Still, the sense of temporal and qualitative unity, of a single voice that orders the whole, is if anything greater than in the previous book. Everything seems to be refracted through the medium of a prose which tends to blur distinctions."

36. Ibid., p. 133.

37. Woolf, *A Writer's Diary*, p. 98: "The lyric portions of *To the Lighthouse* are collected in the 10-year lapse and don't interfere with the text so much as usual."

7. Afterword

1. David Daiches, *The Novel and the Modern World*, rev. ed. (1960; rpt. Chicago: Phoenix Books, 1967), p. 11.

2. Percy Shelley, *Poetical Works*, ed. Thomas Hutchinson (1905; rpt. London: Oxford, 1967), p. 424 (lines 284–87).

3. D. H. Lawrence, *The Rainbow* (1915; rpt. New York: Viking, 1961), p. 167.

4. Robert Langbaum, *The Poetry of Experience* (1957; rpt. New York: Norton, 1963), p. 25. Further references are included in the text.

5. James Joyce, *A Portrait of the Artist as a Young Man* (1916; rpt. New York: Viking, 1968), pp. 252–53.

6. Northrop Frye, *A Study of English Romanticism* (New York: Random House, 1968), p. 31.

Index